The Falling Rate of Profit
and the Great Recession of 2007–2009

Historical Materialism Book Series

The Historical Materialism Book Series is a major publishing initiative of the radical left. The capitalist crisis of the twenty-first century has been met by a resurgence of interest in critical Marxist theory. At the same time, the publishing institutions committed to Marxism have contracted markedly since the high point of the 1970s. The Historical Materialism Book Series is dedicated to addressing this situation by making available important works of Marxist theory. The aim of the series is to publish important theoretical contributions as the basis for vigorous intellectual debate and exchange on the left.

The peer-reviewed series publishes original monographs, translated texts, and reprints of classics across the bounds of academic disciplinary agendas and across the divisions of the left. The series is particularly concerned to encourage the internationalization of Marxist debate and aims to translate significant studies from beyond the English-speaking world.

For a full list of titles in the Historical Materialism Book Series available in paperback from Haymarket Books, visit: www.haymarketbooks.org/ series_collections/1-historical-materialism.

The Falling Rate of Profit and the Great Recession of 2007–2009

A New Approach to Applying Marx's Value Theory and its Implications for Socialist Strategy

Peter H. Jones

Haymarket Books
Chicago, IL

First published in 2021 by Brill Academic Publishers, The Netherlands
© 2021 Koninklijke Brill NV, Leiden, The Netherlands

Published in paperback in 2022 by
Haymarket Books
P.O. Box 180165
Chicago, IL 60618
773-583-7884
www.haymarketbooks.org

ISBN: 978-1-64259-332-7

Distributed to the trade in the US through Consortium Book Sales and
Distribution (www.cbsd.com) and internationally through Ingram
Publisher Services International (www.ingramcontent.com).

This book was published with the generous support of Lannan
Foundation and Wallace Action Fund.

Special discounts are available for bulk purchases by organizations and
institutions. Please call 773-583-7884 or email info@haymarketbooks.org
for more information.

Cover art and design by David Mabb. Cover art is a developed from
*Painting 57, Rhythm 69, (William Morris Block Printed Pattern Book, with
Hans Richter Storyboard*, developed from *Richter's Rhythmus 25* and
Kazimir Malevich's film script *Artistic and Scientific Film—Painting and
Architectural Concerns—Approaching the New Plastic Architectural System*).
Paint and wallpaper on canvas (2007).

Printed in the United States.

10 9 8 7 6 5 4 3 2 1

Library of Congress Cataloging-in-Publication data is available.

Contents

Preface

This book is a largely unchanged version of my PhD thesis, which I started to write in 2009. At the time, I had two aims: to explain the causes of the economic crisis, but above all to push value theory beyond lofty theorisations into a tool for empirical analysis. I was dissatisfied with a certain attitude, still prevalent among Marxists, that sees the concepts Marx develops in *Capital* as of exclusively philosophical and historiographical interest, rather than as the outlines for a coherent system of quantitative analysis radically different from mainstream approaches.

I am certainly not the first to have felt this frustration or to have pursued this kind of project. But most other attempts have started from the premise that Marx's system suffers from a fundamental logical contradiction regarding the relationship between values and prices. I came to this project aware that, since at least the 1980s, Marxists have shown that this contradiction is the result of particular interpretations of Marx's work, and that other interpretations are far more plausible. I was also aware that surprisingly little work takes this as its starting point: and, indeed, that attempts to show that Marx's work does not suffer from a major inconsistency have met with a certain hostility from those committed to more 'orthodox' interpretations. One motivation for this work was to show that more is at stake here than defending Marx's honour: once we clear away the roadblocks created by misinterpretations of Marx, we can make real progress in applying his system to empirical analysis.

Looking back nine years since I began the project, and four years since completing it, I think it largely achieved its aim. Unfortunately, it has not yet started the kind of debate I might have hoped for. In part this has been because, up until now, my PhD thesis has only been available online. Although it attracted considerable attention for a work that is perhaps too academically oriented, it has taken some time to come out in book form.

Since finishing the thesis, I have continued to work on value theory. If I were to write the book again from the beginning, I would make some substantial changes; but then it might take a further few years for any book to be released, further delaying productive debate. It can also be useful for others to see how an approach develops over time, and why it develops. So rather than rewriting the book, I have chosen to write this preface, which I hope succeeds in being more interesting than a mere plan for making revisions. It addresses three issues: the need for a dual system interpretation of Marx's value theory (the most technical section); Marx's concepts of value and of productive labour; and the connection between the falling rate of profit, the potential durability of reforms, and the transition to socialism.

A Temporal Dual System Interpretation

I am no longer persuaded that a single system interpretation does justice to the distinction Marx makes between prices and values, or can deal with situations where prices may not exist at all, but value certainly does (especially under state capitalist production). The main point apparently in favour of a single system interpretation is that it appears to allow for both the sum of prices to be equal to the sum of value, and for the sum of surplus value to be equal to the sum of profits. But as I argue in the thesis, total surplus value and total profits cannot generally be equal once we allow for the existence of the financial system in any case, even under a single system interpretation. The key question is whether the sum of surplus value *explains* the sum of profits that appears to capitalists (and, indeed, the different forms in which it appears), after taking into account all the transformations that prices and financial transactions entail. As long as it remains temporal, I think a dual system interpretation passes this test.

I hope to write more about this in the future. For the moment, readers should note that the first chapter of this book makes the interpretive evidence for a single system interpretation appear rather stronger than it is. In particular, in the book I take Marx's statement that the result of the capitalist's production 'is a commodity that contains surplus-value, and therefore an excess value over and above its cost price' to mean:[1] Value of the commodity = surplus value it contains + cost price.

In fact, all Marx's passage implies is that if a commodity contains surplus value, its value *exceeds* its cost price. It does not say that this excess is always equal to surplus value. In all but the strangest cases, it remains true for a temporal dual system interpretation that if a commodity contains surplus value, its value exceeds its cost price (and here Marx is considering commodities sold at their prices of production, not cases where differences between prices and values are unusually large). The passage I quote therefore does not rule out either a single or a dual system interpretation, contrary to my previous argument. I have chosen to leave my overstatement unchanged in the text of the book so that readers can see the basis for my former view.

---

1   Marx 1981, p. 265.

Other passages support a dual system interpretation against a single system interpretation. Earlier in the same paragraph Marx famously warns that:

> the cost price of a commodity, in which the price of production of other commodities is involved, can also stand above or below the portion of its total value that is formed by the value of the means of production going into it. It is necessary to bear in mind this modified significance of the cost price, and therefore to bear in mind too that if the cost price of a commodity is equated with the value of means of production used up in producing it, it is always possible to go wrong.[2]

Classically this has been interpreted as an admission of error on Marx's part: that he should have transformed the inputs in his example into prices of production, rather than leaving them at prices equal to values, and that therefore he is admitting to using an approximation with which it is possible to 'go wrong'.

In fact, Marx is saying it is possible to 'go wrong' if one supposes, *in all cases*, that the portion of the cost price accounted for by consumed means of production and the value of the means of production consumed are equal. He has chosen to show us the special case in which they *are* equal, and is warning us that this is, in fact, a special case. The example he gives of how to calculate prices of production is therefore not an approximation. Nor is it chosen for reasons of convenience. This special case is interesting because it illustrates the real, historical transition that takes place from commodities selling at values to commodities selling at prices of production.

Once this one-off historical transition is complete, and prices of production are an established fact, commodities bought at prices of production at the end of one period are used to produce commodities that sell at prices of production at the end of the next period. Hence, one's calculation would 'go wrong' if one continued to equate the value of means of production used up with the (constant capital portion of) the cost price, even in cases where inputs are bought at prices differing from values.

Andrew Kliman construes this passage as evidence for a single system interpretation. He argues Marx was saying it is possible to 'go wrong' if one supposes that, in Kliman's words, 'the value of means of production and the sum of value advanced as capital' are equal.[3] If Marx really were saying that these two magnitudes were not always equal, this could indeed be evidence for a single system

---

2 Ibid.
3 Kliman 2007, p. 106.

interpretation. But Marx never refers to 'the sum of value advanced as capital' in this passage; this is Kliman's own (mis)construal of Marx's meaning.

Marx himself says that it is the constant capital portion of 'the cost price of a commodity' and 'the value of means of production used up in producing it' that are not always equal, just as dual system interpretations insist. Moreover, Marx is clearly referring to the value *transferred* to the commodity by the means of production (and not only to the value of the means of production at the time they were produced, as a single system interpretation would need him to be saying), since he says 'the cost price of a commodity, in which the price of production of other commodities is involved, can also stand above or below *the portion of its total value that is formed by* the value of the means of production going into it'.[4] It is in fact single system interpretations that 'go wrong' in the way Marx warns against: they always equate the constant capital portion of the cost price of a commodity with the value of means of production transferred to the commodity. The issue has created so much confusion because Marx never supplies us with a numerical example showing cases where inputs are bought at (last period's) prices of production rather than at values, so we left with only his description of how the calculation would 'go right'.[5]

---

4   Marx 1981, p. 265. Emphasis added.
5   The 1861–63 Manuscript includes further strong evidence for a dual system interpretation:
     It is clear that the conversion of value into cost price works in two ways. First, the profit which is added to the capital advanced may be either above or below the surplus value which is contained in the commodity itself, that is, it may represent more or less unpaid labour than the commodity itself contains. This applies to the variable part of capital and its reproduction in the commodity. But apart from this, the cost price of constant capital – or of the commodities which enter into the value of the newly produced commodity as raw materials, *matières instrumentales* and instruments and conditions of – may likewise be either above or below its value (Marx 1994, p. 352).
     So does another passage in *Capital* III:
     We have already seen that the divergence of price of production from value arises for the following reasons:
     (1)   because the average profit is added to the cost price of a commodity, rather than the surplus-value contained in it;
     (2)   because the price of production of a commodity that diverges in this way from its value enters as an element into the cost price of other commodities, which means that a divergence from the value of the means of production consumed may already be contained in the cost price, quite apart from the divergence that may arise for the commodity itself from the difference between average profit and surplus-value.
     It is quite possible, accordingly, for the cost price to diverge from the value sum of the elements of which this component of the price of production is composed, even in the case of commodities that are produced by capitals of average composition. Let us assume that the average composition is $80_c + 20_v$. It is possible now that, for the actual individual capitals that are composed in this way, the $80c$ may be greater or less than the value of c,

If Marx had explored such examples, he might have been more careful not to give the impression that it is always necessary for the sum of profit to be equal to the sum of surplus value. In the book, I explore why, once we introduce finan-

---

the constant capital, since this c is composed of commodities whose prices of production are different from their values (Marx 1981, pp. 308–9).

Kliman argues these passages do not count as evidence for either interpretation, by relying on the contention that Marx was discussing aggregate prices and values across the whole economy:

The single-system interpretation is supposedly incompatible with these passages because it denies that differences between inputs' prices and values cause a commodity's price to differ from its value. Note, however, that Marx does not refer to 'the divergence of *a commodity's* price of production from *its* value' or 'the conversion of a commodity's value into its [price of production].' He might instead be contrasting an *economy* in which commodities exchange at values to an *economy* in which they exchange at prices of production. This reading eliminates the apparent problem, since the single-system interpretation affirms that prices in the latter economy will differ from prices (= values) in the former for two reasons – because profit differs from surplus-value and because inputs' prices and values differ (Kliman 2007, pp. 108–9, original emphasis).

Yet the passages in question refer explicitly to '*the* commodity', '*a* commodity' and '*the* price' (emphasis added), though Kliman did not quote these phrases. Moreover, the passage from the 1861–63 Manuscript is a commentary on a remark by Bailey concerning the determination of the value of *individual commodities*, not a comparison between two economies. Similarly, the passage from *Capital* III ends by making it clear that Marx's remarks apply 'even in the case of commodities that are produced by capitals of average composition', i.e. to commodities produced by 'actual individual capitals' that make up less than the entire economy. Hence these passages are only consistent with a dual system interpretation.

Alejandro Ramos M. argues Engels left a crucial passage out of the final version of the *Capital* III manuscripts, that supposedly is only consistent with a single system interpretation. Unfortunately this English language article does not include a translation of the passage, so I will quote the crucial part in the original German:

Nehmen wir wie in der ursprünglichen Entwicklung des Kostenpreises (*Capitel* I) Kostenpreiß = Werth des in der Production der Waaren vorgeschossenen Capitals, so haben wir folgende Gleichungen:

Werth = Kostenpreiß + Mehrwerth. $W = K + m$.

oder *Profit*, als identisch   oder = $K + p$ (quoted in Ramos M. 1998, p. 60).

Although my German leaves a great deal to be desired, it seems to me the sentence introducing these equations specifies that they only apply under the condition that the cost price ('*Kostenpreiß*') is equal to the value of the capital advanced ('*Werth des in der Production der Waaren vorgeschossenen Capitals*'), and hence tell us nothing about the contentious cases where prices and values differ. Moreover, they could only apply under such conditions, since they state that value (W, *Werth*) = cost price (K) + surplus value (m, *Mehrwerth*) = cost price (K) + profit (p); i.e. that profit is equal to surplus value. Ramos M. interprets p as 'produced profit' to try to avoid this inconsistency with his interpretation, but the passage never uses this term, and Marx routinely uses the symbol p for profit with its ordinary meaning (i.e. appropriated profit). The passage therefore repeats results Marx has stated elsewhere, which may well be why Engels left it out.

cial transactions, we must allow for the possibility that even 'ordinary looking' measures of the sum of profit contain a substantial portion of profit that does not arise from surplus value: that is, profit that is 'fictitious' in the sense that it does not embody the production of real commodities. But in fact, even if we assume these profits away by assuming away financial transactions, the proposition that surplus value is the source of all real profit does not actually depend on the proposition that the two sums are equal. The issue can be best understood if we consider all the use values that comprise the surplus product (i.e. all the use values used for investment, and consumed by unproductive classes and unproductive workers). The surplus product requires a certain quantity of socially necessary labour time (SNLT) to produce, and this must be equal to surplus value for Marx's theory of exploitation to make sense.

But if, for example, prices for luxuries and investment goods are especially high relative to values, and prices for means of subsistence bought by workers are especially low, a surplus product with a given total value (and, for argument's sake, let us say a given quantities of use values of various types) will have a larger total price than if prices for the same surplus product were low relative to its value. In the former case, supposing all commodities are sold and there is no hoarding, the sum of profit will be larger than in the latter. But in both cases we are considering exactly the same surplus product, which requires exactly the same SNLT to be produced. One perhaps could say that in 'price terms' workers appear more exploited in the former case than in the latter; but clearly in value terms, and in the terms that matter objectively, the level of exploitation in both cases is the same. In both cases, workers and capitalists end up with an identical bundle of use values, which require an identical quantity of SNLT to produce. The demand that Marx's theory arrive at the result that the sum of profit is equal to the sum of surplus value therefore in fact makes a coherent theory of exploitation impossible.

It is legitimate to demand that Marx's theory *explain* how surplus value is the source of real profit; i.e. profit that purchases real output. The theory elucidated above does just this. It shows that the sum of real profit is the product of the sum of surplus value, measured in SNLT, and the average ratio of prices paid for the surplus product to the SNLT that produced the surplus product. Since this latter ratio can be different from the ratio of prices paid for the necessary product to the SNLT required to produce it (and, for that matter, from the same ratio for constant capital bought to replace depreciated constant capital), the sum of surplus value (measured in units of currency, e.g. by multiplying by the ratio of prices to SNLT for the economy as a whole[6]) need not be equal to

---

6   Here, we could stipulate that the sum of surplus value measured in currency be equal to the

the sum of profits. But the reason for the difference is explained by the theory. Rather than leaving a 'gap' into which someone might insert some other explanation for the origin of real profit, Marx's theory shows how any difference in the quantities arises from differences in prices relative to values (before we consider the effects of financial transactions[7]). Furthermore, Marx has a general theory for explaining these differences themselves: his theory of the transformation of values into prices of production.

My shift to a dual system interpretation may sound as though it must drastically revise the method for empirical analysis the book outlines. In fact its empirical consequences should be very modest. Under a temporal dual system interpretation, there must be a distinction between rates of profit measured in price terms, and rates of profit measured in value terms. Marx's hypothesis of the tendency of the rate of profit to fall then becomes the proposition that not only does the underlying price rate of profit tend to fall, but that this fall is determined by a fall in the underlying value rate of profit. The book should therefore be read as testing the first part of this hypothesis, but not the second (though it is very unlikely that the second would be untrue if the first is true). Regarding this test, the only difference the dual system interpretation should make is in measuring the monetary expression of labour time (MELT), which is used as a measure of inflation. The measure used in the book should tend to underestimate the decline of the rate of profit during the 1970s, and overestimate any growth afterwards, or underestimate any decline.[8] It is therefore

---

sum of profit. But then we would be allowing surplus value, as measured in currency, to vary with relative prices, even in cases (such as this) where the sum of prices remains the same, and the SNLT required to produce the surplus product (and the rest of output) remains the same. Hence we would lose the crucial connection between surplus value and exploitation. We would also be saying that, with respect to surplus value, SNLT converts to currency at a different ratio than for the rest of output.

7   Once we allow for the existence of fictitious profits as a result of financial transactions, a source of profit other than surplus value does indeed appear to exist. The problem for the capitalists is that, insofar as profit is produced this way, it does not increase the size or value of the surplus product, except insofar as it allows them to increase the rate of surplus value. Hence its fragility as a source of profit. In this respect, although the profit may be perfectly 'real' to the capitalist who obtains it at the individual level, across society as a whole it in fact constitutes a form of nominal profit.

8   Specifically, the denominator of the MELT should measure the labour time transferred to output by fixed capital depreciation at values, i.e. the labour time that was necessary to produce each use value, rather than at start of year prices. (Under a single system interpretation 'socially necessary labour time' is redefined such that it means the socially necessary labour time that was actually required to produce the use value, plus the labour time 'transferred' by the difference between this and the price paid for the use value, after converting that price to a labour time measure by dividing by the MELT). It is reasonable to suppose that fixed capital

likely that if the measure of the MELT were altered in the way I have proposed, the conclusion regarding the failure of the rate of profit to recover substantially since the crisis of the 1970s would be strengthened. Readers should also note that the book gives similar results using more conventional (and completely different) measures of inflation, indicating that the differences involved here are not that great.

The direction of the likely effects on the decomposition of changes in the rate of profit could be assessed with similar reasoning, but again its magnitude is unlikely to be large. Theoretically, it means that value measures of all the concepts also exist alongside the price measures that the book defines (e.g. a value composition of capital measured in value terms, alongside a value composition of capital measured in price terms). Again, I hope to develop these definitions in future work, but there are unlikely to be major theoretical problems in working 'backwards' from the definitions in price terms to defin- itions in value terms.[9] To put the issue in context, the unresolved problem of measuring value transfers between the US and other countries is likely to be much more substantial empirically (bearing in mind that it is the price rate of profit *after transfers* that matters most for explaining crises, as is argued in the book).

---

tends to be produced under a higher average value composition of capital than for commod- ities generally, hence it is reasonable to suppose that prices tend to stand higher than values for fixed capital. This would mean that the denominator of the MELT used in the book is an overestimate every year. As depreciation of fixed capital tends to grow relative to the rest of output, this would mean the overestimate of the denominator of the MELT gets larger every year in proportion to the numerator. Hence growth in the MELT itself would be underestim- ated. Nominal measures of the rate of profit tend to overestimate the real rate of profit where there is inflation. Because it tends to underestimate inflation, this effect therefore tends to overestimate the real rate of profit. This overestimate is worse when the rate of inflation is higher. Hence, during the period of higher inflation that prevailed in the 1970s, the approach should give a greater overestimate for the rate of profit than it gives at other times when the rate of inflation is more 'normal'.

9   Regarding labour power, we now need to distinguish the value of labour power (which is the sum of values of the commodities consumed by workers in order to be able to go to work) from workers' costs of (re)producing labour power (the sum of prices of the same commod- ities) from the price of labour power (the wage). The underlying rate of profit in price terms uses a numerator that subtracts workers' costs of producing labour power from the total price of net output.

Productive Labour, Value and Directly Social Labour

The chapter on productive labour is also worth revisiting. The crucial point it makes is that whatever grey areas exist in distinguishing productive from unproductive labour, when we come to consider surplus value after unproductive expenditures, those grey areas essentially make no difference to the result. Hence the calculation of the underlying rate of profit is almost entirely unaffected by these theoretically contentious issues. On the issues themselves, however, the chapter appears to adopt a more narrow interpretation of the meaning of productive labour under the capitalist mode of production (and under other modes of production) than I would now argue is justified.

As I explore in the chapter, Marx criticises Adam Smith for having two different conceptions of productive labour: (1) labour that produces a physical object, that can be sold at a later time (as opposed to what we now think of as 'services'), and (2) labour that augments the capital of a capitalist. Marx points out that these conceptions are incompatible, since services can augment capital, but do not produce a physical object. Marx himself adopts conception (2), and rejects conception (1). But elsewhere in *Capital*, Marx says labour involving merely selling commodities, or making financial transactions, does not count as productive labour, even if it makes a profit for the capitalist in question. Because this labour does not produce use value – i.e. it does not produce an object *or a service* that is capable of satisfying human need or functioning as a use value that is a necessary input into production – it is not productive labour. Marx concludes that, in these cases, profit is transferred from productive sectors, and shows how this process takes place (by either adding a retail margin to prices of production, or appropriating a portion of profit of enterprise as interest). I therefore conclude, in the chapter, that Marx requires productive labour power, bought by a capitalist, to both produce a profit for the capitalist who purchases the labour power, and to produce a use value. Effectively, Marx ends up adopting Smith's two criteria, but changes each into a necessary condition (rather than making both sufficient conditions), and modifies criterion (1) to incorporate services that constitute a use value.

An important question this leaves unanswered is: what constitutes productive labour under other modes of production? There is a deeper logic for the two criteria Marx uses that my text overlooked. Criterion (1) can obviously be applied to any kind of labour, performed at any time in history, while criterion (2) is only asking whether this labour produces a profit for the person who buys the labour power in question. Surely it is correct to say that labour that produces a use value is always productive in an absolute sense, regardless of the circumstances in which it is performed.[10] But it may not be productive *of cap-ital*; i.e. it may not produce *profit*. In *Capital*, Marx is answering the specific question: what kind of labour produces profit? The answer is: labour that is both productive in an absolute sense (i.e. that produces some kind of use value) and that is performed by someone who sells their labour power to someone who sells the product of their labour.

Marx himself makes this clear enough:

> In considering the labour process, we began by treating it in the abstract, independently of its historical forms, as a process between man and nature (see Chapter 5). We stated there: 'If we look at the whole [labour] process from the point of view of its result, the product, it is plain that both the instruments of labour and the object of labour are means of production, and that the labour itself is productive labour.' And in note 8 we added further: 'This method of determining what is productive labour, from the standpoint of the simple labour process, is by no means sufficient to cover the capitalist process of production.'[11]

Note what this is *not* saying. It is not saying that, under all modes of production, only labour that produces a profit can be productive labour (an obvious absurdity). Nor is it even saying that, during the era of the capitalist mode of production, the only productive labour is labour that satisfies criteria (1) and (2).

An interesting case here is teachers and medical staff in public schools and hospitals. Clearly they perform labour that produces a use value, most of the time (e.g. when they are not complying with bureaucratic requirements). In this fundamental sense, they are productive workers. But, usually, they do not produce a profit for anyone.

One page on from the passage quoted above, Marx is typically interpreted as denying that public school teachers are productive workers:

> Yet the concept of productive labour also becomes narrower. Capitalist production is not merely the production of commodities, it is, by its very

---

10   What if a product is wasted: i.e. it is left unconsumed, or it functions as a use value less
      productive than intended (e.g. it is used as scrap)? In such cases, surely it makes sense
      to say that the labour expended on the product is *wasted* productive labour, rather than
      saying that because the product is not used, the labour in question retroactively becomes
      unproductive labour as such.

11   Marx 1976, p. 643.

essence, the production of surplus-value. The worker produces not for himself, but for capital. It is no longer sufficient, therefore, for him simply to produce. He must produce surplus-value. The only worker who is productive is one who produces surplus-value for the capitalist, or in other words contributes towards the self-valorization of capital. If we may take an example from outside the sphere of material production, a schoolmaster is a productive worker when, in addition to belabouring the heads of his pupils, he works himself into the ground to enrich the owner of the school. That the latter has laid out his capital in a teaching factory, instead of a sausage factory, makes no difference to the relation. The concept of a productive worker therefore implies not merely a relation between the activity of work and its useful effect, between the worker and the product of his work, but also a specifically social relation of production, a relation with a historical origin which stamps the worker as capital's direct means of valorization. To be a productive worker is therefore not a piece of luck, but a misfortune.[12]

The standard interpretation of this passage is faulty for a number of reasons. First, surely Marx here is discussing what is necessary for a worker to be both productive *and* productive of profit. He is not saying that, with the emergence of capitalist relations of production, the schoolmaster who does not work for the capitalist ceases to perform productive labour in an absolute sense. This would be to suppose that the emergence of capitalist relations of production somehow changes the definition of what it means to produce a use value.

Comprehension of this passage is further stifled if we succumb to the temptation to suppose Marx is comparing a state-employed teacher with a privately-employed one (at a time when state schools did not even exist in the UK). In fact Marx is probably comparing a self-employed teacher – one engaged in what Marx calls 'simple commodity circulation' or 'simple commodity exchange', or what Engels later calls 'simple commodity production' – with one hired by a capitalist.[13] Whereas a teacher employed by a capitalist enriches their employer, a schoolmaster who runs their own school and sells their own services does not. In general, *Capital* becomes difficult to understand unless the reader grasps that simple commodity exchange really took place to some extent throughout human history, and that its increasing importance was a precursor

---

12   Marx 1976, p. 644.
13   Marx 1976, p. 260; Marx 1981, p. 474; Engels in Marx 1981, p. 1037.

to capitalist relations of production.[14] A state-employed teacher is something different again, because (a) rather than selling the product of their labour, they sell their labour power (like an 'ordinary' worker employed by a capitalist), but (b) their employer does not sell the product of their labour either.[15]

To answer the question of whether teachers in public schools produce *value*, we therefore have to go back to a first principles discussion of value theory, which should also be of broader interest. Roughly three concepts of 'value' exist amongst Marxists. Concept (a) treats the concept of value as identical to the concept of socially necessary labour time. According to this approach, value is a transhistorical concept: one could say, on this approach, that all SNLT that produces a use value produces value. Apparent evidence for this approach includes Marx's letter to Kugelmann:

> Every child knows that any nation that stopped working, not for a year, but let us say, just for a few weeks, would perish. And every child knows, too, that the amounts of products corresponding to the differing amounts of needs demand differing and quantitatively determined amounts of society's aggregate labour. It is SELF-EVIDENT that this necessity of the distribution of social labour in specific proportions is certainly not abolished by the specific form of social production; it can only change its form of manifestation. Natural laws cannot be abolished at all. The only thing that can change, under historically differing conditions, is the form in

---

14   Under capitalist relations it continues to exist, but in a form subsumed under capitalist relations of production: see more on this below.

15   The case of the self-employed is also discussed in the chapter, but it is worth adding the following here. If the social value of what a self-employed producer produces is equal to its price, then clearly they cannot produce a surplus value that anyone but themselves can appropriate (a case Marx discusses explicitly). But if the social value of what they produce and the price it sells for are different, then the value they produce clearly either contributes to aggregate surplus value appearing as profit, or subtracts from it. In the most common case, the self-employed work with less advanced equipment than the businesses that buy labour power that they compete with. Hence they tend to produce less value per hour than their competitors; i.e. the social value of what they produce is less than its individual value. This is not a value transfer as such. But if, in addition, the social value of what they produce is above the price it sells for, then they produce surplus value that contributes to the sum of profits. Therefore, the self-employed who work in industries with relatively low value compositions of capital (which is the more common case) do in fact produce surplus value. Clearly when Marx seems to say they never produce surplus value, he is in fact assuming prices are equal to values (as he does throughout most of *Capital* I), as he could not have explained the way in which they do produce surplus value without having already given an account of the transformation of values into prices (i.e. without having given 'the science before the science').

which those laws assert themselves. And the form in which this proportional distribution of labour asserts itself in a state of society in which the
interconnection of social labour expresses itself as the private exchange
of the individual products of labour, is precisely the exchange value of
these products.

Where science comes in is to show how the law of value asserts itself.
So, if one wanted to 'explain' from the outset all phenomena that apparently contradict the law, one would have to provide the science before the
science.[16]

This interpretation only holds up if we suppose the 'law of value' refers to the
'natural law' that social labour must be distributed in definite proportions. But
what phenomena could possibly contradict a natural law such as this (even
seemingly), which is known by every child? Clearly by 'law of value' Marx is
actually referring to 'the form in which this proportional distribution of labour
asserts itself *in a state of society in which the interconnection of social labour
expresses itself as the private exchange of the individual products of labour*' (i.e.
the law determining how the proportional distribution of labour is determined
under commodity production), and not the mere definitional truth that social
labour must be distributed in some way or other under all forms of society.
Engels also explicitly rejects the proposition that value production will continue under socialism in *Anti-Dühring*.[17]

Concept (b) treats value as something that is only produced under the capitalist mode of production. Yet commodities have been produced for millennia,
and Marx himself gives us many examples of the production of commodities
prior to capitalism:

> In the ancient Asiatic, Classical-antique, and other such modes of produc-
> tion, the transformation of the product into a commodity, and therefore
> men's existence as producers of commodities, plays a subordinate role,
> which however increases in importance as these communities approach
> nearer and nearer to the stage of their dissolution. Trading nations, prop-
> erly so-called, exist only in the interstices of the ancient world, like the
> gods of Epicurus in the *intermundia*, or Jews in the pores of Polish soci-
> ety.[18]

---

16   Marx 1988, pp. 68–9, original emphasis.
17   Engels 1987, p. 294.
18   Marx 1976, p. 172.

Capitalist relations of production are only one specific way in which commodities can be produced. Their key feature is typically that not only the product of labour, but labour *power* is commodified. Hence the capitalist mode of production expresses *a further development* of the commodity form, both historically and logically, beyond 'ordinary' or 'simple' commodity exchange. Since Marx clearly identifies the law of value with the production of commodities generally, concept (b), although common, is an implausible interpretation of what Marx meant by 'law of value'.

This bears on the perennial question of how to understand the first chapters of *Capital*. Because Marx starts by saying '[t]he wealth of societies in which the capitalist mode of production prevails appears as an "immense collection of commodities"', it is often assumed that the first chapters of *Capital* (and the text as a whole) exclusively investigate the capitalist mode of production.[19] Marx's decision to begin by investigating the commodity is then presented as resembling the approach taken by a modern mainstream economics textbook, where one first starts with abstract and unrealistic assumptions, and then moves closer to 'reality' by relaxing them; where 'reality', in this case, is understood to be fully fledged capitalist society. In fact, Marx starts by telling us wealth under capitalism takes the form of commodities in order to explain his decision to begin by exploring the commodity itself generally, initially in the simpler and more abstract form it really takes historically, *before* it embraces labour power. Prior to the commodification of labour power, commodities were produced under a wide range of circumstances: e.g. by pre-class societies, by slaves, by peasants experiencing varying kinds of bondage, working collectively or as a family unit, or by independent craftspeople owning their own means of production. Early on in *Capital* Marx wants to examine 'simple commodity circulation' by abstracting away *these* differences.

Alex Callinicos cites the following passage as evidence that Chapter 1 of *Capital* I deals exclusively with commodity production under capitalism:

> the product wholly assumes the form of a commodity only – as a result of the fact that the entire product has to be transformed into exchange-value and that also all the ingredients necessary for its production enter it as commodities – in other words it wholly becomes a commodity only with the development and on the basis of capitalist production.[20]

---

19   Marx 1976, p. 125.
20   Marx 1989b, v. 32 p. 265, cited in Callinicos 2014, p. 136.

But the quotation is clearly discussing what is necessary for the product to *wholly* assume the form of a commodity, and does not state that *part* of the product never takes the form of a commodity prior to capitalism (the other passage Callinicos cites restates the same view: that '[o]nly on the basis of capitalist production does the commodity become the *general form* of the product').[21] As Marx points out in the preceding quotation, commodity production rarely *dominated* social relations prior to the emergence of capitalist society. Where commodities were produced, sometimes use values bought from the proceeds from selling them were the main way the people who produced them reproduced their existence, and sometimes they were not.[22] Marx begins *Capital* by distilling the essential logic of the history of the development of 'simple commodity exchange' because the capitalist mode of production is the expression of the most thorough and all-embracing development of commodity production generally. In his view, it is necessary to first understand the commodity in its 'simple' form, which is a form in which it really existed: hence, Marx explains the fundamental concepts concerning the operation of the law of value prior to assuming labour power is sold as a commodity.[23]

---

21   Marx 1989b, v. 32 p. 301, cited in Callinicos 2014, p. 136, emphasis added.

22   This point would be devastating to Marx's project if the early chapters of *Capital* I were a strange condensed history of the entirety of all forms of human production prior to capitalism, but as in fact these chapters are only focused on exploring the commodity form as it has really existed, Marx is happy to make this observation himself:

> this relationship of reciprocal isolation and foreignness does not exist for the members of a primitive community of natural origin, whether it takes the form of a patriarchal family, an ancient Indian commune or an Inca state. The exchange of commodities begins where communities have their boundaries, at their points of contact with other communities, or with members of the latter. However, as soon as products have become commodities in the external relations of a community, they also, by reaction, become commodities in the internal life of the community. Their quantitative exchange-relation is at first determined purely by chance. They become exchangeable through the mutual desire of their owners to alienate them. In the meantime, the need for others' objects of utility gradually establishes itself. The constant repetition of exchange makes it a normal social process. In the course of time, therefore, at least some part of the products must be produced intentionally for the purpose of exchange. From that moment the distinction between the usefulness of things for direct consumption and their usefulness in exchange becomes firmly established. Their use-value becomes distinguished from their exchange-value. On the other hand, the quantitative proportion in which the things are exchangeable becomes dependent on their production itself. Custom fixes their values at definite magnitudes (Marx 1976, p. 182).

23   Callinicos also endorses I.I. Rubin's objection to Marx's claim that the distinction between labour and labour power applies transhistorically (Callinicos 2014, p. 172). I do not understand why many Marxists agree with Rubin on this point, but it seems to express a certain

The reader uninitiated in Marxological debates should be warned that this
is not a fashionable interpretation. Chris Arthur criticises Engels for introducing the term 'simple commodity production' and reading this back into Marx's

---

allergy to using transhistorical categories of analysis generally (even though Marx often
does so: e.g. the concept of 'species being'), and perhaps also an understandable desire to
side with Rubin against the Stalinist misinterpretations he was opposing. But Marx's own
concepts make perfect sense: the distinction between the ability to work (labour power)
and the expenditure of the ability to work (labour) surely applies to all human labour,
regardless of whether or how it is bought or sold. It is essentially, and quite correctly, a
'physiological' distinction. Capitalist relations of production are typically distinguished
by the *commodification* of labour power, which is *not* a physiological process; hence value
is not produced transhistorically, *contra* Stalinist misinterpretations. Rubin then uses his
misreading to tie himself in knots regarding Marx's distinction between abstract and concrete labour, out of concern to offer an alternative to interpretations of the labour theory
of value that require a 'physiological equality' between various different types of concrete
labour. *Marx's* labour theory of value requires no such equality: it says that, where value
is produced, it is created by the expenditure of socially necessary labour time. Time is not
'physiological', nor does the expenditure of labour time always produce value. For Marx,
all labour is at once abstract and concrete, whether or not it produces value: its concrete
quality is what it does ('tailoring', 'weaving') and its abstract quality is how long it takes.
Under socialism, all labour will of course continue to have both an abstract and a concrete
quality. The allocation of labour time between tasks will also remain important, at least
under the lower phase (and even once labour becomes life's prime want we will probably
still need to plan to do work, unless perhaps machines eliminate all necessary labour); but
the allocation of labour time will not be carried out through the mediation of the law of
value.
    Revealingly, when discussing his position that abstract labour only appears as a cat-
egory under commodity production, Rubin tells us he is not sure this is Marx's position: 'I
[Rubin] also pointed out ... that this equation of labour acquires a very particular social
form in commodity production [this is correct – P.J.] and therefore makes way for the
appearance of a completely new category, that of abstract labour [this is incorrect – P.J.].
I think that Marx regarded the question in this way, although we have no clear statement
by him on the subject' (Rubin 1978, p. 113). In fact Marx discusses what he means by the
term 'abstract labour' often enough in *Capital*, but Rubin effectively disagrees with the
way Marx uses the term. Rubin has to turn similar somersaults to try to make Marx say
the opposite of what he means with respect to the distinction between labour and labour
power:

> In the above-mentioned section of *Capital*, Marx does, in fact, seem to give a basis
> for the interpretation of abstract labor precisely in a physiological manner. 'Product-
> ive activity, if we leave out of sight its special form, viz., the useful character of the
> labor, is nothing but the expenditure of human labor-power. Tailoring and weaving,
> though qualitatively different productive activities, are each a productive expendit-
> ure of human brains, nerves, and muscles, and in this sense are human labor'. And,
> in concluding, Marx stresses this idea still more sharply: 'On the one hand all labor is,
> speaking physiologically, an expenditure of human labor-power, and in its character of
> identical abstract human labor, it creates and forms the value of commodities. On the

work, when Marx himself never uses it.[24] But Marx himself uses the term 'simple commodity exchange' or 'simple commodity circulation' often enough, and what is exchanged must also have been produced. In *Capital* III, Marx tells us explicitly that *Capital* I Chapter 3, at least, deals with 'simple commod-

---

other hand, all labor is the expenditure of human labor-power in a special form and with a definite aim, and in this, its character of concrete useful labor, it produces use-values'. Supporters as well as opponents of Marx find support in the cited passages and understand abstract labor in a physiological sense. The first repeat this definition, not analyzing it critically. The others bring against it a whole series of objections and sometimes they make of this the starting-point for the refutation of the labor theory of value. Neither the former nor the latter notice that the simplified conception of abstract labor (which was presented above), at first glance based on a literal interpretation of Marx's words, cannot in any way be made consistent with the entirety of Marx's theory of value, not with a series of individual passages in *Capital* (Rubin 1973, pp. 134–5).

This quotation is a textbook example of wishful interpretive method: Rubin hides his disagreement with Marx's own unambiguously stated concepts by describing those who agree with them as falling prey to a 'simplified', 'uncritical', 'literal' reading. Essentially, in his justified struggle against Stalinist physiological conceptions of *value*, Rubin conflates Marx's concepts of labour power, abstract labour and value, and tries to impose his own meaning on them. If Rubin had instead read Marx more carefully (and more literally!), he would have found plenty of ammunition against the view that labour always produces value (some of which I have cited above). Regarding this passage, when Marx says 'in its character of identical abstract human labor, it creates and forms the value of commodities', this does not imply Marx says labour *always* creates value; he could be saying (and I think he is saying) that *in cases where* labour creates value, it is able to do so by virtue of its (transhistorical) character of being abstract labour, which is the result of the physiological expenditure of labour power.

Alfred Sohn-Rethel's related argument that value relations involve a 'real abstraction' (a term Marx never uses) piles on further confusions (1978, p. 20). The abstract quality of labour is always perfectly real: it might really take 10 weeks to plough through value-form theory and find oneself as confused as when one started. The production of value is also perfectly real: a use value produced for exchange really is produced for the sake of what can be obtained in exchange for it, and not for the direct purpose of satisfying need. Sohn-Rethel may be unconsciously borrowing from both Marx's concept of a 'real subsumption' of labour (which means something quite different: essentially, that contrary to a merely formal subsumption, the relations of production in question have come to change the way a use value is produced, concretely), and evidently also from Rubin's misinterpretation of Marx's concept of abstract labour.

I am in favour of making intellectually creative use of Marx's work (and indeed anyone else's) where this serves a useful purpose, but where this involves misinterpreting the meaning of central concepts, and those misinterpretations gain general currency, the risk is readers will lose the ability to understand Marx's text using his own terms. Rubin can be more than excused for this, as he was not writing in a climate where openly disagreeing with Marx was possible, and his correct emphasis on the fact that *value production* is not transhistorical constituted a brave struggle against a crude Stalinist mystification.

24   Arthur 2004, p. 19.

ity circulation'.[25] If one supposes Engels is saying that Marx is assuming all producers *always* own their own means of production in the early chapters of *Capital*, then there might be grounds for criticising Engels's introduction of the term: since Marx refers only to simple commodity *exchange* or *circulation*, and this includes cases where means of production are not owned individually. But I have not seen any evidence that Engels makes this argument.

A related claim is that 'simple commodity production' never existed. If this claim means no one has ever owned their own means of production and mainly lived from the proceeds of selling use values produced for exchange, it constitutes a strong historical claim contradicted by evidence and basic common sense: it not only writes out of the historical record the existence of the mediaeval artisan, but also individual producers who own their own means of production and sell their output on the market today. If this claim means individual ownership of the means of production cannot give rise to the law of value, again what appears to be a sceptical attitude turns out to involve strong and implausible historical claims. In a society where the producers make only a small surplus, and keep little or none of that for themselves, for producers dependent on selling and buying for their subsistence it becomes a matter of life and death to try to ensure that the part of their product that they exchange sells near or above its value, and that the commodities they buy with those proceeds are bought near or below their value. If any other outcome persists, they will either perish or have to find another trade. For producers buying things they could otherwise produce themselves, it would rarely make sense to pay a price such that the labour time they give up in the form of the commodities they sell exceeds the labour time they would otherwise spend producing the use value they want directly, unless conditions were exceptional (e.g. they had more of a perishable commodity than they could use, and they were not partial to alcohol). There are of course interesting cases where one might imagine prices not being proportional to values, e.g. if a guild were successful in restricting the output of a particular commodity, and it was difficult or impractical for non-specialists to produce. Such cases are ordinary enough examples of how the operation of the law of value is affected by monopoly and rent. If the objection to 'simple commodity production' is that it implies a linear story of the development of the commodity, I do not see why this should be the case: the degree of commodification of production has suffered many setbacks historically, most obviously with the decline of the Roman Empire, a setback

---

25   Marx 1981, p. 436.

that was probably ultimately necessary to make space for the widespread emergence of capitalist relations of production, and hence the further development of the commodity form. Commodification has also been connected to a range of different relations of production, and not just to relatively free individual producers owning their own means of production. If the claim that 'simple commodity production' never existed means that it never constituted a distinct mode of production, then this could be an opening for a useful discussion of what Marx means by the concepts 'mode of production' and 'relations of production'.

Unfortunately, Arthur never advances an alternative theory of prices prior to the emergence of capitalism, and seems to share commodity form theorists' reluctance to construct such a theory generally, even under capitalism. Readers are entitled to ask whether a theory that does not theorise the main way in which the law of value functions (movements in price) has much to tell them about that law itself, either historically or today. In seeking to collapse the distinction between value and price, value form theory also takes us in a direction strikingly similar to that taken by the neoclassical 'revolution'; but without, so far, giving us the benefit of a quantitatively determined system open to criticism. Scientific enquiry depends not only on scepticism, but also on making bold conjectures, as Marx does throughout *Capital*.

Individual producers of commodities also played a crucial historical role in laying the basis for the emergence of capitalist relations of production, and in influencing the politics of the early socialist movement. Urban petty-bourgeois producers were the main agents of the French Revolution, and the political base of Proudhonism. Hence their main concerns were rates of interest, taxes and rent, and obtaining a 'fair' price for their products against competition from the larger capitalist producers who were displacing them. They should be distinguished from the petty-bourgeoisie who were rising with the emerging capitalist society, who were mainly the ones who were not producers as such (e.g. lawyers and professionals). Marx's famous critique of commodity fetishism is surely aimed both at theory that mystifies capitalist relations of production and at Proudhon's theory glorifying simple commodity exchange by individual producers. Petty-bourgeois producers are the most important example in *Capital* of people who depend on and then are ruined by the operation of the law of value before and after the emergence of the capitalist mode of production.

Concept (c) recognises that commodities were produced prior to capitalism, and therefore treats the law of value as applying to all use values produced for exchange, throughout history. This is nearest to the truth, but still merits further discussion.

For Marx, value is usually produced 'where individual labor ... exists in an indirect fashion' (see footnote 27 below for the exception).[26] Marxists have called this 'indirectly social labour'. Labour is *directly* social if it exists as social labour due to the conscious allocation of labour between tasks, across a group of people, for the purposes of satisfying human needs (including investment for meeting future need). Labour that produces a use value for exchange is *in*directly social because its existence as a branch of social labour (i.e. labour that, if performed, entitles the owner of the use value to obtain use values produced by others) depends on a social process (selling commodities) that is not consciously controlled as a whole. Indirectly social labour produces value because in order to count as social labour, this labour must take the form of value. That is, it must take a form in which it counts as social labour by virtue of how much what it produces is *worth*, as determined by a process that is not consciously controlled as a whole. Directly social labour does not produce 'value' as such, because it counts as social labour to the extent that it is defined as such by a consciously conceived plan. How much the *product* of this labour is 'worth' is not relevant.[27] The *Critique of the Gotha Programme* puts this most clearly:

> Within the collective society based on common ownership of the means of production, the producers do not exchange their products; just as little does the labour employed on the products appear here as the value of these products, as a material quality possessed by them, since now, in contrast to capitalist society, individual labour no longer exists in an indirect fashion but directly as a component part of the total labour.[28]

---

26   Marx 1989a, p. 85.

27   An exception here is labour time spent producing commodities which function as a universal equivalent (which, in Marx's time, were gold and silver: arguably today no commodity as such fulfils this function). When gold and silver were money, labour producing gold and silver counted as directly social labour because its result was already exchangeable for any other product of social labour. Labour that produces ordinary commodities, on the other hand, must first be exchanged for money, and only then can other products of social labour be obtained, supposing a universal equivalent exists. In cases of barter, prior to the formation of any universal equivalent at all – i.e. prior to the existence of any commodity that is readily accepted as payment regardless of whether the person wants to use the commodity itself – no commodity counts as social labour immediately because anyone who wants to obtain something in exchange for what they own or produce must first find someone else who wants it.

28   Marx 1989a, p. 85. It would be easy but fallacious to suppose this counts as evidence for the view that value is only produced under capitalist relations of production. Capitalist society is the highest expression of the development of the commodity form, so it makes sense

Value is also crucial to the famous comparison Marx makes in *Capital* I, Chapter 1 between 'a society of commodity producers' and 'an association of free men, working with the means of production held in common'. For the sake of comparison, Marx supposes that the latter society uses each individual's labour time as the measure according to which means of subsistence are divided between the producers.[29] This means labour time functions as the measure according to which means of subsistence are divided in both societies (if we assume actual labour time is equal to socially necessary labour time, which is by no means generally the case). But in the one society, labour time serves this function 'in accordance with a definite social plan'; in the other, the producers 'treat their products as commodities, hence as values, and [only] in this material form bring the individual, private labours into relation with each other as homogeneous human labour'. Hence, under socialism, social relations towards both labour and the products of labour are 'transparent in their simplicity'; while in the latter society, 'labour is expressed in value', and hence becomes a subject fit for mystifying theorisation.[30]

The sceptical reader of *Capital* might ask, if this comparison between what elsewhere Marx makes clear is an example of the lower phase of communism and a society of commodity producers is apparently so close, then why bother struggling to get there?[31] A concern for having transparent and simple social relations does not quite seem enough to justify it. In fact, the differences are sharper than a superficial reading might suggest.

First, a society of commodity producers who owned their own means of production would in fact be very different from the capitalist mode of production. This is roughly what petty-bourgeois utopians, such as Proudhon, wanted to achieve. Such a change would indeed be substantial, by eliminating the sale and purchase of labour power, which is the basis for exploitation under the capitalist mode of production. But it would also be impossible to reach, in a society where the forces of production have developed to the point where they need

---

for Marx to contrast it to socialism here when explaining why value production does not exist under socialism. It does not follow that *only* capitalism can be contrasted to socialism in this way, and Marx does not say this.

29 Marx makes it clear that another method of dividing means of subsistence might also work. As it happens, his example fits the description what he later calls 'the lower phase of communism'; in the higher phase, which also involves directly social labour, the principle involved is 'from each according to their ability, to each according to their need', so there is no need for labour time to determine the division of the product. Marx 1989a, p. 87.

30 Marx 1976, pp. 171–3.

31 I am using the terms 'socialism' and 'communism' as equivalents, as Marx usually does.

to be worked by groups of people; and it would be reactionary to try to shrink the means of production back to an appropriate scale for individual producers.

Second, and more importantly for present purposes, under the lower phase of communism, the producers decide, collectively, what to produce. Only labour that fits within the specifications of a plan counts as directly social labour and entitles the person who performs it to withdraw use values from those that have been produced in common. Rather than what is to count as social labour being established in an indirect fashion, e.g. through commodity exchange, it is decided in advance, through a plan. This is what distinguishes the lower phase of communism from labour *money* proposals, e.g. Gray's labour bank. Marx's labour vouchers, like Owen's, are not money.[32]

Marx does not insist dogmatically on labour vouchers under communism, because, for him, the higher phase of communism involves the abolition of this 'bourgeois right' in favour of the principle: from each according to their abilities, to each according to their needs.[33] Even prior to the higher phase there would surely be cases where labour vouchers are not appropriate: e.g. for use values already produced plentifully enough that they can be made available for free (e.g. public transport), or for use values society decides should immediately be made available on the basis of greatest need (e.g. healthcare). In this way, we can see how, as the forces of production develop further under the lower phase of communism, as people's needs cease to be shaped by alienation and advertising, and as more work was of a kind people wanted to do, the lower phase would grow into the higher phase as the distribution of more types of use value would not need to be regulated, and more work could be done without needing an incentive to do it. Whether the higher phase would require abundance in the full sense of the term is debatable: people might no longer need an incentive to work even before all undesirable work is eliminated and before all 'higher needs' are met. Marx is sensibly non-specific on this question, but sensibly specific on the need for a stage between the capitalist mode of production and the higher phase in which there is a planned economy and money no longer plays an important role.

The lower phase of communism is also the point by which the state has withered away, and classes no longer exist.[34] It therefore cannot be reached

---

32 A series of discussions held by the Marxist Humanist Initiative helped to clarify these points. Marx 1970, pp. 83–6; Marx 1976, p. 188.

33 Marxists who scoff generally at all 'bourgeois rights' would do well to remember that Marx thought they needed a place at the centre of the organisation of society under the lower phase of socialism.

34 Lenin argues the state does not wither away until the higher phase of communism is

overnight. The stage preceding it is Marx and Engels' much maligned (and much misunderstood) 'dictatorship of the proletariat'. For Marx and Engels, the 'dictatorship of the proletariat' simply means the proletariat holding governmental power through its representatives and carrying out measures in the interests of the proletariat, i.e. socialist measures. As Hal Draper argues convincingly at length, dictatorship did not have the meaning for Marx and Engels that it has now.[35] Marx and Engels did not allow for any method of implementing socialist measures other than democratically: given the emancipation of the working class must be its own act, and working people make up the immense majority of society, anything else is a contradiction in terms. They never abandon their orientation in the Manifesto that the path to socialism involves 'winning the struggle for democracy', and in numerous places they argue that universal suffrage must be fought for and retained.[36] They favour

---

reached ('the state has not yet completely withered away, since there still remains the safeguarding of "bourgeois law", which sanctifies actual inequality. For the state to wither away completely, complete communism [by which Lenin clearly means the higher phase] is necessary', Lenin 1964, p. 472). But in the *Critique of the Gotha Programme* Marx argues: '[*b*]*etween* capitalist and communist society there lies the period of the revolutionary transformation of the one into the other. Corresponding to this is also a political transition period in which the state can be nothing but *the revolutionary dictatorship of the proletariat*', and this is in a piece that clearly states that communism as such begins with the lower phase of communism (Marx 1989a, p. 95, emphasis altered). For Marx, the lower phase of communism therefore constitutes the point at which classes no longer exist; and of course Marx and Engels's theory of the state emphasises that the state only exists under class society. Engels states explicitly:

> As soon as there is no longer any social class to be held in subjection ... a state is no longer necessary. The first act by virtue of which the State really constitutes itself the representative of the whole of society – the taking possession of the means of production in the name of society – this is, at the same time, its last independent act as a State. State interference in social relations becomes, in one domain after another, superfluous, and then dies out of itself; the government of persons is replaced by the administration of things, and by the conduct of processes of production (Engels 1989, p. 321).

Nowhere does either Marx or Engels refer to the need for a state as such (i.e. a repressive apparatus) to enforce rules regarding distribution right up until the higher phase: this is Lenin's own conception. Prior to abundance the potential for theft obviously remains, but Marx and Engels's prediction is effectively that a repressive apparatus will no longer be necessary to enforce laws such as this once classes no longer exist. Laws were enforced by pre-class societies prior to the emergence of a state, so there is a strong basis for predicting this can be done under communism prior to reaching abundance.

35   Draper 2011, pp. 77–93.
36   An entire book could probably be written on Marx and Engels's attitude to universal suf-

a more strongly democratic state than exists currently, incorporating the key measures taken by the Paris Commune: recallable representatives paid average workers' wages elected by universal suffrage, who are to carry out the func-

---

frage, but it is clear enough that they support it strongly and see it as very powerful, potentially in contradiction with capitalist relations of production.

Engels's writings on the subject are unambiguous, and not only after Marx's death. In material that functions as a draft programme for the Communist League and as a draft of the Manifesto ('Principles of Communism', 1847), he argues:

In America, where a democratic constitution has already been established, the communists must make the common cause with the party which will turn this constitution against the bourgeoisie and use it in the interests of the proletariat – that is, with the agrarian National Reformers (Engels 1976, p. 356).

The Manifesto itself (written in 1848) is less specific, but as part of its focus on winning the struggle for democracy states that the Communists 'labour everywhere for the union and agreement of the democratic parties of all countries' (Marx and Engels 1976b, p. 519). Also in 1848, Marx and Engels issue a leaflet ('Demands of the Communist Party in Germany') that includes the demand for universal suffrage (Marx and Engels 1977, p. 3).

In *The Class Struggles in France* (1850), Marx appears to adopt a more ambivalent attitude towards universal suffrage. Here, he is positive:

The classes whose social slavery the constitution is to perpetuate – proletariat, peasantry, petty bourgeoisie – it puts in possession of political power through universal suffrage. And from the class whose old social power it sanctions, the bourgeoisie, it withdraws the political guarantees of this power. It forces the political rule of the bourgeoisie into democratic conditions, which at every moment help the hostile classes to victory and jeopardize the very foundations of bourgeois society (Marx 1978a, p. 79).

But here he argues:

Universal suffrage had fulfilled its mission. The majority of the people had passed through the school of development, which is all that universal suffrage can serve for in a revolutionary period. It had to be set aside by a revolution or by the reaction (Marx 1978a, p. 137).

An article he writes in response to the rise of the Chartists (1855) helps to clarify his position:

two-thirds of the population of France are peasants and over one-third townspeople, whereas in England more than two-thirds live in towns and less than one-third in the countryside. Hence the results of universal suffrage in England must likewise be in inverse proportion to the results in France, just as town and country are in the two states. This explains the diametrically opposite character which the demand for universal suffrage has assumed in France and England. In France the political ideologists put forward this demand, which every 'educated' person could support to a greater or lesser extent, depending on his convictions. In England it is a distinguishing feature roughly separating the aristocracy and bourgeoisie on the one hand, and the people, on the other. There it is regarded as a political question and here, as a social one. In England agitation for universal suffrage had gone through a period of historical development before it became the slogan of the masses. In France, it was first introduced and then started on its historical path. In France it was the practice of universal suffrage that failed, whereas in England it was its ideology ... [Universal suffrage in England] is

tions currently enacted by the bureaucracy as well as function as legislative bodies. This is what they mean by 'smashing the state': this is not a violent project. Contrary to popular belief, nowhere do either Marx or Engels argue that

---

the Charter of the people and implies the assumption of political power as a means of satisfying their social needs. Universal suffrage, which was regarded as the motto of universal brotherhood in the France of 1848, has become a battle cry in England. There universal suffrage was the direct content of the revolution; here, revolution is the direct content of universal suffrage (Marx 1980, p. 242).

The most plausible interpretation is that Marx's 'objection' to universal suffrage in France was only that it was too weak as a demand: he did not *oppose* it, but he thought that it was at once too utopian (it could not last in a genuine way in the conjuncture at the time) and not 'utopian' enough (it did not demand socialism). The context is important here: in France, the parliament elected by universal suffrage had rendered itself ineffectual and set above itself a president elected by universal suffrage (Louis Napoleon) who went on to seize power in a dictatorship (in our sense of the term) sanctified by universal suffrage plebiscites of very questionable legitimacy. Hence, the practice of universal suffrage in France failed (essentially because the proletarian forces were not able to win over the peasantry, and a divided bourgeoisie settled for the rule of a strong man). If Marx ever *did* mean his statement that universal suffrage needed 'to be set aside' to apply generally, it is clearly a view he revises based on the experience of the Chartists.

In 1871, Marx praises the Paris Commune for introducing universal suffrage against a dictatorship (in our sense) in wartime (Marx 1986, p. 331). He never advocates giving extra weight to the votes of 'real proletarians', or refusing to hold elections on the grounds that the proletariat must rule as a dictatorship, or anything of that sort. If Marx had thought an insurrection against a government elected by universal suffrage was a good idea, then surely in his strongest polemic against state fetishism, the *Critique of the Gotha Programme* (1875), he would have argued this. But what he actually does is continue to advocate for a 'democratic republic' as the form *in* which the class struggle has to be fought out (not something to be overthrown), in the context of a critique of petty-bourgeois democrats who wish merely to establish democracy without also campaigning for socialism: 'vulgar democracy, which sees the millennium in the democratic republic and has no suspicion that it is precisely in this last state form of bourgeois society that the class struggle has to be definitively fought out' (Marx 1989a, p. 96). For Marx and Engels insurrection was permissible to *establish* democracy against absolutist rule; they never advocate it to overthrow a democratically elected government (including a constitutional monarchy).

Note that Marx and Engels were writing at a time when the power imbalance between the military and ordinary people was very different to today. The modern state has access to weapons with a devastating destructive power that can be wielded by a small core of loyal troops, including remotely. The Arab Spring has demonstrated the disastrous consequences of allowing a struggle to become militarised, even in relatively weak states, since more powerful states are likely to become involved. On the other hand, the Arab Spring has also shown that peaceful strikes and protests can bring down dictatorships in the right circumstances, as they did in Egypt, and with more lasting success in Tunisia.

Nor is Marx and Engels' emphasis on democracy the basis for a 'stages' theory. Even in relatively backward Germany in 1850, they want the Communists to struggle for socialist measures to be implemented from the outset, through democratic organs once they exist

power should be snatched from a government elected by universal suffrage. Moreover, Engels states explicitly that where there is universal suffrage, and the

---

(Marx and Engels 1978, p. 287). This is what they mean by making the revolution perman-ent: not *stopping* the push for socialist reforms once having achieved a democratic state. Similarly, in 1882 they argue for making communal forms of ownership in Russia the dir-ect starting point for socialism along with a democratic socialist revolution in the West, not pausing for a period of capitalist development before taking socialist measures (Marx and Engels 1989, p. 426).

During and after the 1850s, Engels understandably makes the most frequent references to the importance of universal suffrage, since he was tasked with writing the more political material while Marx was working on *Capital*. I find it inconceivable that there could have been a substantial difference between Marx and Engels on this question without it being referenced in their correspondence; clearly, in the following examples, Engels speaks for both he and Marx:

[1850] The working classes will have learned by experience that no lasting benefit whatever can be obtained for them by others, but that they must obtain it themselves by conquering, first of all, political power. They must see now that under no circum-stances have they any guarantee for bettering their social position unless by Universal Suffrage, which would enable them to seat a Majority of Working Men in the House of Commons (Engels 1978a, p. 275).

[1850] [U]niversal franchise in an England two-thirds of whose inhabitants are industrial proletarians means the exclusive political rule of the working class with all the revolutionary changes in social conditions which are inseparable from it (Engels 1978b, p. 298).

[1870] In England, the bourgeoisie could get its real representative, Bright, into the government only by an extension of the franchise, whose consequences are bound to put an end to all bourgeois rule (Engels 1985, p. 97).

Engels continues to argue for universal suffrage democracy after Marx's death, here in his critique of the SPD's 1891 'Erfurt Programme':

If one thing is certain it is that our party and the working class can only come to power under the form of a democratic republic. This is even the specific form for the dictat-orship of the proletariat, as the Great French Revolution has already shown (Engels 1990a, p. 227).

The phrase 'democratic republic' here clearly refers to all forms of democratic election of the state, and not only to a workers' state (though it refers to that too). At the end of the nineteenth century the phrase 'democratic republic' meant roughly what it means now. A democratic republic would become 'the dictatorship of the proletariat' simply if the pro-letariat exercised power within it: e.g. if a proletarian party was elected to government and carried out socialist measures. A democratically elected government under a consti-tutional monarchy would also qualify: Engels puts the UK in the same category as France and the US (Engels 1990a, p. 226).

Engels reiterates his and Marx's view on the democratic republic in an article the Italian press 1892:

All of governmental, aristocratic and bourgeois Germany reproaches our friends in the Reichstag for being republicans and revolutionaries. Marx and I, for forty years, repeated ad nauseam that for us the democratic republic is the only political form in

parliament exercises real power (rather than, for example, being *de facto* sub-ordinate to a monarch), the socialist revolution can and should be completed

---

which the struggle between the working class and the capitalist class can first be uni-versalised and then culminate in the decisive victory of the proletariat.

The honourable Mr. Bovio is surely not so naive as to believe that an emperor of Germany would draw his ministers from the socialist party and that, if he so desired, he would accept the conditions – implying abdication – without which those ministers could not count on the support of their party? (Engels 1990b, p. 271).

Hence even Draper gives the phrase 'dictatorship of the proletariat' a stronger mean-ing than at least Engels intended (and probably Marx too). He interprets the phrase to mean only a workers' state (i.e. the state after having been smashed), counterposing this to 'ordinary' parliamentary democracy, when Engels above is allowing for a workers' gov-ernment under a parliamentary democracy also to be an example (Draper 2011, pp. 115–16). The workers' government would surely need to be carrying out socialist measures to qual-ify.

In the same article Engels also clarifies his attitude towards violence under the regime of the Kaiser:

For a start, I have never said the socialist party will become the majority and then proceed to take power. On the contrary, I have expressly said that the odds are ten to one that our rulers, well before that point arrives, will use violence against us, and this would shift us from the terrain of majority to the terrain of revolution (Engels 1990b, p. 271).

Clearly Engels expected the German absolute monarchy to use violence against the social-ist party rather than let it reform away absolutist rule through a majority in the Reichstag (a prediction that proved correct). But note that even here, where there was no real demo-cratic rule, Engels' conception is that the parliamentary road to socialism would only be abandoned in response to violence from the other side. It surely follows that Engels not only thinks the peaceful path to socialism was *open* in countries with a democratic consti-tution, *but that it should be followed*, provided the other side does not use violence to pre-vent a socialist government coming to power in violation of the constitution. Even here, under the current balance of forces between ordinary people and the military, challenging an illegitimate government with violence is unforgivably irresponsible and dangerous.

The Paris Commune succeeded, at one stroke, in establishing a democratic republic, in constituting the dictatorship of the proletariat, and in smashing the state (by making its representatives recallable, etc.). But if the same uprising had occurred against a democrat-ically elected government (under a constitutional monarchy or otherwise), its character would have been very different. Nowhere do Marx or Engels license an insurrection to establish democracy against democracy, on the (fallacious) grounds that only in this way can the state be smashed (or, indeed, on any grounds). This kind of insurrection cannot solve the problem of establishing its own legitimacy. Prior to seizing power, support for the transfer of power to whatever new organs of democracy are proposed has always been and will almost certainly always be limited to a minority, since the rest of the population will ask why those who are seeking power do not demand (or even wait for) a new election and run in it. Moreover, without winning an election before taking power, there is no way for a majority to participate in and sanction the overthrow of the government that won

peacefully.[37] This is a vision of a democratically elected government democrat-
ising the unelected parts of the state, so that the state may in turn be used by
ordinary people as an instrument for taking democratic control over the means
of production.

---

the current legitimate election. At this fundamental level such an act is inconsistent with
Marx and Engels' project of workers' self-emancipation. The practical consequences are
also likely to be unforgivably disastrous.

37   In the critique of the 'Erfurt Programme' Engels argues:
    One can conceive that the old society may develop peacefully into the new one in
    countries where the representatives of the people concentrate all power in their hands,
    where, if one has the support of the majority of the people, one can do as one sees fit
    in a constitutional way: in democratic republics such as France and the USA, in mon-
    archies such as Britain, where the imminent abdication of the dynasty in return for
    financial compensation is discussed in the press daily and where this dynasty is power-
    less against the people. But in Germany where the government is almost omnipotent
    and the Reichstag and all other representative bodies have no real power, to advocate
    such a thing in Germany, when, moreover, there is no need to do so, means removing
    the fig-leaf from absolutism and becoming oneself a screen for its nakedness (Engels
    1990a, p. 226).
Lenin fails to understand the significance of this passage, downplaying it by emphasising
the word 'conceive' and claiming Engels only intends it to apply to states that are 'very free'
(Lenin 1964, p. 449). This ignores the fact the Engels explicitly cites the examples of the US,
France and the UK as places where a peaceful path is open, and that he explicitly cites the
absolutist monarchy in Germany as the reason the parliamentary road to socialism should
not be advanced as a principle under those conditions. He surely only says no more than
that a peaceful revolution can be *conceived* because he is not confident that, even in a state
where there are full democratic rights, non-socialists will continue to respect these rights
if a socialist government is elected. That is, he holds the view that if there is an attempt
to depose a democratically elected government through a *coup d'état*, it is permissible
to resist it. Even here, under contemporary conditions, allowing a struggle to depose an
illegitimate government to become militarised or violent is unacceptably dangerous.
    Marx and Engels also do not rule out that a workers' government may need to use a
state's repressive functions against those who forcefully oppose the legitimacy of a democratically elected government and the measures it takes; something all states have the legal
power to do currently. They argue these positions against anarchists who think the state
can be dispensed with immediately, against *putschists* pursuing conspiracies, and against
opportunists who refuse to even imply the need to end absolutist rule; but never against
people committed to respecting the legitimacy of what we now consider to be 'ordinary'
democratic elections.
    Perhaps *State and Revolution* could be forgiven for overemphasis if Lenin's argument
were directed only against the opportunist position held by the SPD at the time (which
faced an absolutist monarchy and had even supported WWI); but in fact it becomes a justification for the *Comintern* refusing to stick to the path of contesting democratic elections
for the purposes of winning power, regardless of their legitimacy (instead mainly contesting them for propaganda purposes), and, crucially, ignoring this path in Germany after the
fall of the Kaiser.

For Marx, the lower phase of communism marks the *completion* of the socialist revolution. This is the point at which there is no longer a capitalist class who may resist democratic rule, and indeed no class divisions at all, hence the point at which the repressive functions of the state are no longer needed and wither away. So whereas communist or socialist measures are part of 'the real movement which abolishes the present state of things',[38] the lower *phase* of communism is the first destination. If it is to lead to the lower phase of communism, a democratic government and a democratised state must make conscious efforts to get there. That means progressively bringing value production under planned, democratic control, for the purposes of meeting need. Hence, value production will recede under a workers' state and be insignificant or non-existent at the point of reaching the lower phase of communism.

Marx may have seen indirectly social labour as equivalent to labour that produces a use value for exchange, i.e. a commodity. Other possible cases had largely not emerged when he wrote *Capital*, and *Capital* does not consider the role of the state in detail. Engels makes clear that state ownership of the means of production does not automatically mean an end to the unplanned nature of capitalist production.[39] Even as Marx formulates them, however, the concepts of value production and production for exchange are not identical. In my view, the labour performed by workers in the arms industry in the former Soviet Union was indirectly social because its existence as branch of social labour depended on producing a product that could compete with arms produced elsewhere, in a process that was not consciously controlled as a whole. More generally, labour performed by workers in the Soviet Union in industries supplying the arms industry, and contributing to producing means of production, was indirectly social labour because, although it (very imperfectly) took place according to a (despotic) plan, the overriding purpose of that plan was to compete militarily with the West (including through developing industry).[40]

Like 'ordinary' capital accumulation, and unlike the satisfaction of human need, this has a limitless quality to it. Human beings' needs change with history, but they are not limitless; as one can verify by observing the personal consumption habits of even the most profligate members of the super-rich. Like

---

38   Marx and Engels 1976a, p. 49.

39   From *Anti-Dühring* (1878): 'the transformation, either into joint-stock companies, or into state ownership, does not do away with the capitalistic nature of the productive forces' (Engels 1987, p. 265).

40   A similar argument will be familiar to many readers: it is first put by Raya Dunayevskaya, and later by Tony Cliff. Cliff puts more emphasis on military competition, Dunayevskaya on the accumulation of means of production for its own sake. Dunayevskaya 1988, pp. 212–40; Cliff 1974, pp. 118–233.

the accumulation of arms, the accumulation of means of production has no real limits if it is not consciously planned to meet future need. This is because means of production can be used for producing (and bought in order to produce) more means of production; or, indeed, means of destruction.[41]

To return to our original question, what about labour performed by public sector workers producing use values? Where this labour produces a product that directly satisfies human need, with no exchange involved, it surely qualifies as directly social labour. The motivation for making this labour directly social may not be 'pure': clearly capitalist states have an interest in reproducing labour power that is healthy and educated enough to meet the requirements of its purchasers. But it nevertheless exists as a branch of social labour based on a conscious decision to meet human need, that working-class people regularly have to struggle defend.

There are interesting intermediate cases that hopefully help to illustrate the concept. Public transport, for example, rarely covers its costs with fares, and usually its providers (whether a public agency or private company) are obliged to service routes that would never be serviced otherwise. In this respect, the labour performed by state-employed public transport workers exists as a branch of social labour regardless of what it is 'worth'. Where it is privatised, there is a company that hires the workers in order to make a profit, but the profit made by companies in these cases typically comes out of a mixture of taxation revenue and fares. In such cases, insofar as a route 'stands on its own two feet' as a profit-making operation, without subsidy, it counts as indirectly social labour; but otherwise, the only reason the labour on the route is performed is as the result of conscious decision to meet human need. Other 'user pays' public services fall into the same category: in some cases, the fees might

---

41   An economy planned to meet human need would still need to invest in expanding the stock of means of production, in order to meet future need. It seems likely a society organised in this way would have to strive consciously to ensure *enough* of the total product was set aside for this purpose. Under the capitalist mode of production, the tendency is for far too much of the product to be invested in expanding means of production (and to expand it in ways that harm future generations by damaging nature, and that are oriented to fulfilling the needs of those who need it least). This is because the balance between meeting current need and meeting future need is not consciously regulated; it is a product of how much workers are exploited, how much surplus value is wasted on unproductive labour and unproductive uses of inputs (especially arms), and the degree of capitalists' personal profligacy. The decisive factor in determining Soviet decision making regarding accumulation was a combination of the drive to maximise military output, and the drive to maximise industrial production that had the potential to be used for military purposes in the event of a war; hence it had the limitless quality of capital accumulation even though profit making played a marginal role in investment decisions.

be high enough that the service would be viable on a for-profit basis, but in others the service would not exist except for the conscious decision to provide it. The concept of directly social labour does not mandate that there be no payment involved, nor does it make any evaluation of whether the decision itself was democratic or dictatorial (in the contemporary sense of the word), or in whose interests it was made. Hence although understanding what it means for labour to be directly social is crucial for understanding Marx's concept of the communist mode of production, the two concepts are not equivalent. Nor is directly social labour necessarily 'a good thing' in all cases; it is of course possible to make poor decisions regarding what is to count as directly social labour, and/or to make those decisions poorly or undemocratically.[42]

To the question: 'do public sector workers produce value?' we can therefore respond: mostly 'no', but it depends. Fortunately, it does not matter for calculating the rate of profit in price terms, even the underlying rate of profit. If a public sector worker produces value, but the output is not sold, then there is no surplus value that can be appropriated as profit as such, as there is no transformation of the value they produce into a price. The reproduction of the public sector worker's labour power still needs to be met out of commodities produced elsewhere (whether or not they produce value), and this must be subtracted from the total product when calculating what the book calls 'surplus value less unproductive expenditures' (which now must be translated to: 'underlying profit after unproductive expenditures'). If a fee is charged for what they produce, then we have to be careful not to count both the fees and the cost of labour power and inputs used up. But the accounting I have used only ever counts the costs themselves, never the fees, because this is how the national

---

42   Nor can the concept be stretched to cover any subsidy whatsoever: an ordinary bread subsidy might cause more labour time to be spent producing bread than would be otherwise, but if people bought less bread, bread factories would produce less of it. Hence it does not cause any labour to exist as a branch of social labour on a directly social basis. A state provided user pays service is usually different. For example, in the Australian Capital Territory, the territory government runs the buses directly, and covers the difference between costs and fares itself. If bus patronage declined significantly, cuts to services would not follow automatically. Undoubtedly some people would favour making cuts, while others would question why bus patronage had declined, what this meant for efficient transportation in Canberra, and would look into how people could be encouraged to stop driving their cars. If the bus service were privatised, this would not necessarily be different. Probably the operators of the bus service would ask the government for their minimum service requirements to be reduced or their subsidy to be increased, or threaten to cancel their contract, and a similar political process would take place: though this time with a large private company's interests contending alongside.

accounts also operate. If the public sector worker does not produce value at all, then by definition (and in practice, because there is no sale of their output) no value can be appropriated as profit.[43]

The Falling Rate of Profit and the Transition to Socialism

The book does not go into great detail regarding the implications of its analysis for socialist strategy. One reason for this is that, logically, strategy (and tactics) should follow from an understanding of reality, rather than the other way around; and there was only so much that could be tackled within the scope of a single PhD thesis aimed primarily at understanding reality. Hence the thesis only included a few paragraphs reproducing the conclusion most commonly drawn from a falling rate of profit explanation of economic crisis: that it implies nothing short of rapid, worldwide economic transformation will be successful. Desirable though such a transformation might be, if it is the only way we can reasonably hope to achieve socialism, it implies achieving socialism is much less likely than it would otherwise be.

Typically those who take a more optimistic view do so on the basis that there is 'plenty' of profit to be redistributed, and therefore an ordinary social-democratic programme can be the starting point for a transition to socialism. The reverse side of the medal is that economic crises are not an inherent feature of the capitalist mode of production, and hence part of the justification for the transition to socialism is lost. Getting to socialism also therefore becomes a kind of act of will: something that is desirable, but not necessary to overcome the contradiction between the development of the forces of production and

---

43   When does a 'fee' become a price paid for an ordinary commodity? The national accounts distinguish 'ordinary' government employment from employment in state run enterprises (which they term 'government enterprises'), where a state-run enterprise is defined as one that sells most or all of its output. This is not a bad working definition, and the national accounts do not allow us to make a different one in any case. The calculations in the book now exclude state-run enterprises from all measures of the rate of profit, because state-run enterprises in the US are not generally under pressure to make commercial rates of return (generally their surplus net of depreciation is actually negative). In a country where state-run enterprises made up a significant portion of the economy it would be important to calculate and report the rate of profit for state-run enterprises separately for most analytical purposes, e.g. to understand movements in the rate of growth. The thesis included an error regarding the treatment of state-run enterprises (with a marginal effect on the results) that has now been corrected. Effectively, the thesis unintentionally allocated the entire (but very small relative to the private sector) output of state-run enterprises to surplus value.

capitalist relations of production. More fundamentally, a strategy premised on relatively high rates of profit seems likely to fail if profit rates are not in fact high.[44]

My PhD thesis took aim at these arguments, and it was correct to do so; but was it correct to therefore conclude that winning durable reforms is unlikely while capitalism continues to exist? What had not occurred to me, at the time of writing the thesis, was the possibility of winning reforms that address the connection between low and falling rates of profit and economic crisis, as a path to achieving a transition to socialism. The idea is that planning has the potential to mitigate the reproduction crises caused by the falling rate of profit (and perhaps even to limit their severity by anticipating them) even before that planning itself constitutes the lower phase of socialism as such, and before it embraces the entirety of world production. Unlike an orthodox Keynesian approach, this planning would need to focus on regulating production and investment directly, and not merely on state monetary and fiscal policy. This planning also could and should reduce unproductive expenditures, by progressively superseding the need for advertising, the financial system, supervisory labour, etc. The agency of this planning might be worker-controlled industry, it might be a workers' government, or it might be both. Insofar as this were achieved, it would constitute a (partial) overcoming of the central contradiction between the development of the forces of production and capitalist relations of production; that could, in turn, lead to a further overcoming of this contradiction if the approach proved itself in practice. Hence, rather than being 'mere' reforms, these could constitute revolutionary reforms: i.e. reforms that take on a self-reinforcing logic, leading to a revolution in the relations of production. They would therefore qualify as 'socialist measures'. The most consequential change I have made to the text since it was originally written is to allow for this possibility.

Politically, this makes clear that electing a workers' government could be a step towards socialism. In democracies as they are ordinarily defined, where majority support can translate into governmental power through winning an election (i.e. most states in the world), I also think it is the *only* possible and justifiable route to socialism, given the emancipation of the working class must be its own act.[45] Typically this is thought of as counterposed to the rule of workers' or people's councils, but I see no reason for this: if councils form, why not

---

44   This is certainly not an argument *against* redistribution, but, rather, an attempt to understand how redistribution (and much more) can be won and held onto.

45   Outside democracies the rule of a socialist government would also need to be legitimated by holding an election as soon as possible.

extend them and make them the basis for a universal franchise electing councils of recallable delegates to whom state power is transferred, through a refer-
endum? It is also typically thought of as counterposed to smashing the state,
but again, why should it be? In principle, a workers' government could reorgan-
ise the functioning of the bureaucracy and armed forces of the state as much
as was necessary to bring it under full democratic control: there is no reason,
in principle, why a commune state could not even be brought into existence
this way (whether taking such steps immediately is sensible is another question entirely). Clearly such far-reaching transformations would not be 'easy',
nor something that could be implemented through government decree in a
vacuum from class struggle. But refusing to gain the legitimacy of winning
genuine elections would be unpardonable, particularly as it brings the risk of
starting a civil war. Historically, of course, socialists have not always had the
advantage of the existence of elections where majority support really can translate into governmental power. Marx's reflections on the Paris Commune apply
to the experience of workers' seizing power from a dictatorship (in our sense of
the word) in wartime, as do the Bolsheviks' theorisations of the Russian Revolution of 1917.[46]

---

46   The failure of the Third International is at least in part attributable to the attempt to export
the Bolshevik model of revolution to political conjunctures where it was inappropriate,
e.g. the March Action in Germany, and the Bolsheviks' related insistence, shared by Stalin
and Trotsky, that they could not survive in a 'holding pattern' (such as the NEP) without
(a) quickly winning power elsewhere (Trotsky's assumption) or (b) rapidly and brutally
industrialising the country (Stalin's assumption, and to a lesser extent also Trotsky's). A
little patience could have gone a long way, and perhaps better Marxist economic theory
applicable to state policy could have gone even further.

   Another apparent argument against winning an election is that it rules out workers
coming to power due to a mass strike. But this supposes, amongst other things, that mass
strikes can only ever last a short time, and that they cannot themselves be the catalyst
for an election. The recent experience in Greece indicates that in fact mass strikes can
be a regularly common occurrence during a crisis; and even though they did not trigger
an election immediately, they were *the* major contribution to bringing a party to power
that had never held it before. May 1968 showed that mass strikes can also trigger an election relatively quickly. But in neither case did a workers' party exist with majority support
for a programme that could both address the immediate issues that triggered the political crisis and constitute a step towards socialism. SYRIZA capitulated after promising the
impossible: debt relief while staying in the Eurozone (which is quite different from saying it should have unilaterally left the Eurozone). If it had sought a better mandate for
seeking power, it might have been able to deliver more. But essentially all the alternative
plans for overcoming the crisis rested on Keynesian assumptions. Can Marxist assumptions be made an alternative basis for policy in the here and now, and not only 'after the
revolution'? Surely the answer is 'yes', but answering this question in detail depends on
first extending Marxism as a tool of empirical analysis.

Even if it turns out that reforms cannot mitigate the consequences for the working class of economic crises due to the falling rate of profit, the arguments regarding elections still apply. But a workers' government would need to move more quickly towards planning and winning the struggle to elect workers' governments elsewhere, presenting itself more starkly with the problem of the 'leap of faith', and increasing the range of scenarios in which it fails. There is a certain tendency amongst Marxists to suppose that planning *as such* takes away all the effects attributed to the falling rate of profit. Fundamentally, the falling rate of profit is the expression, under capitalist relations of production, of the development of the forces of production, which is embodied in the growth of means of production relative to living labour. All else being equal, a higher accumulation of means of production tends to reduce the rate of economic growth (measured in quantities of use values), regardless of whether production is carried out on a for-profit basis.[47] Planning cannot change this. Planning could raise the rate of growth by devoting more labour time to investment, and less to meeting immediate need; but whether it should try to do this in developed economies is very doubtful (if we want to achieve aims such as a shorter working day and reign in environmental destruction). What planning undoubtedly *should* try to do is to eliminate waste created by unproductive expenditures, crises, and disproportions; above all, the waste of human creative potential due to unemployment. To do this effectively, it will need to rely on accurate information and analysis, including accurate information about parts of the economy over which it does not have control, during the transition between capitalism and the lower phase of socialism.

Under the capitalist mode of production so far, planning on a large scale has only ever been used for making profits or maximising the output of a few types of use value. Public healthcare and education have proved adept at producing healthcare and education (without doing much for giving workers control over their own workplaces). The autocratic system in the former Soviet Union proved 'adept' at industrialising a country at brutal pace by forcing high rates of production of building materials and weapons; it proved less adept at meeting people's consumption needs beyond providing the basics (when it chose to do even that); and it proved equally if not more disastrous for maintaining

---

47   If, in terms of SNLT, the stock of accumulated means of production is large relative to output net of depreciation, as happens as the forces of production develop, then for any given percentage of net output devoted to investment, it will lead to a smaller percentage increase in the stock of means of production than it would otherwise, hence a smaller increase in net output next period than otherwise, unless the rate of productivity increase per unit of SNLT due to innovation increases sufficiently to compensate.

a healthy natural environment. The Chinese state has proved 'adept' at using planning mechanisms to create large profit-making enterprises and a highly unequal and autocratic society. What none of these examples have achieved (or indeed aimed for) is successful planning across a wide variety of types of industry, on a path towards taming and eliminating 'the market' (or, more accurately, indirectly social labour), in a way that expands democratic control over the economy.

This is not simply a political challenge. We need the technical and intellectual tools with which to carry out this type of planning successfully. It will not do to leave the completion of tasks such as this until 'after the revolution'; or, worse, to claim that it is 'undemocratic' or 'substitutionist' to work on proposals for how workers could direct their own activity towards getting to socialism.[48] Work has been done in this general direction. But the most interesting attempt to show how planning could work democratically on a large scale other than Marx's, Parecon, suffers from not really demonstrating how the transition from capitalism to Parecon could come about.[49] Rather than unify a detailed quantitative analysis of how capitalism functions with a plan to transcend it, it engages in the legitimate and related task of imagining how society could function once capitalism has already been transcended.

To understand how reforms might be able to address the symptoms of the falling rate of profit, as part of the transition towards the lower phase of socialism, it will help to understand, in detail, *why* low and falling rates of profit lead to crises. I think the thesis broke new ground in this respect in proposing a method for understanding the connection between the rate of profit and rates of return on financial assets: financial markets are clearly the main 'transmission belt' for translating low and falling rates of profit into economic crises, via financial crises. As its conclusion alluded to, however, the thesis did not really explore the use value side of the contradiction between use value and value, which is fundamental to Marx's theory of crisis.

To do this, I think Marxists need to revisit the reproduction tables in *Capital* II.[50] Debate regarding these has never really got beyond the question of whether Marx was saying (or implying, in spite of his intentions) that capitalism does not generate enough demand to sell all its commodities, or whether his argument that it can sell all its output is correct. As Rosa Luxemburg must

---

48   Nor can Marx be marshalled into saying we should never think about how to get socialism. This unavoidably involves thinking about what socialism might look like, as Marx does on several occasions, most fully in the *Critique of the Gotha Programme* (Marx 1989a).

49   Albert 2003.

50   As I have started to do in some draft work, Jones 2017 and Jones 2018.

have sensed, the problem with the latter position (which, *contra* Luxemburg, is undoubtedly the correct one) is: why did Marx bother with his reproduction tables in order to show, apparently, that capitalism can reproduce itself smoothly? It could have been to underline the importance of a falling rate of profit explanation for crises. But a crisis is, fundamentally, a crisis of reproduction: a situation in which commodities (including, crucially, labour power) remain unsold. A complete explanation of economic crisis in terms of a falling rate of profit needs to show how the falling rate of profit is connected to a breakdown in reproduction.[51] This cannot be done without understanding the relationships between various sectors of the economy, and how unplanned investment creates disproportions between them. Since investment is mainly directed by financial markets, this depends on an adequate theorisation of financial markets, which in turn depends on an adequate understanding of rent.

This implies the need for a theory capable of quantification and susceptible to testing, just as Marx pioneers with his reproduction tables. I think the potential to make progress on such a theory is strong. It is very easy to adopt a posture that is sceptical of quantification by drawing on justified opposition to the way that capitalism reduces everything to numbers. But the former does not follow from the latter. The way to oppose capitalism successfully is not to refuse to understand how the system works, but to use our understanding of it to help get rid of it and replace it with something that works better.

May 2018
Canberra, Australia

---

51 Grossman understands the need to do this, but his own work does not achieve it as far as I am aware. In his *The Law of Accumulation and Breakdown of the Capitalist System*, Grossman shows how a schema devised by Bauer leads to a 'breakdown', contrary to Bauer's intentions. The 'breakdown' consists in one of Bauer's assumptions no longer being able to be met: specifically, the system 'breaks down' because the rate of accumulation cannot remain as high as Bauer assumed it must remain. This certainly demonstrates a contradiction between Bauer's interpretation of his schema and the schema itself. But it does not illustrate an actual economic crisis, since, in reality, there is no reason for the rate of accumulation to remain constant as Bauer assumes. Grossman 1992, pp. 59–129.

Tables and Figures

Tables

Figures

Advice to Readers

This book aims to do two things: to develop an interpretation of Marx's value theory and to apply this to analysing the causes of the 2007–09 Great Recession in the United States. Combining general theory and concrete analysis in this way is, I hope, the most productive way to do both, but it does mean readers mainly interested in the causes of the recession may be put off by the more theoretical material that comprises most of the book. Most of the concrete analysis is in Chapters 7 and 8, and one alternative is to read these first and then judge whether the results of the theoretical framework are strong enough to justify reading the earlier chapters.

The emphasis on developing a framework that can be applied using the national accounts also means there is some technical material that readers interested in value theory at a more general level may find less immediately relevant. I have relegated the material discussing statistics to appendices wherever possible, and it should be possible to follow the theoretical arguments without necessarily following their relationship to the accounting.

The book is a revised version of a PhD thesis of the same name, written at the Australian National University in Canberra and completed in November 2014.

CHAPTER 1

Marx's Value Theory and the Law of the Tendential Fall in the Rate of Profit

The Great Recession has again confirmed Marx's prediction that economic crises are inevitable under capitalism. Yet Marx's most developed explanation for *why* this is the case – his law of the tendential fall in the rate of profit (LTFRP) – is not widely accepted, even among Marxists.

Marx's broader value theory suffers an arguably worse fate. Its fundamental premises are endlessly debated and reinterpreted, but, with important exceptions, this often delivers few concrete analytical insights. Perhaps as a result, *Capital* is often consulted for its famous quotations, its literary merits, its method, its philosophy, and even sometimes its conclusions; but the quantitative value theory on which these conclusions are based is almost as widely neglected or rejected as the LTFRP.

This book builds on the work of a small but growing number of Marxists whose temporal single system interpretation (TSSI) of Marx's value theory aims to recover this aspect of Marx's thought. The TSSI refutes two influential allegations of internal inconsistency against Marx's system: the transformation problem, and the Okishio Theorem. Both have done major damage to the credibility of Marxist ideas.

The Okishio Theorem claims that profit-increasing technological change cannot lead to a falling rate of profit in the way Marx describes.[1] If it were true, then logically it would entail rejecting not only Marx's LTFRP, but also the crisis theory he develops on that basis, an important aspect of Marx's historical materialism, and one part of the case for revolutionary socialist politics.

The transformation problem has been even more damaging, since it appears to show that Marx's *entire* value theory is internally inconsistent. If this were true, it would invalidate Marx's explanation of how the working class is exploited under capitalism, and most of the rest of his analysis in *Capital*.

Understandably, much energy has been expended debating the significance of these problems or trying to solve them (though not always usefully). There is also a mutually reinforcing relationship between the lack of confidence these

---

1 Okishio 1961.

critiques have created and what Alan Freeman has called 'Marxism without Marx': the attempt to divorce Marx's conclusions from his economic analysis.[2]

Yet refutations of these critiques have existed since the 1980s. They have demonstrated that the transformation problem and the Okishio Theorem depend on a misrepresentation of Marx's theory that is still prevalent: that he was trying, or should have been trying, to construct an equilibrium model of the capitalist economy. If we drop this assumption, the TSSI demonstrates that Marx's procedure for transforming values into prices is not guilty of the inconsistency his critics allege, and the Okishio Theorem does not refute Marx's LTFRP.[3]

The TSSI therefore clears the way for significant progress to be made towards understanding Marx's political economy on its own terms, extending it, and using it for empirical analysis. In particular, it makes the quantification of Marx's value theory a much more viable endeavour; since, if Marx's value theory can be quantified on an internally consistent basis, it is much more likely to be a useful framework through which to analyse economic statistics. So far, however, most work on the TSSI has remained at the level of high value theory.

This work takes these breakthroughs as its starting point for an analysis of the dynamics of the rate of profit. Specifically, it uses Marx's value theory to develop a new method of measuring the rate of profit, the cause of its hypothesised tendency to fall, the factors counteracting this and their effect on the rate of profit, and the connection between the rate of profit and financial rates of return. It applies this to data for the US economy, with a focus on testing whether Marx's LTFRP can explain the causes of the Great Recession.

Parts of the book are unavoidably technical. It uses some mathematics, but this does not go beyond high school level algebra (e.g. there are no matrices or vectors). The more difficult aspects describe how the US national accounts are used to construct the measures mentioned above, but it should be possible to understand the general argument without following every detail of the accounting.

The book is structured as follows. This chapter discusses the most relevant parts of the vast literature devoted to Marx's value theory and the rate of profit, both as background and to take positions on the most important points of controversy over how to interpret and test Marx's law. The first section starts with overviews of explanations of the falling rate of profit before Marx, and the signi-

---

2   Freeman 2010, p. 652.
3   Kliman 1988; Freeman and Carchedi 1996; Carchedi 2009; Kliman and Freeman 2009; Kliman and McGlone 1988; Carchedi 1984; Giussani 1991. Kliman 2007 is the best starting point and summarises the debates.

ficance of the LTFRP for Marx and for socialist strategy. Then it considers how to interpret the LTFRP: over what time period Marx supposes it applies and whether it predicts future movements in the rate of profit. The second section discusses the three most important *theoretical* objections to the LTFRP – the transformation problem, the Okishio Theorem, and the charge that it is indeterminate – and the persuasive arguments that have been made against them.

The next three chapters set out a new method for measuring the rate of profit and explaining its movements. Chapter 2 raises a problem with existing temporal approaches to measuring the rate of profit: that their historical cost measures of fixed capital cannot allow for the devaluation of existing capital, even though this rightly plays a crucial role in their interpretations of the LTFRP. It argues that valuing capital advanced at input prices addresses this issue, and is consistent with a TSSI. This includes a numerical example which shows that the Okishio Theorem only 'works' if profit is mis-measured by valuing inputs at output prices. It also gives a method for quantifying the effect of the cheapening of constant capital on the rate of profit, and how this relates to measuring surplus value, plus a hypothesis concerning the relationship between the pre-production price rate of profit, the rate of accumulation and the rate of growth of output.

Chapter 3 goes further into measuring the effects of the counteracting factors to the falling rate of profit and it gives a method for measuring the effect of the rising organic composition of capital (OCC). It argues the OCC is not the ratio of the stock of constant capital to the annual wages bill (a flow), as is usually thought, but the ratio of the stock of constant capital to the *stock* of variable capital. This means it can only be measured after calculating the turnover time of variable capital. It also gives a method for doing this. This forms the basis for decomposing changes in the rate of profit (ROP) in terms of changes in the OCC, the cheapening of new capital, the devaluation of pre-existing capital, changes in the turnover time of variable capital, and changes in the rate of surplus value.

Chapter 4 raises problems with existing definitions of the numerator of the rate of profit. It repeats Gillman's argument that rather than defining the ROP as $s / (c + v)$, it should be defined as $(s - u) / (c + v)$, where 'u' is certain unproductive expenditures of surplus value. It then shows why the common view that $(s - u)$ is equal to after-tax profits from production is not correct. It argues the difference between the two has a deeper theoretical significance: it shows that a value theory approach implies the need to account for the difference between 'non-fictitious' profits and the profits actually recorded by businesses and investors. The chapter then gives a method for measuring non-fictitious profits using the US national accounts.

This raises the question of what *fictitious* profit is, and how it can be produced. Chapter 6 argues it is the result of the expansion of fictitious *capital* in excess of the expansion of actual capital. But to give the necessary background for this argument, Chapter 5 discusses Marx's views on finance and the rate of profit. Chapter 6 then builds a framework for quantifying the relationship between the average non-fictitious rate of profit and the average rate of return on fictitious capital. It also explains how this relates to movements in interest rates and share markets, and the way in which 'excessive' fictitious profits can create the conditions for property and stock market bubbles and crashes.

Finally Chapter 7 presents the results from applying these techniques to US data, with a particular focus on how they can help us to explain the causes of the Great Recession and the relevance of Marx's LTFRP, and Chapter 8 draws some conclusions concerning the predictive power of Marx's analysis in *Capital*.

1   The Development of the LTFRP and Its Significance

1.1   *The Falling Rate of Profit before Marx*

Among the classical political economists it was widely believed that the rate of profit had a long-term tendency to fall. This conjecture was consistent with the limited evidence they had. Though Adam Smith acknowledges it 'must be altogether impossible' to calculate 'average profits of stock' using the statistics available to him, he argues 'the progress of interest ... may lead us to form some notion of the progress of profit'. He finds that interest rates in England had been declining since at least the reign of Henry VIII. He also observes that the more developed European countries (England and Holland) tended to have lower interest rates than the less developed (France and Scotland), which in turn had lower interest rates than the colonies. He draws the conclusion that the average rate of profit in a country is mainly a function of its level of development.[4]

Smith seems to argue this is a result of intensifying competition leading to rising wages:

> The increase of [capital] stock, which raises wages, tends to lower profit. When the stocks of many rich merchants are turned into the same trade,

---

4 Smith 1976, pp. 105–16.

their mutual competition naturally tends to lower its profit; and when there is a like increase of stock in all the different trades carried on in the same society, the same competition must produce the same effect in them all.[5]

On the other hand, Smith also thinks that the end result of this process would be a combination of *low* wages and low profits:

> In a country which had acquired that full complement of riches which the nature of its soil and climate, and its situation with respect to other countries allowed it to acquire; which could, therefore, advance no further, and which was not going backwards, both the wages of labour and the profits of stock would probably be very low.[6]

Here he instead seems to explain falling profits in terms of a limit to the level of a country's development imposed by a combination of its natural conditions and its competitive position.

Ricardo takes up these same themes but combines them into a more coherent explanation (if still an implausible one). He argues the rate of profit tends to fall because of declining marginal productivity in agriculture: a higher population requires more food, which requires agriculture to expand to cover less fertile land. This pushes up the labour time required to produce the food and clothing needed by workers, which pushes up wages, pushing down the rate of profit. While, for him, this downward 'gravitation' of the profit rate is checked by technological improvements in agriculture and manufacturing, the overall tendency is nevertheless downwards.[7]

He expresses the same concern as Smith over where this process will lead:

> The farmer and the manufacturer can no more live without profit than the labourer without wages. Their motive for accumulation will diminish with every diminution of profit, and will cease altogether when their profits are so low as not to afford them an adequate compensation for their trouble.[8]

---

5   Ibid.
6   Ibid.
7   Ricardo 2001, pp. 71–84.
8   Ibid.

Ricardo calls this the 'stationary state'. For him, invoking its spectre has a political purpose: to argue that the English state cannot afford its system of poor relief.[9]

For J.S. Mill, the invocation of the stationary state has a slightly different political purpose. He argues an end to accumulation will naturally eliminate some of the nastier aspects of capitalism: it promises an end to the 'trampling, crushing, elbowing, and treading on each other's heels' associated with striving for wealth. Whereas '[h]itherto it is questionable if all the mechanical inventions yet made have lightened the day's toil of any human being', a combination of laws limiting inheritance rights, policies restricting population growth and an end to the accumulation of capital promises a world in which 'industrial improvements would produce their legitimate effect, that of abridging labour'.[10]

1.2   *Marx's Contribution and His Crisis Theory*

Marx does not conduct his own empirical investigation into movements in the rate of profit, and it seems unlikely he would have had access to much better data than Smith if he had tried.[11] His critique of the classicals concerns *why* the rate of profit falls, and what this implies about the stability of capitalist social relations.

The most counter-intuitive aspect of Marx's LTFRP is that increasing productivity tends to *lower* the rate of profit. This seems particularly strange if we assume no change in real wages, as both Ricardo and Marx did. Surely increases in productivity should make it cheaper to produce the commodities that make up the real wage, tending to increase the rate of profit? As mentioned, Ricardo acknowledges that this is true in manufacturing, but retreats to the implausible position that not only does productivity in agriculture decline over time, but that the effect this has on the labour time required to produce each workers' means of consumption is larger than the effect of increasing productivity in manufacturing.

Marx, on the other hand, argues that the development of industry *does* tend to reduce the labour time required to reproduce labour power, *and* to increase the ratio of surplus value to productive workers' wages. He calls this 'the production of relative surplus value'.[12] But he points out, against Ricardo, that the

---

9   Ricardo 2001, pp. 58–70.
10   Mill 2009, pp. 589–96.
11   Though he does investigate movements in the interest rate further, e.g. Marx 1981, p. 684.
12   Marx 1976, pp. 429–91.

ratio of profits to wages is not the only determinant of the rate of profit.[13] The rate of profit is the ratio of profits to the *whole* of the capital advanced by the capitalist, including the cost of raw materials, machinery, structures and equipment ('constant capital'), and not just outlays on wages ('variable capital').

As capital accumulates, Marx famously argues there is a tendency for the stock of constant capital to grow faster than variable capital. Because the only source of profit is surplus value, and because surplus value is only produced by workers (who are employed in numbers proportional to capitalists' spending on wages) there is a tendency for the rate of profit to fall over time.[14] In this way, Marx takes a premise which he shares with classical political economy – that labour is the only source of new value – and shows how it leads to a better explanation for falling profit rates; replacing what he calls Ricardo's retreat into 'organic chemistry' with an analysis of how capital accumulation unintentionally changes social relations. Marx attaches great significance to this explanation. In the *Grundrisse*, he calls it 'the most important law of modern political economy, and the most essential for understanding the most difficult relations' because it can explain why economic crises must necessarily recur under capitalism.[15]

The classical political economists did not identify the link between the falling rate of profit and economic crises. Like the neoclassicals today, they subscribed to versions of the dogma that the market is inherently self-correcting and harmonious. The most well-known of these has become known as 'Say's Law': the idea that 'supply creates its own demand', as Keynes summarised it.[16] Ricardo holds a soft version of this doctrine, which leads him to rule out the possibility of any prolonged general inability to sell output.[17] In its hardest version, Say's Law can be taken to mean that because every purchase is also a sale, total purchases must always be equal to total sales – and therefore even momentary crises are impossible.

Marx's critique of Say's Law is the starting point for his analysis of crises. He points out that although it is true that every purchase for one person is a sale for another, every transaction is an exchange of a commodity *for money* (excluding barter). During a crisis, the immediate problem is that there are many who want to exchange their commodities for money ('sellers'), but relatively few who want to exchange their money for commodities ('buyers'). That is, people

13   Marx 1973, p. 753.
14   Marx 1981, pp. 317–38.
15   Marx 1981, p. 749.
16   Keynes 1936, pp. 18–19.
17   Ricardo 2001, pp. 209–16.

hold onto their money, and unsold commodities pile up. As Marx stresses, this is only a *description* of what a crisis is: it only shows that 'the possibility of crises' is inherent in the form of the commodity. It does not say *why* they occur.[18]

At the next level of concreteness, Marx argues

> the ultimate reason for all real crises always remains the poverty and restricted consumption of the masses, in the face of the drive of capitalist production to develop the productive forces as if only the absolute consumption capacity of society set a limit to them.[19]

This looks like evidence that Marx is an 'underconsumptionist': i.e. that he thinks the cause of crises is low wages. But as Marx understood, 'the poverty and restricted consumption of the masses' is a *permanent* feature of capitalism, and does not explain why reproduction sometimes proceeds more or less 'smoothly', and at other times collapses into crisis.

Like the critique of Say's Law, the masses' restricted consumption explains one of the conditions that make crises *possible* under capitalism. During a crisis, there are too many sellers and not enough buyers, so commodities pile up unsold, and factories go idle. At such moments, production and consumption fall well short of the 'absolute consumption capacity of society'. If *that* set the only limit to the development of the productive forces, there would be no crisis. Here Marx is polemicising against the view that such crises are due to an *absolute* excess of productive capital (i.e. an excess relative to need), rather than an excess in relation to the *capacity* and (for the wealthier) *willingness* to buy output.

In *Capital* II, where Marx examines the reproduction process in most detail, he forcefully repudiates underconsumptionism:

> It is a pure tautology to say that crises are provoked by a lack of effective demand or effective consumption. The capitalist system does not recognise any forms of consumer other than those who can pay, if we exclude the consumption of paupers and swindlers. The fact that commodities are unsaleable means no more than that no effective buyers have been found for them, i.e. no consumers (no matter whether the commodities are ultimately sold to meet the needs of productive or individual consumption). If the attempt is made to give this tautology the semblance of

---

18   Marx 1976, pp. 208–9.
19   Marx 1981, p. 615.

greater profundity, by the statement that the working class receives too small a portion of its own product, and that the evil would be remedied if it received a bigger share, i.e. if its wages rose, we need only note that crises are always prepared by a period in which wages generally rise, and the working class actually does receive a greater share of the part of the annual product destined for consumption. From the standpoint of these advocates of sound and 'simple' (!) common sense, such periods should rather avert the crisis. It thus appears that capitalist production involves certain conditions independent of people's good or bad intentions, which permit the relative prosperity of the working class only temporarily, and moreover always as a harbinger of crisis.[20]

Marx's *own* crisis theory is the LTFRP. Whereas bourgeois political economy tended to see the declining rate of profit as a gradual slide into stasis, Marx argues it is an unstable process that brings about its own negation. To show why, he considers an extreme, hypothetical case of an 'absolute overproduction of capital'; a situation in which 'no further additional capital could be employed for the purpose of capitalist production', i.e. to produce additional surplus value. At this point any new capital must compete for a share of a fixed or even declining mass of profits. This would happen when the working population could not supply any more labour time (full employment) and the rate of surplus value could not be increased in the short-term (as Marx points out, these two conditions go together: if there is full employment then it is difficult for capitalists to push down wages). Again, note that Marx is considering an extreme case for illustrative purposes: in reality, absolute full employment never happens under capitalism.[21]

The full employment assumption implies that the new capital can only begin to operate by employing existing workers, meaning that 'one portion of the capital would lie completely or partially idle'. For the old capital, this would mean a decline in the mass of surplus value appropriated, since some of the fixed mass of surplus value is now appropriated by the new capital. That is, '[t]he valorization of the old capital would have experienced an absolute decline'. Marx argues 'this kind of actual devaluation of the old capital would not take place without a struggle' over which portion of the existing capital is to lie idle. The resolution of the crisis, and the return to a '"healthy" movement of capitalist production' then depends on the *devaluation* of capital restoring the

---

20   Marx 1978b, pp. 486–7.
21   Marx 1981, p. 360.

rate of profit (a process which is the focus of Chapter 2). Marx also discusses how the stagnation in production associated with the crisis leads to unemployment, declining wages and hence a rising rate of surplus value. This 'prepares the ground for a later expansion of production – within the capitalist limits.'[22]

Farjoun and Machover provide an alternative but complementary account of the link between the falling rate of profit and economic crises. They point out that because the tendency for the rate of profit to equalise across industries and enterprises is never realised completely in practice, there will always be variation in the rates of profit made by different firms. This means that when the average rate of profit falls, some firms' rates of profit may become negative, or at least fall low enough that they cannot meet payments on their debt. This creates the possibility of a credit crisis, a slump in investment, and/or a recession.[23]

1.3   *The Significance of the LTFRP*

This link between the falling rate of profit and economic crises is a crucial aspect of Marx's historical materialism, and one that has been under-appreciated by Marxists. In the *Grundrisse*, Marx argues this explanation of crisis makes the LTFRP 'the most important law from the *historical* standpoint' because it explains how capitalism becomes a fetter on the further development of the forces of production:

> The growing incompatibility between the productive development of society and its hitherto existing relations of production expresses itself in bitter contradictions, crises, spasms. The violent destruction of capital not by relations external to it, but rather as a condition of its self-preservation, is the most striking form in which advice is given it to be gone and to give room to a higher state of social production.[24]

In his *Law of the Accumulation and Breakdown of the Capitalist System*, Henryk Grossman explains how the falling rate of profit expresses this contradiction quite directly. Under any mode of production, the development of human productivity can be expressed by the quantity of means of production, M, set in motion by the expenditure of each unit of human labour power, L. Under capitalism, this growth takes the specific form of a growth in the value composition of capital (the ratio of c to v). According to Marx's law, it is precisely growth in

---

22   Marx 1981, pp. 360–4.
23   Farjoun and Machover 1983, pp. 163–6.
24   Marx 1973, pp. 749–50, emphasis added.

this ratio which pushes down the rate of profit and necessitates a crisis: i.e. it is precisely capitalism's success at developing human productivity which brings its continued reproduction into crisis.[25]

The LTFRP is also the basis for an argument in favour of socialism. Without it, we can still observe from experience that economic crises have been a recurrent feature of capitalism, as Marx and Engels do in the Manifesto.[26] But this does not explain whether they will occur in the future, or how this might be prevented. If, for example, the real cause of a particular crisis is not the falling rate of profit, but low wages, this suggests that the crisis could be overcome on terms favourable to the working class if it fought for higher wages alone. Similarly, if the underlying cause is financial speculation, the solution to the crisis is to reform the financial system. In both cases, the fight for socialism becomes a kind of 'added extra': a fight which may be worth pursuing for moral reasons, but which is not necessary in order to avert future crises and allow for the unfettered development of the productive forces. As Grossman puts it, 'we abandon the materialist basis of a scientific argument for the necessity of socialism, the deduction of this necessity from the economic movement'.[27]

However, the most important 'non-coercive' mechanism through which capitalist social relations are reproduced today is the pressure to make a profit. If profit rates are high, this can suggest a certain 'breathing space' exists for reforms to be won within the system, according to a certain strategy. Specifically, it suggests that there is plenty of surplus value available for a left-wing government to appropriate and spend on improving workers' living standards and nationalising the means of production. It also suggests that state- or worker-controlled industries could co-exist with other capitalist firms without coming under strong pressure to increase productivity and keep wages low, because their margins would be large enough to accommodate this. But if the average profit rate is low, this suggests that major reforms that rely exclusively on redistribution either would be impossible, or, if they were implemented, they would throw the capitalist economy into crisis. In other words, it suggests that major reforms of this type won by the workers' movement would not last long while capitalism continues to exist.

However, this does not rule out the possibility of winning and holding major reforms tailored to address a reality of low profit rates: specifically, reforms that simultaneously improved workers' living standards and that reduced waste created by capitalist relations of production (along with redistributing profit to

---

25   Grossman 1992, pp. 29–34.
26   Engels and Marx1976b, pp. 489–90.
27   Grossman 1992, p. 56.

workers). If it is done effectively, economic planning could be used to reduce or eliminate waste due to disproportions and as a manifestation of crises, and serve as a step towards achieving socialism. This requires a theory that not only accurately describes the causes of economic crises in general terms, but also can be used for detailed empirical analysis.

As the workers' movement seems a long way from completing a socialist revolution, the relevance of these strategic dilemmas can seem limited. It can also be tempting to think that the political and moral arguments for socialism will suffice, without the need for their economic counterpart. The Bolsheviks, for example, led a workers' revolution without a clear understanding of the tendency of the rate of profit to fall or value theory. But after they took power this was a significant liability. For example, with the isolation of the revolution there was an extensive debate over how long they would need to 'hold out' before the next crisis hit the advanced economies, which would have benefitted from a better understanding of the LTFRP.[28]

Crisis theory is also intimately related to Marxist theories of imperialism. In the early twentieth century, arguments over political economy often took the form of a contest between underconsumptionist theories (e.g. Kautsky, Luxemburg, Varga and Stalin) and theories that began from the unevenness and disproportionality of capitalist development (e.g. Hilferding and Trotsky); and the various theories of imperialism constructed at this time were formed on variations of either of these foundations.[29] A better understanding of *Marx's* crisis theory and movements in the rate of profit may prove a more fruitful starting point for a contemporary Marxist theory of imperialism.

If used properly, an analysis of movements in profit rates is also perennially important for understanding the *current* state of the capitalist economy and how it is likely to change: that is, for developing *perspectives*. Even for small groups of socialists, political activity that is informed by accurate perspectives is much more likely to be well-directed and successful.

1.4   *Interpreting Marx's Law*

There is debate over what Marx means by a 'tendency' for the rate of profit to fall. This debate is important, because in order to test *Marx's* law, we must first accurately interpret it.

Essentially there are three positions. The most widely held is the simplest: that Marx's law predicts that, over the long term, the average rate of profit will

---

28   Day 1981.
29   Day 1981, pp. 1–39.

tend to fall. Most versions of this interpretation allow for some variation in the rate of profit over the short-term.

In one of the first attempts to test the law using statistical data, Gillman adopts this position. He argues that Marx distinguishes between cyclical movements in the rate of profit, which can be caused by a range of factors, and a long-term 'secular decline', to which the law refers. According to Gillman, this is how, for Marx, the law is supposed to explain why economic crises not only occur and recur, but tend to intensity over time.[30]

Anwar Shaikh adopts a similar interpretation. He proposes a tendency for what he calls the 'basic' rate of profit to decline over the history of capitalism. His 'basic' rate of profit is what the rate of profit would be if fixed assets were used at full capacity. He argues that this basic rate will fall even during boom years.[31] This is a potentially interesting hypothesis, but Shaikh does not demonstrate that it is an implication of *Marx's* LTFRP; which, as we will see below, incorporates the claim that the rate of profit recovers after crises.[32]

Sweezy also adopts the secular decline interpretation of the law, but argues that Marx fails to show that this would occur in practice. In particular, he argues that Marx never manages to show why a rising rate of surplus value could not prevent the rate of profit from falling over the long term. Another way of putting his point is that Marx failed to show that increases in the rate of surplus value are a mere counteracting factor and not the over-riding *tendency*.[33]

Heinrich has recently revived a version of this argument, but goes one step further. He argues that, for Marx, 'the increase in the rate of surplus-value as a result of an increase in productivity is not one of the "counteracting factors", but is rather one of the conditions under which the law as such is supposed to be derived.' So, according to Heinrich, even if we grant Marx the assumption that the counteracting tendencies have no effect, Marx still failed to show that 'in the long term ... the rate of profit must fall'. We will address this criticism below.[34]

In their polemic against Heinrich, Kliman et al. argue that this objection is based on a misinterpretation of Marx's law. They argue that Marx's law 'is not a *prediction* of what must inevitably happen, but an *explanation* of what does happen'.[35] Specifically, they argue Marx's law says that

---

30   Gillman 1957, pp. 5–6.
31   Shaikh 1992, pp. 176–9.
32   Mage also subscribes to the secular decline interpretation: Mage 1963, p. 111.
33   Sweezy 1949b, pp. 101–5.
34   Heinrich 2013.
35   Kliman et al. 2013, p. 4.

the capitalist mode of development of the forces of production – accumu-
lation of capital accompanied by labour-saving technical change that in-
creases productivity – is the dominant cause, in the long run, of the fall in the
rate of profit. The rate of profit falls only under particular circumstances,
and it can fall for other reasons, such as rising wage rates, but if and when
it does exhibit a long-term decline, the capitalist mode of development
of the forces of production is the dominant cause of that decline.[36]

This turns the secular decline interpretation on its head. According to this interpretation, rather than predicting that the rate of profit will fall in the future,
Marx's law *as such* explains why the rate of profit falls *in the case that* it falls. It
follows that if the rate of profit rises, this does not count as evidence against this
version of 'Marx's law'. Periods of a rising rate of profit would simply be outside
the domain of explanation of the law as such. If we wanted to find evidence to
try to refute this version of 'Marx's law', we would have to find cases in which
the rate of profit exhibits a 'long-term decline', but establish that it fell for some
reason other than the accumulation of capital accompanied by labour-saving
technical change.

Thus on Kliman et al.'s interpretation, Marx's LTFRP is a much less ambi-
tious hypothesis than it is usually understood to be. As Carchedi and Roberts
point out, it says precisely nothing about whether economic crises are likely
to continue to occur under capitalism, because it says nothing about whether
the rate of profit is likely to fall in future.[37] Based on other work they have published, Kliman and Freeman clearly also do believe that recurrent crises *are*
likely under capitalism, and that the rate of profit *is* likely to fall, but according
to their interpretation these are not predictions of Marx's 'law as such'.[38]

In response to this interpretation, it is first necessary to point out that
whether or not Marx's law *itself* incorporates a prediction, Marx *does* say,
more than once, that the rate of profit *actually tends to fall.* For example, after
presenting a numerical example in which the rate of profit falls as the ratio of
constant to variable capital rises, Marx says '[t]he hypothetical series we constructed at the opening of this chapter therefore expresses the actual tendency
of capitalist production'.[39] He also says: '[a]s the capitalist mode of production
develops, so the rate of profit falls, while the mass of profit rises together with

36   Kliman et al. 2013, p. 5, their emphasis.
37   Carchedi and Roberts 2013a.
38   Kliman 2011; Freeman 2012.
39   Marx 1981, p. 318.

the increasing mass of capital applied'.[40] Moreover, Marx *must be* committed to the proposition that the rate of profit tends to fall over at least some time period if it is to be a useful basis for a theory of crises. So, whether or not we consider this proposition part of what they call the 'law as such', it needs to be true for their 'law as such' to have any relevance. It is therefore difficult to understand why Kliman et al. attach so much importance to this particular interpretative issue.

Moreover, if Marx *had* wanted to insist that the claim that the rate of profit actually tends to fall is not a part of his law of the tendential fall in the rate of profit, then surely he would have explained this quite specific use of language very carefully and transparently, even when writing a draft manuscript. The fact that he does not do so strongly favours the interpretation that the law itself incorporates the prediction that the rate of profit actually tends to fall.

However, there is also the question of the length of time over which the law applies. Reuten and Thomas argue Marx does not advance a single, coherent position on this question. In the *Grundrisse*, Marx holds the position that the rate of profit falls over the long term, which they see as a 'naturalistic' inheritance from classical political economy. Later, especially in the manuscripts that become *Capital* III, they argue Marx adopts a cyclical interpretation: that the rate of profit falls in the lead up to crises, and rises afterwards. They even suggest Marx could have replaced the name he himself chooses for his law in Volume 3 ('the law of the tendential fall in the rate of profit') with the 'theory of the rate of profit cycle'.[41]

As we have seen, there is nothing 'naturalistic' about Marx's position in the *Grundrisse*; it is precisely in the *Grundrisse* that Marx develops an explanation for the falling rate of profit in terms of social relations and pours scorn on Ricardo's retreat to 'organic chemistry'.

Reuten and Thomas' claim that Marx 'reformulates' his law is similarly thin. In fact, in both the *Grundrisse* and *Capital* III, it is clear that Marx thinks there is both a tendency for the rate of profit to fall as capitalism develops, *and* that there is a cyclical movement. As Reuten and Thomas acknowledge, the idea that crises allow the rate of profit to recover by devaluing capital is already present in the *Grundrisse*, alongside the idea that the rate of profit nevertheless tends to fall in the long term:

---

40   Marx 1981, p. 356.
41   Reuten and Thomas 2011.

These contradictions, of course, lead to explosions, crises, in which momentary suspension of all labour and annihilation of a great part of the capital violently lead it back to the point where it is enabled [to go on] fully employing its productive powers without committing suicide. Yet, these regularly recurring catastrophes lead to their repetition on a higher scale, and finally to its violent overthrow.[42]

In *Capital* III Marx repeats both positions. In the sections discussing the law itself, it is true that he focuses on the cyclical movement:

The devaluation of the elements of constant capital, moreover, itself involves a rise in the profit rate. The mass of constant capital applied grows as against the variable, but the value of this mass may have fallen. The stagnation in production that has intervened prepares the ground for a later expansion of production – within the capitalist limits.
    And so we go round the whole circle once again.[43]

But elsewhere in the Volume 3 manuscripts, he maintains the position that the rate of profit tends to fall with the development of the productive forces. Note also that Marx refers to the rate of profit in a single country:

Since we have seen that *the level of the profit rate stands in inverse proportion to the development of capitalist production*, it follows that the higher or lower rate of interest in a country stands in the same inverse proportion to the level of industrial development, particularly in so far as the variation in the rate of interest expresses an actual variation in the profit rate.[44]

Are these two positions consistent? First note that the passage immediately above is not exactly equivalent to a 'declining trend' position. The development of capitalist production does not necessarily proceed in a linear fashion in a single country over time. Even on a world scale, the development of the forces

---

42   Marx 1973, p. 750.
43   Marx 1981, pp. 363–4.
44   Marx 1981, p. 481, emphasis added. This passage was not added into *Capital* III by Engels, it comes directly from the original manuscript: 'Da man gesehn, daß die Höhe der Profitrate in umgekehrtem Verhältniß zur Entwicklung der capitalistischen Production steht, folgt daher, daß höhrer oder niedrer Zinsfuß in einem Lande dasselbe umgekehrte Verhältniß zum Stand der industriellen Entwicklung hat – so weit die Verschiedenheit des Zinses wirklich Verschiedenheit der Profitrate ausdrückt' (Marx 1992, pp. 432–3).

of production can stagnate due to economic slumps or could even, in theory, be sent backwards for a time. But as long as the development of the productive forces *does* recover the rate of profit should have a tendency to fall over the long term, according to Marx's formulation.

A possible problem with this position is that, as Kliman argues, a severe crisis could in theory devalue so much capital that afterwards the rate of profit rises to a new high.[45] If this did not coincide with the physical destruction of the forces of production (or, at least, if it did not coincide with very much destruction), then both the rate of profit and the level of capitalist development might reach all-time highs after the crisis. Then, even if the profit rate recommenced its 'ordinary' rate of decline, this may not lead to a falling trend over the long term. Another crisis might then be triggered that allowed the rate of profit to recover to a level up to or exceeding the previous high. Under such a scenario, the rate of profit rate might indeed move in a cycle with no secular trend, or even have an upward trend. We will deal with this objection in the next chapter.

In any case, there is no *inconsistency* between Marx's positions that the rate of profit tends to fall as capitalism develops and that devaluation causes it to move cyclically. Together, they imply a 'downward spiral' interpretation of Marx's law. This is the version of the law this work will test.

Though both are testable propositions, the cyclical movement is easier to investigate, because it does not require data stretching across the whole history of capitalism. Note that Marx's theory does not predict just *any* cyclical movement in the rate of profit; it predicts that the rate of profit will fall in the lead up to crises, and recover with the destruction or devaluation of capital.[46] Arguably this is the most important aspect of Marx's law, because it forms the most immediate basis for his explanation of crises. So the main focus of the work will be on testing this proposition. However, Chapter 7 also uses less reliable data to investigate whether there is a long-term downward trend in the rate of profit, and whether this is also reflected in a long-term tendency for the rate of interest to decline.

In both cases we will look at US data only. This is mainly to keep the scope of the work manageable. But it also raises the question of whether Marx's law applies to the rate of profit in a single country. Some argue that, in theory, Marx's law applies to the average rate of profit across the world as a whole.[47]

---

45   Kliman 2011, pp. 25–6.
46   As is discussed in Chapter 5, this must also be distinguished from Marx's theory of the business cycle, which covers a shorter time period.
47   Roberts 2012.

Estimates of the average rate of profit in a single country would therefore only express the effects of Marx's law imperfectly.

However, in his list of counteracting factors, Marx includes 'foreign trade'.[48] We also saw above that Marx himself refers to the relationship between the rate of profit and the level of development in a single country. This raises some difficult questions which Marx does not address: to what extent do rates of profit equalise across borders? How do we account for international transfers of surplus value? Chapter 4 discusses these a little further, but they cannot be addressed properly in the context of a study of the average rate of profit in the US alone.

2   Criticisms of the Law

2.1   *Indeterminacy*

As mentioned, Sweezy and Heinrich object that Marx does not conclusively demonstrate that the effect of the rising organic composition of capital will tend to outweigh the effect of the rising rate of surplus value. At various stages in his argument it is true that Marx assumes away the effect of the rising rate of surplus value, in order to focus on other aspects of movements in the profit rate.[49] But elsewhere in *Capital*, especially in Volume 1, Marx argues there is a tendency for the rate of surplus value to rise.[50] Moreover, it is important for Marx to at least show that it is *probable* that the effect of the rising organic composition of capital will outweigh the effect of a rising rate of surplus value, otherwise there is no basis for his prediction that the rate of profit tends to fall.

Although it is not developed at length, Marx sets out the essentials of this argument. Whereas, in previous examples, Marx has assumed that the rate of surplus value is constant, in the section of Volume 3, Chapter 15 ('Development of the Law's Internal Contradictions') headed 'The Conflict Between the Extension of Production and Valorization', he points out that 'the development of productivity ... takes a double form – firstly, there is an increase in surplus labour, i.e. a shortening of necessary labour-time, the time required for the reproduction of labour-power; secondly, there is a decline in the total amount of labour-power (number of workers) applied to set a given capital in motion.'[51] The first is what Marx calls the production of relative surplus value; the second

---

48   Marx 1981, pp. 344–7.
49   Marx 1981, p. 318.
50   Marx 1976, pp. 429–636.
51   Marx 1981, p. 355.

is an expression of the rising value composition of capital. He argues their combined effect on the rate of profit will be the following:

> In so far as the development of productivity reduces the paid portion of the labour applied, it increases surplus-value by lifting its rate; but in so far as it reduces the total quantity of labour applied by a given capital, it reduces the number by which the rate of surplus-value has to be multiplied in order to arrive at its mass. Two workers working for 12 hours a day could not supply the same surplus-value as 24 workers each working 2 hours, even if they were able to live on air and hence scarcely needed to work at all for themselves. In this connection, therefore, the compensation of the reduced number of workers provided by a rise in the level of exploitation of labour has certain limits that cannot be overstepped; this can certainly check the fall in the profit rate, but it cannot cancel it out.[52]

To understand this argument, we first need to explain what Marx means by 'a given capital'. When explaining movements in the average rate of profit, Marx often considers what they would mean for a single, representative capital of value 100 with an average value composition of capital, average rate of surplus value and average rate of profit. Above, Marx considers what happens when the number of workers employed by this average, given capital falls from 24 to 2: i.e. if the ratio of capital advanced to workers grows 12 times larger. In this case, Marx points out that even if we assume each worker initially produces only two hours of surplus value each day, implying a very low initial rate of surplus value, this still gives a total of 48 hours surplus labour. Unless they did not need to eat or sleep, there is no way that two workers could ever supply that much surplus labour. Even if they worked 12 hours a day and 'lived on air' (i.e. earned zero wages, implying an 'infinite' rate of surplus value), they would still only supply 24 hours of surplus labour, and the rate of profit would fall by half.

The underlying reason for this is, as Marx says, that the ratio of capital advanced to hours worked can rise indefinitely, whereas the surplus value that a given worker can supply in a day has absolute limits. Shaikh shows that this means '[f]or *any* combination of rates of rise of s/v and C/l [where 'l' is employment], one can easily show that the basic rate of profit [i.e. the ROP assuming full capacity utilisation] will inevitably fall'.[53]

---

52   Marx 1981, pp. 355–6.
53   Shaikh 1992, pp. 177–8.

This does not *guarantee* that the rate of profit will fall over any given time period. If we assumed a sufficiently slow rate of increase in the ratio of capital advanced to workers, then a rising rate of surplus value could make possible a rising rate of profit over 100 years, 500 years, or any time period we choose, with the inevitable fall coming afterwards. But Marx clearly comes to the reasonable conclusion that such cases are unlikely to occur in practice: i.e. that the rate of profit will tend to fall over time periods that are relevant.[54]

Similarly, there is no *guarantee* that the ratio of capital advanced to workers will increase over time. Marx conjectures that it will, but he acknowledges 'counteracting factors'. In particular, as will be discussed in Chapter 3, the effects of the cheapening constant capital due to technical progress and the shortening turnover time of variable capital tend to push up the rate of profit; and again, in the abstract, we could construct examples in which this outweighs the effect of a rising OCC.

But again, the fact that Marx never *proves* that the effect of the rising OCC must generally outweigh these counteracting factors does not imply that movements in the rate of profit are 'indeterminate'. It is impossible to prove, *a priori*, that the rate of profit *must* fall over any given period. All Marx could establish was that it was *likely* that the tendency of the rate of profit to fall explained crises in the past, based on the combination of the limited evidence available to him and his own attempt to understand the most important tendencies of capitalist development; and that it was *likely* that this would lead to future crises.

Indeed, this is all we can reasonably expect from practically *any* proposition in the social sciences. If it were possible to predict the future with certainty there would be no point in doing so. Ultimately, then, the validity of the law can only be decided with reference to statistical evidence. However, this evidence must be arranged and interpreted in a fashion as consistent as possible with Marx's system. The next criticism we will consider concerns that system as a whole.

2.2   *The Transformation Problem*

As mentioned above, the transformation problem has done considerable damage to the credibility of Marx's value theory, on which the LTFRP is based. It has also spawned an enormous literature. Here we will confine ourselves to outlining the problem itself, and discussing how the allegations of internal inconsistency made against Marx's solution to it have been shown to be false.

---

54   Marx 1981, pp. 341–2.

A version of the transformation problem is implicit in Ricardo, and Marx examines it in *Theories of Surplus Value*.[55] The general problem is how to reconcile the idea that labour is the source of value with the equalisation of profit rates across firms and industries.

For *Marx's* value theory, the problem takes the following specific form. The value of a commodity is the socially necessary labour time (SNLT) necessary to produce it. Capitalists are able to make profits because one particular kind of commodity – human labour power – can produce more value than it costs to reproduce and purchase. Workers also need material to work with. This is the product of past human exertion (what Marx calls 'dead labour') combined with natural resources. Marx argues that these materials only pass on the value of the SNLT that they embody – they do not create new value. So the only source of surplus value is 'living labour': i.e. the new productive labour performed over a given period.

If labour values directly determined prices, as Marx mostly assumes in *Capital* I, and the surplus value produced by workers in each branch of industry therefore directly determined profits in that branch, then branches with a below average ratio of constant to variable capital would make above average rates of profit. However, if this were true in practice, the situation would not last long. Seeing the above average rates of profit on offer, capitalists would focus their new investments on branches with relatively low compositions of capital, and output in these branches would therefore grow relatively fast. At prices equal to values this would lead to an oversupply of the commodities produced by these branches, and these capitalists would be forced to lower their selling prices, while the reverse would be true in branches with relatively high value compositions. This means there is a tendency for prices to move towards levels at which they equalise rates of profit across branches. Marx calls these 'prices of production'.[56]

Marx illustrates the problem using a numerical example. He assumes five different branches of production, each with different compositions of capital, but with the same rate of surplus value. His first two tables show that, if commodities sell at prices equal to their values, then the branches with higher compositions of capital will earn lower rates of profit than branches with lower compositions.[57]

Then he shows how this situation would be altered if the total surplus value were instead distributed among branches such that their rates of profit

55   Marx 1951, pp. 249–50.
56   Marx 1981, pp. 241–53.
57   Marx 1981, p. 255.

were equal. In this case, the commodities produced by the capitals of higher than average composition would sell for prices higher than their values, and the commodities produced by the capitals of lower than average composition would sell for prices lower than their values; that is, these prices would effect a transfer of value from the lower composition capitals to the capitals with higher compositions. If actual prices are equal to these prices of production, then '[t]he various different capitals here are in the position of shareholders in a joint-stock company' – i.e. each capitalist appropriates profits in proportion to the capital they advance, and not profits equal to the surplus value produced by the workers they employ.[58]

In his numerical example, Marx takes the values of the capital advanced by each branch of production to be known data. Specifically, he assumes that inputs are purchased at their *values*, but outputs are sold at their prices of production. This solution to the transformation problem has been a constant source of controversy since it was published.[59] Here we will outline the strongest and most influential objection to it, that of Ladislaus von Bortkiewicz, and how TSSI Marxists have refuted it.

Bortkiewicz's critique tries to show that Marx's transformation procedure suffers from 'internal contradictions', because it is incompatible with simple reproduction.[60] To do this, Bortkiewicz relies on two false premises. The first is that Marx's example assumes simple reproduction. In fact Marx never says this, so technically Bortkiewicz's attempt to demonstrate internal contradictions falls at the first hurdle. Nevertheless, for Marx's transformation procedure to be valid generally, it should be possible to use it to construct examples that *are* compatible with simple reproduction, so we cannot dismiss the issue this easily.

Bortkiewicz's second false premise is the real source of the difficulties Marxists have had with the transformation problem. Under the influence of the emerging school of equilibrium economics, *Bortkiewicz* imposes the condition on *Marx's* procedure that input prices are equal to output prices. That is, he makes it a condition that prices do not change over time.

Taken together, these premises are equivalent to demanding that Marx's transformation procedure conform to the standards of an equilibrium model of prices. Bortkiewicz recognises that this is foreign to Marx's approach, which he sees himself as 'correcting':

---

58   Marx 1981, pp. 256–8.
59   For histories of this controversy, see Kliman 2007, pp. 41–54 and Freeman 2010b.
60   Bortkiewicz 1952, p. 9.

Marx always proceeds *arithmetically*: he assumes certain quantities to be known and deduces from them, by a series of successive operations, the unknowns which interest him ...

[T]he Marxian method rest[s] on an unfounded view of the character of economic relations. Alfred Marshall once said of Ricardo 'He does not state clearly ... how, in the problem of normal value, the various elements govern one another *mutually*, and not *successively* in a long chain of causation.' This description applies even more to Marx ...

Modern economics is beginning to free itself gradually from the successivist prejudice, the chief merit being due to the mathematical school led by Léon Walras.[61]

However, there is no reason to consider Marx's successivist procedure a 'prejudice' in need of 'correction'. It simply amounts to the idea that one thing causes another in a temporal sequence: that prices paid for inputs today will affect the prices and values of the output they are used to produce in the future.

It is in fact Bortkiewicz's alternative starting point that rests on an unfounded view of the character of economic relations. In reality, prices change over time. Imposing an equilibrium model of price and value determination onto this reality effectively implies that the prices and values of inputs today are *retroactively determined* by the prices and values of outputs produced and sold in the future. Bortkiewicz and other equilibrium theorists are entitled to construct models on this basis if they want to: after all, it is impossible to construct any theory without making some simplifying assumptions. However, they are *not* entitled to require that *Marx's* theory share their unrealistic abstraction, and declare it inconsistent for failing to do so. This is setting up and knocking down a straw man. As we will see, the (probably unintentional) genius of Bortkiewicz's article is that not only does he make his straw man look so convincing that even Marxists have confused it for the real thing, after knocking it down he kindly offers us a 'corrected' version which some Marxists decided to adopt.

This 'correction' is deeply flawed. By imposing the conditions that input prices are equal to output prices, and that input values are equal to output values, Bortkiewicz creates two separate systems of simultaneous equations: a value system and a price system. This makes the value of a commodity proportional to both the labour time spent producing it *and its constant capital inputs*,

---

61   Bortkiewicz 1952, pp. 23–4.

stretching back to inputs that are 'wholly the result of direct labour'.[62] It follows that the value of one commodity relative to another is in no way determined by the price system. From this starting point, it is only possible to maintain one of Marx's two aggregate equalities: that the total price of output is equal to its total value, or that total profit is equal to total surplus value. Imposing both creates an internal inconsistency.

Bortkiewicz and many Marxists after him think this is a problem with Marx's theory. In fact it only demonstrates that Marx's theory is inconsistent with Bortkiewicz's equilibrium approach. In other words, Bortkiewicz's attempt to show that Marx's *non*-equilibrium approach is *internally* inconsistent fails because it smuggles in Bortkiewicz's own equilibrium assumption. There is also something quite arbitrary about the way in which Bortkiewicz relates his value system to his price system. Values do not do any real explanatory work: some aggregate of values is just deemed to be equal to some aggregate of prices. As Kliman observes, many 'solutions' to the transformation problem take just this form, often accompanied with textual evidence for why Marx thought that their favoured aggregate equality was more important than the others.[63]

When he republished Bortkiewicz's critique in English translation, Sweezy presented it as a vindication of Marx's theory. He argued that Bortkiewicz's purpose was to eliminate 'relatively superficial errors ... to show that the core of [Marx's] system was sound'.[64] The form of his 'solution' then became the basis for the simultaneous, dual system interpretation that dominated Marxist economics for most of the twentieth century, and still remains influential today.

For example, Anwar Shaikh and Ahmet Tonak base their detailed procedure for converting national accounts into Marxist categories on this type of interpretation. For Shaikh and Tonak, every commodity has a value and a price. Value is the number of average socially necessary labour hours that would be necessary to replace the commodity, and price is the amount of money paid for the commodity. Fixed constant capital passes on value based on its depreciation rate multiplied by the number of labour hours it would take to replace it under current technology. For them, unlike Marx, value is always measured in labour hours (or weeks, years, etc.), and price in currency.[65]

Under this interpretation, the transformation problem is presented as an empirical question: to what extent is there variation in prices that is not ex-

62   Bortkiewicz 1952, p. 18.
63   Kliman 2007, pp. 160–1.
64   Sweezy 1949a, pp. xxviii–xxix.
65   Shaikh and Tonak 1994, pp. 78–87.

plained by variation in values? There is no other way to present the problem, since their system of values is not even scaled such that some aggregate of values is equal to some aggregate of prices: the two systems are measured in different units, and are completely separate. Thus they cite studies that find that price and value magnitudes have small absolute average deviations (12% or less) and high correlations, and argue that this demonstrates that the transformation problem is not empirically significant.[66]

But this bears little relationship to Marx's theory. First, as discussed above, the starting point of Marx's transformation procedure is that individual prices do diverge from values, and profits diverge from surplus value for individual capitals, because there is a tendency for rates of profit to equalise across capitals with unequal value compositions. For Marx, this was a real feature of capitalism worth investigating, not just a minor technical question. Shaikh acknowledges that he differs from Marx in this respect.[67]

Second, correlation is a measure of the extent to which two variables move together. Values and prices share a large quantitative component in common: cost price (or cost price and cost value for dual system interpretations). In the controversies over the transformation of values into prices this is generally not disputed. So when we calculate the correlation between values and prices, we should *expect* it to be high, since a large part of the test is picking up on whether both values and prices do in fact share this element. Effectively, this measure of correlation allows dual system proponents to marshal the fact that cost price is a shared element as evidence for their theory, when in fact it is a proposition shared by almost every economic theory. Using two different methods to correct for this, Kliman finds no support for the hypothesis that value per dollar of cost explains variation in price – and, in one model, finds that including this variable (along with costs) actually reduces the predictive power of the model.[68]

This dual system interpretation came under attack in the 1980s. The so-called 'New Interpretation' was one challenger. Under the 'old' dual system interpretation, the price of labour power is the wage, while the value of labour power is the sum of the values of commodities bought by workers to reproduce their labour power. Foley, Duménil and others argue that in fact the wage is equivalent to *both* the value and the price of labour power.[69] This means that the total value of labour power purchased over a year (V) is equal to the wages

---

66   Shaikh and Tonak 1994, pp. 141–4.
67   Shaikh and Tonak 1994, p. 64.
68   Kliman 2007, pp. 200–1.
69   Foley 1982; Duménil 1983.

bill. By then imposing the condition that the sum of surplus value (S) is equal to the sum of profit, the New Interpretation also gets the result that new value added (S + V) is equal to the total price of the net product. However, this is not the same as *Marx's* stipulation that the sum of the prices of *gross* output be equal to the sum of their values.

Single system interpretations take this same idea but apply it to *all* inputs, not just labour power. That is, they assume constant capital also passes on value to output based on its price and not its original value. The equality of the total value and total price of gross output then follows, along with the equality of total surplus value and total profit.

For each individual commodity, however, its price can differ from its value. To understand why, we need to introduce the concept of the Monetary Expression of Labour Time (MELT).[70] This is usually calculated as the ratio of the total price of the net product to total employment or hours worked (though the next chapter discusses how this is modified under a temporal interpretation). It therefore gives a measure of the value added by an 'average' hour of labour time.[71] The value of a commodity can then be defined as the cost of the inputs used up to produce it plus the product of the MELT and average *direct* labour time required to produce the commodity. In general this will be different from the commodity's price.

Single system interpretations have been produced in both temporal and simultaneist variants, and both can be consistent with Marx's two aggregate equalities.[72] This shows that a single system interpretation of Marx's system can in fact deal with the special case in which input prices are equal to output prices: i.e. a single system interpretation does not rule out the possibility of equilibrium prices *a priori*. The distinctive feature of a *temporal* single system interpretation is that it does not impose this condition as an assumption. According to a temporal approach, the value transferred by inputs is based on their price at the time production commences, whether or not this turns out to be equal to prices when outputs are produced.

One strong reason to prefer a temporal approach is that, if we want a value theory that can explain crises, it does not seem very sensible to *assume* equilibrium. Another crucial advantage of the temporal interpretation is that it is the only approach that is consistent with Marx's LTFRP, as will be discussed

---

70   Ramos M. 2004.

71   Ideally this would be a measure of the value added by an hour of *socially necessary* labour time at the average skill level.

72   For simultaneist versions, see Wolff, Roberts, and Callari 1982; Lee 1993; Moseley 1993.

below. But there is also direct textual evidence for a TSSI. Shortly after present-ing his transformation procedure, Marx anticipates Bortkiewicz's objection that he 'fails' to transform the value of inputs into prices of production:

> It was originally assumed that the cost price of a commodity equalled the value of the commodities consumed in its production. But for the buyer of a commodity, it is the price of production that constitutes its cost price and can thus enter into forming the price of another commodity. As the price of production of a commodity can diverge from its value, so the cost price of a commodity, in which the price of production of other commod-ities is involved, can also stand above or below the portion of its total value that is formed by the value of the means of production going into it. It is necessary to bear in mind this modified significance of the cost price, and therefore to bear in mind too that if the cost price of a commodity is equated the value of the means of production used up in producing it, it is always possible to go wrong. Our present investigation does not require us to go into further detail on this point. It still remains correct that the cost price of commodities is always smaller than their value. For even if a commodity's cost price may diverge from the value of the means of pro-duction consumed in it, this error in the past is a matter of indifference to the capitalist. The cost price of the commodity is a given precondi-tion, independent of his, the capitalist's, production, while the result of his production is a commodity that contains surplus-value, and therefore an excess value over and above its cost price.[73]

This passage is usually seen as evidence of sloppiness on Marx's part: that he should have explored the implications of relaxing the assumption that the cost price is equal to the value of inputs used up to produce the commodity, but wrongly thought that this was not a significant issue. In retrospect we can say that if Marx *had* given a numerical example of this sort it would have saved Marxists a great deal of confusion. But in fact Marx does tell us enough to deal with the more general case. He tells us that the result of the capitalist's produc-tion 'is a commodity that contains surplus-value, and therefore an excess value over and above its *cost price*'. That is:

Value of the commodity = surplus value it contains + cost price.

---

73   Marx 1981, pp. 264–5.

This conception of surplus value is only consistent with a single system interpretation. According to a dual system interpretation, he *should* have said that the surplus value of a commodity is an excess over and above the *value of the commodities used to produce it*, i.e.:

Value of the commodity = surplus value it contains + value of inputs (including labour power) used to produce it.

The passage above also supports the view that Marx was a temporalist. Marx tells us '[t]he cost price of the commodity is a given precondition, independent of his, the capitalist's, production'. But if he were a simultaneist, then he should have said that the cost price of the capitalist's inputs is mutually determined with the price of outputs, and not a given precondition.[74]

2.3 *Productivity Improvements and the Rate of Profit*

This section surveys two related criticisms of Marx's explanation of the relationship between productivity improvements and the rate of profit. The first is a common intuitive objection to the LTFRP: if productivity improvements tend to lower the average rate of profit, then why would capitalists choose to introduce them? Marx addresses this issue. His answer is that even though, as a class, capitalists suffer a lower average rate of profit, the individual businesses that are first to introduce a cost-reducing technique benefit from what is now called a 'first mover advantage'. This is because, when the new technique is introduced, the price of output in that branch does not generally fall immediately to the price of production associated with the new technique. For a time, the first movers compete side-by-side with businesses using older, less productive techniques; meaning that, generally, the price of output will remain somewhere between the price of production determined by the older techniques and the price of production determined by the new one.[75] This means the first movers can sell their output above (and potentially well above) their prices of production; so, for a time, they appropriate 'super profits'. These super profits are paid out of surplus value transferred from other businesses.

Note that Marx's explanation here fits easily with a successivist, dynamic approach: the incentive to introduce a new technique depends on there being a period in which profit rates are not equal and prices are not in equilibrium.[76] Moreover, if technological change is more or less continuous, it is likely that

---

74   For more textual evidence in favour of a TSSI, see Kliman 2007, pp. 89–111.

75   See Carchedi 1991, pp. 55–7 for a useful discussion of Marx's theory of price determination.

76   Marx 1981, pp. 373–4.

the 'second movers' will in fact be the 'first movers' to introduce another, still more productive technique when they come to replace their equipment. This would mean that, rather than equalising, each company's profit rate would trace something like the path of a competitor in a downhill leapfrog race: a downward trend punctuated by upward spikes.[77]

The second criticism will we consider is the Okishio Theorem. It claims to show that, assuming no change in the real wage, any technological change that lowers costs per unit cannot lead to a fall in the rate of profit. It will either lead it to increase or to stay the same.[78]

The problem with the Okishio Theorem is its definition of the rate of profit. It is defined such that input prices are equal to output prices: that is, in 'simultaneist' terms. But for any real economy, input prices are never simply equal to output prices. Changing prices are a feature of capitalism; and, crucially, of increases in productivity. It turns out that calculating the rate of profit as though input prices really *are* equal to output prices is equivalent to making an accounting mistake that assumes away the very dynamic of a falling rate of profit followed by devaluation which Marx's law sets out to explain.

For example, suppose a cost-reducing productivity improvement is implemented across the machine-producing sector, and this brings the cost of machines down from $100 at the start of the year to $50 at the end. For owners of existing machines, in a sense this is both good news and bad news. The good news is that when their machines need replacing, this will cost half as much. The bad news is that their existing machines have just halved in value.

A prudent accountant will recognise this as an asset write-down, and charge the change in the value of the machines against both the balance sheet and profits. A less prudent account might hold these machines at their historical cost, ignoring the effect of the change in current prices on both the balance sheet and profits. Only a transparently fraudulent set of accounts would write-down the value of the machines on the balance sheet but fail to charge this loss against profits.

Yet calculating the rate of profit as though input and output prices are equal is equivalent to this third alternative. According to the simultaneist definition of the rate of profit, the stock of capital should be valued at output prices – in this example, $50 – and no charge made against profit for the devaluation of the machines beyond accounting for their ordinary rate of depreciation. The Okishio Theorem is able to 'prove' the profit rate cannot fall because this $50

---

77   Carchedi 1991, pp. 68–90. See Wells 2007 for a comprehensive empirical study of the distribution of rates of profits.

78   Okishio 1961.

loss per machine is subtracted from the denominator of the rate of profit but not from the numerator.

As will be discussed in the next chapter, Marx *did* think that one effect of productivity improvements was to cheapen the elements of existing and newly produced capital advanced. But he conceived of this as a process in time, where capital must first be advanced at the prices prevailing at the start of the production period, and is only devalued when those prices actually change. This difference is crucial, because in reality technological development is a continuous process. In the example above, if there were to be no change in productivity in the second year, then the rate of profit defined in pre-production price terms *would* rise to the same level as the simultaneist 'rate of profit' for the first year (since pre-production prices for the second year are just the output prices of the first year). But for the rate of profit to fall, the law presupposes continual development of the productive forces: i.e. it presupposes continual increases in productivity. When this stops happening, during a slump or a crisis, the law predicts the rate of profit will *rise*.[79]

Using temporal measures of the rate of profit, many numerical and algebraic examples have been given that refute the proposition that cost-reducing technological change can never cause the rate of profit to fall.[80] However, as will be discussed in the next chapter, a problem with these measures of the rate of profit is that they measure fixed assets at *historical cost*. This rescues the idea that productivity improvements can cause the rate of profit to fall at the expense of eliminating the possibility for the devaluation of existing capital to cause it to rise. In the next chapter, we will show that if inputs are instead valued exclusively at pre-production prices, we can allow for the possibilities of both the devaluation of existing capital and a falling rate of profit due to productivity increases.

---

79   After writing this text, I discovered another problem with the Okishio Theorem, the discussion of which so far only exists in draft form. Jones 2018 gives a numerical example in which cost-reducing, labour-saving technical change leads to a decline in the rate of profit even when it is (mis-)measured in simultaneist terms. This shows that even cost-reducing technical change that is not continuous can lead to a rate of profit that falls and then stays lower than initially. This does not eliminate the possibility for the rate of profit to rise as a result of devaluation due to crisis (i.e. a change in relative prices unrelated to technical change), or indeed for certain types of technical change (e.g. of the kind discussed in the text above) that are not continuous to result in a decline followed by an increase in the rate of profit once technical change ceases.

80   Kliman 2011, pp. 127–32; Ernst 1982; Kliman 1988; Freeman and Kliman 2000; Kliman and McGlone 1999.

3   Summary

This chapter has argued that it matters for Marx's historical materialism and socialist strategy whether the rate of profit has a tendency to fall, and that TSSI Marxists have shown that attempts to demonstrate internal inconsistency of Marx's LTFRP have failed. But as the next three chapters will argue, although temporalism must be the starting point for any coherent quantitative interpretation of Marx's value theory, there are problems with the existing interpretations that we need to rectify.

Devaluation

There is a connection between correctly measuring the rate of profit and understanding its dynamics. One key question is how to conceptualise 'devaluation' – that is, the loss of value due to movements in prices. But there is a problem with the way existing temporal interpretations deal with this issue. Kliman, Freeman, Carchedi and Roberts all rely on versions of the idea that the capital stock in the denominator of the rate of profit should be valued at the original prices paid to purchase the assets ('historical cost'). This effectively rules out the possibility that the value of the capital stock inherited from previous years can be affected by falling prices for similar assets, and leads to a situation where assets in the capital stock which are the same (or very similar) but were bought at different times are valued at different prices. Importantly, it rules out the possibility for the rate of profit to recover as a result of writing down capital values due to economic crises.

This chapter shows that a temporal interpretation of Marx's value theory (and hence solving the transformation problem) does not rely on using historical cost valuation. Crucially, the Appendix shows that the *only* reason the Okishio Theorem appears to rule out the possibility of cost-reducing technical change leading to a falling rate of profit is that it is based on mis-measuring profit by valuing inputs at output prices.[1] As long as we do not make this mistake on the numerator of the rate of profit, any of the three plausible methods for valuing the capital stock – historical cost, 'current cost' at input prices, or even 'current cost' at output prices – can allow for the combination of a falling rate of profit and cost-reducing technical change. So there is no reason to rule out Marx's law *a priori*, even if we value the capital stock at current cost, and hence allow for devaluation.

The chapter also shows how to calculate the Monetary Expression of Labour Time (MELT) in a way that is consistent with temporalism. This gives a measure of inflation based on a labour theory of value that avoids the inconsistencies other methods create, and allows us to measure devaluation.

---

1 Though Jones 2018 (draft work) gives another counter-example to the Okishio problem that shows a hitherto unrecognised way in which cost-reducing technical change can lead to a falling rate of profit, even if it is not continuous.

1   Formalisms, Models and Method

Before setting out the counter-example to the Okishio Theorem and the method for measuring devaluation some general discussion of method is necessary. Most of economics revolves around models: systems of equations which take data inputs (independent variables) and turn them into predictions, or dependent variables. Generally, the test of a good model is how well its predictions fit with observations, though models can also play a more theoretical role.[2]

As the last chapter outlined, Marx makes many predictions in *Capital*: e.g. that as the forces of production develop the organic composition of capital will tend to rise, and the rate of profit will tend to fall. Not all of these predictions are necessarily quantifiable but some of them – such as the LTFRP – clearly are or at least should be quantifiable in principle, if they are to have any meaning.

When reading the work of contemporary mainstream economists, we do not expect to encounter any great difficulties deciphering what their models refer to. This is because they generally refer to variables which are already defined under existing statistical frameworks, such as the national accounts, and these have been designed to facilitate the measurement of variables of interest to neoclassical and Keynesian economists.[3] But when reading the classical political economists we have to bear in mind that these frameworks did not exist, and we should not read them back into their work. The lack of a national accounting framework meant the classicals had to either draw on 'common sense' concepts, concepts borrowed from other political economists or accountants, or create their own concepts through which to express their arguments and predictions.

When reading Marx we need to be especially vigilant about clarifying the nature of the concepts he is referring to. As he warns us:

> Vulgar economics actually does nothing more than interpret, systematize and turn into apologetics the notions of agents trapped within bourgeois relations of production. So it should not surprise us that precisely in the estranged form of appearance of economic relations that involves these *prima facie* absurd and complete contradictions – and all science would

---

2   For example, the model in the Appendix is not intended to predict anything, just to show that a certain combination of outcomes is possible.

3   Some more esoteric variables used by neoclassical economics, such as utility, do pose considerable measurement difficulties, but in the case of utility this is a product of the doubtful existence of the 'object' itself.

be superfluous if the form of appearance of things directly coincided with their essence – that precisely here vulgar economics feels completely at home, these relationships appearing all the more self-evident to it, the more their inner connections remain hidden, even though they are comprehensible to the popular mind.[4]

One way to express the problem of clarifying concepts (as it relates to quantifiable phenomena) is that before we can formulate models and predictions, we first need an accounting framework within which to express models and predictions. This is what Freeman terms a 'formalism'.[5] Unlike a model, a formalism itself does not imply testable hypotheses or make predictions, but gives a conceptual 'language' through which models can be constructed, predictions made and results reported.

For example, Shaikh and Tonak's *Measuring the Wealth of Nations* includes both a Marx-inspired model and a Marx-inspired formalism. Their formalism gives a method for, among other things, calculating the SNLT embodied in different types of output according to a simultaniest definition, which they call the *value* of the commodity.[6] This is not a prediction which can be tested, just a method for transforming the national accounts into a set of observations. They then investigate how closely these observations fit with a particular *model*: specifically, that prices tend to be proportional to their measures of values.[7] This model is often thought to constitute Marx's theory of value (though in fact Marx's discussion of the transformation of values into prices of production specifically repudiates this).

Veneziani criticises the TSSI for *assuming* that Marx's aggregate equalities are true, rather than constructing a model which yields these equalities as predictions.[8] But this is a category error. Since a TSSI is a formalism, and not a model, it is not supposed to make predictions. It is instead a framework for arranging economic data in a way which aims to be both consistent with Marx's value theory and helps us to understand the real connections between the phenomena we are seeking to explain. The 'test' of whether this is a *good* formalism is whether, once we assume its framework, we can give successful explanations and make successful predictions, which may include models. Thus a formalism can usefully be thought of as part of what Lakatos calls the 'hard core' of

---

4   Marx 1981, p. 956.
5   Freeman 1996, pp. 225–6.
6   Shaikh and Tonak 1994, pp. 78–89.
7   Shaikh and Tonak 1994, pp. 141–4.
8   Veneziani 2004.

propositions which are not usually tested directly, but are instead evaluated according to their potential to act as a framework for successful research.[9]

Most of this book works on developing an appropriate formalism within which to test Marx's predictions. Therefore the formalism itself is not something that can be tested. Nevertheless, it *is* possible to specify some desirable features of a formalism *a priori*. First, an internally consistent and coherent formalism is to be preferred over one that is inconsistent or incoherent, because this is an important aspect of what it means for explanation to make sense. This extends to the question of the realism of assumptions. Milton Friedman's infamous justification for the unrealistic assumptions of mainstream economics is that the realism of assumptions does not matter, because in some cases unrealistic assumptions can be the basis for constructing models with as much (or possibly more) predictive power as models that use more realistic assumptions.[10] In other words, reality can be 'as if' the unrealistic model were true. But such cases beg the question *why* the unrealistic model can produce accurate results. If the model builder concedes that their model is 'unrealistic', this concedes that their model is an incomplete explanation of the phenomena they seek to explain. The model builder can only explain why their unrealistic model 'works' with reference to propositions to which they *are* committed, and therefore *do* consider 'realistic'.

In the case of a strict formalism, the question of the realism of its assumptions is posed differently from that of a model. For example, if we want to construct a strict formalism, and we build into it the assumption that input prices are equal to output prices, then the relevant question is not whether this is true 'most of the time' or 'when it matters' or 'under ideal conditions' (as it might be for constructing a model), but whether, *a priori*, they *must* always be exactly equal in reality. Simultaneist formalisms fail this test. Because it has been constructed so that it can be applied to national accounts data, the accounting framework in this work will not always pass this test either, because sometimes we will have to make approximations so that we can work with the available data. But, in general, our aim is to do this as little as possible, so that the formalism can be as effective as possible as a framework within which to test other hypotheses.

Second, since we are also interested in interpreting Marx's value theory, a good formalism should be as consistent as possible with Marx's work. This does not necessarily mean constructing a formalism that is consistent with

9   Lakatos 1968, pp. 168–70.
10   Friedman 1966.

everything Marx ever wrote, because, being a human being, Marx was not immune from making errors or contradicting himself. But it does mean trying to construct an interpretation that is as consistent as possible with Marx's most important arguments and conclusions.

So far this has mainly been a discussion of *our* method of inquiry, and less a discussion of Marx's. Marxists have an understandable tendency to be preoccupied with discussing Marx's method, since, if you believe Marx's method is a successful one, it makes sense to try to understand and emulate it.

As this investigation proceeds, it makes many observations about Marx's method. But it does not contain an extensive treatment of this subject on its own. If Marx had discussed the question of his method in detail, then it might make sense to begin by elucidating Marx's method, in order to help answer other questions of interpretation. But in *Capital* Marx says notoriously little about his method explicitly, so what that method actually is remains a matter of controversy. Hence there is always a danger, when discussions of method precede other questions of interpretation, that an author's specific interpretation of Marx's method becomes a distorting lens through which all of Marx's other statements are viewed. To put the issue more bluntly, it is all too common for Marxists to take interpretations of Marx that they dislike or find inconvenient and declare them to be inconsistent with (their own, contentious interpretation of) Marx's method, rather than confronting the interpretation with Marx's own statements directly.

What *Capital does* give us is the results of Marx's *own* application of his method. If we wanted to remain 'true' to Marx's method, then our job would be to take the theory and predictions Marx develops as a result of this, interpret them correctly and test them. If the process of doing this were to help clarify the nature of Marx's method, then this would be useful too. If Marx's work contained major inconsistencies and gaps then it might be necessary to devote more space to discussing and speculating on the nature of his method in order to go back and see if we can apply it more rigorously than he himself did. But to anticipate the conclusion of this study, we do not find this to be the case.

2   Devaluation and Value

As the last chapter explored, for Marx the average rate of profit tends to trace the path of a downward spiral: as the OCC rises, the rate of profit declines over the long term, but this is punctuated by economic crises, which allow for temporary recoveries in the rate of profit by devaluing the stock of capital. The

Okishio Theorem appeared to show that the main dynamic in this hypothesis (the falling rate of profit) was not possible, at least not if we suppose that capitalists only make investments which reduce their costs per unit of output.

The great merit of existing temporal interpretations is that they not only 'solve' the transformation problem, they show that the Okishio Theorem does not apply to all measures of the rate of profit. But as we will briefly show below, they have purchased this at the cost of measuring rates of profit or defining value in ways that cannot allow for movement in the other direction due to devaluation, at least not in the way Marx describes. The issues involved get to the core of what we mean by (and how we define) value, if we want a definition that makes the movement in the rate of profit that he describes possible.

Note that this is all we want: a definition that makes the movement in the rate of profit that Marx describes *possible*. This is not the same as a definition that guarantees this result in advance, which would be just as problematic as one that rules it out in advance. Of course, the kind of definition we want may not be possible, if Marx's account of the dynamics of the rate of profit contradicts itself, or contradicts his theory of value. One purpose of this work is to show that such a definition is indeed possible.

First, we should point out that the role of devaluation in allowing for a recovery in the rate of profit is not something Marx merely mentions in passing. In *Capital* he discusses it at some length and gives it an important place in his crisis theory:

> The periodical devaluation of the existing capital, which is a means, immanent to the capitalist mode of production, for delaying the fall in the profit rate and accelerating the accumulation of capital value by the formation of new capital, disturbs the given conditions in which the circulation and reproduction process of capital takes place, and is therefore accompanied by sudden stoppages and crises in the production process.[11]
>
> ...
>
> The chief disruption, and the one possessing the sharpest character, would occur in connection with capital in so far as it possesses the property of value, i.e. in connection with capital *values*. The portion of capital value that exists simply in the form of future claims on surplus-value and profit, in other words promissory notes on production in their various forms, is devalued simultaneously with the fall in the revenues on which it is reckoned. A portion of ready gold and silver lies idle and does not

---

11   Marx 1981, p. 358.

function as capital. Part of the commodities on the market can complete their process of circulation and reproduction only by an immense reduction in their prices, i.e. by a devaluation in the capital they represent. The elements of fixed capital are more or less devalued in the same way.[12]

Devaluation is also a counter-tendency to the falling rate of profit outside of periods of crisis, as technological development devalues existing constant capital:

> Also related to what has been said [about the cheapening of constant capital] is the devaluation of existing capital (i.e. of its material elements) that goes hand in hand with the development of industry. This too is a factor that steadily operates to stay the fall in the rate of profit.[13]

Freeman and Kliman have slightly different ways of treating the effect of price changes on the value of the existing stock of capital. Freeman's formalism starts with the axiom that the exchange of commodities, and the price movements that these exchanges create, cannot alter the total value of the stock of commodities that exists across the economy at a point in time. That is, according to Freeman, once value is created by workers in production, it remains part of the total stock of value tied up in commodities until it is destroyed (whether through individual consumption, productive consumption, or destruction or damage through accident or natural disaster).[14] This is his version of Marx's axiom that the sum of values is equal to the sum of prices: i.e. he interprets it as applying not only to the total value of newly produced output, but also to the total value of the stock of commodities inherited from previous periods of production.

The problem with this interpretation is that devaluation is precisely a process whereby existing commodities lose part (or all) of their value. It is therefore hard to see how his approach can allow for the devaluation of existing capital that Marx describes. The closest Freeman's formalism comes to representing this is that it allows for some of the value of commodities owned

12   Marx 1981, pp. 362–3, original emphasis.
13   Marx 1981, p. 343.
14   This does not preclude price changes *transferring* value from one type of commodity to another: e.g. if the price of iron ore rises, while all other prices stay the same, according to Freeman's formalism if there has been no production or consumption a proportion of the total value embodied in all other commodities is transferred to the total value of the stock of iron ore, without any change in the total value embodied in the stock of commodities as a whole.

by capitalists to be *transferred* to non-capitalists, if the prices of commodities owned by businesses falls relative to the value of money. This would indeed devalue the existing stock of capital. But this is not what happens in reality when capital is devalued due to a crisis; generally, non-capitalists do not get richer while capitalists get poorer. Nor is this an effect that Marx describes. Marx describes a process whereby practically all commodities are devalued due to the crisis: above he lists future claims on surplus value (fictitious capital), gold and silver, unsold commodities and fixed capital.

Freeman's formalism also allows for the possibility that capital advanced in *nominal terms* can decline as a result of falling prices for constant capital. But Marx uses the term *value* in the quotation above, which he emphasises. He clearly does not mean a purely nominal decline.

The same criticism applies to using fixed assets at historical cost to measure capital advanced, as Kliman, Carchedi and Roberts do.[15] Kliman himself devotes two sections in a chapter of *The Failure of Capitalist Production* to discussing the importance of devaluation due to crisis for Marx's LTFRP. He writes:

> The LTFRP implies that there is an ever-present tendency in capitalism for labor-saving technical innovation to lower the rate of profit. Yet Marx also argued that this tendency is interrupted and counteracted from time to time by 'the destruction of capital through crises'.
>
> Part of what he was referring to is the destruction of physical capital assets ... But insofar as the theory of crisis is concerned, what matters is the destruction of capital in terms of *value* – the decline in value of physical capital assets as well as the decline in the (fictitious) value of financial assets. Of course, when physical assets are destroyed, their value is destroyed as well, but the predominant factor that causes capital value to be destroyed is falling prices.[16]

But a historical cost measure cannot account for the effect of falling prices on the existing stock of fixed assets. A historical cost measure values each asset at the price for which it was originally purchased (after depreciation). Using a pure historical cost measure (i.e. one which does not adjust for general price inflation), falling prices only influence the nominal value of capital advanced insofar as they affect the prices of *newly produced* assets. The prices at which existing assets are valued must, by definition, remain constant (after allow-

15   Kliman 2011, pp. 102–23; Carchedi and Roberts 2013b, p. 111.
16   Kliman 2011, p. 22.

ing for depreciation). The only way the existing stock of fixed assets could be *devalued* using a pure historical cost measure would be in *relative* or *inflation-adjusted* terms – i.e. relative to the prices of other commodities, or the MELT. But this would require an *increase* in the prices of newly produced commodities, not a decrease. If we use an inflation-adjusted historical cost measure, the effect Marx describes is similarly not possible. The whole point of such a measure would be to leave the inflation-adjusted prices of pre-existing fixed assets unchanged after depreciation, and therefore unaffected by devaluation.

Indeed, Kliman acknowledges that his historical cost measure does not account for devaluation, effectively conceding that the historical cost rate of profit is not the measure of the rate of profit to which Marx's law refers:

> It is true that capital does eventually become revalued according to the cost of reproducing it, and that capital devaluation therefore tends to raise the profit rate. The 'resolution' of the discrepancy between original production costs and current reproduction costs, however, takes place through the many mechanisms of crisis, through the *forcible* adjustment of old values to the new ... The discussion below is confined to the underlying tendency of the profit rate and the unit price, independently of periodic disruptions.[17]

That is, Kliman acknowledges that his historical cost measure of the rate of profit does not take into account the effect of the 'forcible adjustment of old values to the new' that occurs during crises. It is also important to point out that it is not true that devaluation *only* occurs through periodic disruptions and crises. Above we saw that Marx mentions 'the devaluation of existing capital that goes hand in hand with the development of industry' as a factor that '*steadily* operates to stay the fall in the rate of profit', which a historical cost measure of the rate of profit similarly fails to account for.

3   Historical Cost, Input Cost and Output Cost

If the theoretical results of the TSSI depended on historical cost valuation, this criticism would be a major problem, since it would leave the TSSI unable to reproduce Marx's conclusion that crises allow the rate of profit to recover by devaluing capital. Fortunately, the counter-example in the Appendix shows

---

17   Kliman 1988, p. 286.

that this is not the case: the refutation of the Okishio Theorem and the res-olution of the transformation problem do not depend on historical cost valu-ation.

Interested readers are invited to read the appendix and work through the example. Here we will just discuss the result and draw out some of its implica-tions.

First, the polarisation of the debate over how to measure the rate of profit between historical cost and current cost has filtered out some important dis-tinctions between different measures of the 'current cost' of an asset. The rate of profit is a combination of a 'flow' and a 'stock' variable: the numerator is the flow of profits measured over the duration of a period (usually from the beginning of a year to the end) while the denominator is the stock of capital (constant and variable[18]) used to produce those profits. To measure the stock of capital at current prices, we need to take the quantities of each type of use value that exists in the stock (e.g. the quantities of each type of machine used in production) and multiply by current prices. But because prices do not neces-sarily stay constant over the course of a year, we have to decide whether to use the prices that prevailed at the start of the year (the 'input' or 'pre-production' prices in a period-by-period model) or the prices that prevail by the end of the year ('output' prices or 'replacement cost').

Part of the reason these distinctions have been blurred is that most dis-cussions of the Okishio Theorem assume away the existence of fixed cap-ital. In a model with circulating capital only, where the whole stock of cap-ital is fully used up over the course of every period, historical cost and input cost are equivalent. Kliman's counter example to the Okishio Theorem, for example, appears to show that the crucial issue is historical cost versus cur-rent cost, because only his historical cost measure declines as a result of cost-reducing technical change.[19] But because his model does not include fixed capital, a historical cost measure of the rate of profit is equivalent to a meas-ure of the rate of profit which values the capital stock at start of year (input) prices.

Another source of potential confusion is the understandable tendency to apply the same method of valuation to calculating the numerator and the denominator of the rate of profit. Since total profit is the difference between output and the cost of the constant and variable capital *expended* to pro-duce that output, we can also 'choose' whether to value the capital stock at

18   See the next chapter for a discussion of why both variable and constant capital on the
      denominator of the rate of profit are stocks and not flows.
19   Kliman 2007, pp. 120–1.

input prices or output prices for this purpose, so this can look like the same question as whether to value the denominator at output or input prices. This can all become blurred together into a single 'divide' across numerator and denominator between temporalism/historical cost and simultaneism/current cost.

On the question of how best to value the denominator, there are a few competing considerations. If we want a measure of the rate of return a business would make if it held an asset over the course of its life, then historical cost on the denominator is appropriate. But since real businesses can buy and sell assets throughout the course of their lives, this measure has significant limitations. If we want a measure of the actual rate of profit made over the course of a year, then we should use input prices to value the denominator, since this measures the actual price of the assets in question at the time they needed to be owned to use them to start production. If we want to use past data to estimate future profitability, in some cases it might make sense to use end of year prices to value the capital stock, since these are the most recent prices we will have available. But since our aim is to test Marx's law using actual rate of profit data, it makes sense for us to use input prices.

On the question of how to calculate the numerator, the question is much simpler. First, no one, as far as I am aware, argues that fixed capital transfers value to output at its historical cost. For example, Kliman and Freeman's position is that constant capital transfers value to output based on its price at the time production *starts*.[20] As Kliman explains:

> Precisely how much value is transferred from the means of production has been the subject of considerable controversy ... I and other proponents of the temporal single-system interpretation (TSSI) interpret Marx as having held that the amount of value transferred is the amount of value that is needed to acquire the means of production (rather than their own value). The word 'needed' serves to indicate that the amount of value transferred depends upon (a) the current cost, rather than the **historical cost**, or original cost, of the means of production, and (b) the socially average expenditure on the means of production.[21]

Second, of the two possible measures of profit based on current cost, only one is an *actual* (as opposed to a hypothetical) measure of profit. If we calculate

---

20   Freeman 1999, p. 14.
21   Kliman 2011, p. 22, original emphasis.

'profit' by valuing inputs at output prices, we are calculating profit as though it were possible to buy inputs at the end of the production process, rather than at the start. This tells us what profit *would have been* if prices at the start of the year had been the same as they were at the end of the year (i.e. if the economy were in equilibrium). Perhaps for some purposes this could be interesting, but not for empirical analysis.

Unfortunately, this is the measure of profit the Okishio Theorem uses. The counter-example in the Appendix clarifies that the *only* reason the Okishio Theorem appears to show that cost-reducing technical change cannot lead to a falling average rate of profit is that it uses this mistaken definition of profit. If we measure profit based on the cost of inputs *when the capitalists need to own them in order to make output* – i.e. at the start of the production process – cost-reducing technical change can lead to a fall in the average rate of profit *whichever of the three methods* we use to value the capital stock on the denominator.

The last refuge for simultaneists was to argue that the counter-examples to the Okishio Theorem depended on historical cost valuation, and that historical cost valuation was not an appropriate measure of the rate of profit. This counter-example shows that disproving the Okishio Theorem does not rely on historical cost valuation. The claim that the Okishio Theorem says anything about Marx's LTFRP or the movement of any *actual* measure of the rate of profit is therefore incorrect and those who have advanced it should either acknowledge this or refute the argument.

4   Measuring Devaluation

Now we have a measure of the rate of profit that can allow for both devaluation and a falling rate of profit due to cost-reducing technical change, we want a method for measuring the devaluation of fixed capital, and distinguishing this from changes in the value of money (inflation) and 'ordinary' depreciation.

Our first task is to clarify more precisely what depreciation means. Depreciation is often thought of in purely physicalist terms, as the wear and tear that a machine undergoes over the course of its useful life. But there is also depreciation due to obsolescence; what Marx calls 'moral' depreciation. As Marx identifies, this takes two forms: depreciation due to the invention of new, more productive material elements of capital (e.g. faster computers, machines capable of producing more output per worker), and depreciation due to the cheapening of the cost of reproducing the existing material elements of capital (e.g. when a computer or machine becomes cheaper to produce, or if inputs such as iron or steel become cheaper).[22]

One issue of controversy is whether Marx thought that moral depreciation transfers value to output. Kliman argues that Marx's position is that it does not.[23] This is important because the depreciation models used in the US national accounts incorporate a portion of moral depreciation, and if Kliman is right, then, ideally, we would exclude moral depreciation from our calculations.

However, Marx in fact does allow that moral depreciation can transfer value to output. In *Capital* II, Marx argues that fixed capital 'gives up value to the product in proportion to the exchange-value that it loses together with its use-value.'[24] Elsewhere, he indicates that moral depreciation fits this description, when he refers to '[t]he constant improvements which rob existing machinery, factories, etc., of a part of their use-value, and therefore also their exchange-value'.[25] Moral depreciation robs existing machines of part their use value because their use value, for capitalists, is the extent to which they can valorise capital, which is in part determined by the productivity and cost of machines used by other capitalists.

Marx also states *explicitly* that fixed capital transfers value to the product as a result of moral depreciation:

> This process is particularly significant at times when new machinery is first introduced, before it has reached a certain degree of maturity, and where it thus constantly becomes outmoded before it has had time to reproduce its value. This is one of the reasons for the unlimited extension of working hours that is usual in periods of this kind, work based on alternating day and night shifts, so that the value of the machines is reproduced without too great costs having to be borne for wear and tear. If the short working life of the machines (their short life-expectancy *vis-à-vis* prospective improvements) were not counter-balanced in this way, they would transfer too great a portion of their value to the product in the way of moral depreciation and would not even be able to compete with handicraft production.[26]

---

22   Marx 1981, p. 208.
23   Kliman 2010, p. 73.
24   Marx 1978b, p. 237.
25   Marx 1981, p. 208.
26   Marx 1981, pp. 208–9.

Does this mean that *all* moral depreciation transfers value to output? It is possible that this is what Marx had in mind. But if this is the case, it raises the problem of measuring it. If the price of an asset falls, how can we know whether this is due to moral depreciation, devaluation, or ordinary wear and tear? As Freeman points out, we cannot answer this question by examining the physical properties of the asset itself.[27]

Note, however, that the above passage refers to the short life *expectancy* of machines in a period of rapid technological development. This suggests that the crucial issue is how much the capitalists should *expect* depreciation to affect the value of their fixed capital, whatever the cause.[28]

Compare this with the way depreciation is measured in the US national accounts. The BEA's depreciation models try to base their assumptions on information about the prices actually paid for fixed assets when they are bought second-hand.[29] For example, the depreciation schedule for cars is informed by comparing the prices, at a single point in time, for similar types of car made 1 year ago, 3 years ago, 10 years ago, etc.[30] So effectively this is a measure of the rate at which the price of an asset is expected to decline over time (including due to expected moral depreciation), excluding inflation.

This is basically in keeping with Marx's conception of depreciation, if we adopt the expectations-based interpretation proposed above. One difference is that, in his numerical examples, Marx uses straight line models of depreciation, while the US national accounts mostly use geometric models (i.e. they assume the value of fixed assets declines at a constant rate).[31] But Marx does not seem to be wedded to using straight line models:

> The portion of the price which must replace the wear-and-tear of the machinery enters the account more in an ideal sense, as long as the machinery is still at all serviceable; it does not very much matter whether it is paid for and converted into money today or tomorrow, or at any particular point in the capital's turnover time.[32]

---

27 Freeman 1996, p. 254.
28 Note this is different from saying that capitalists' *actual* expectations determine the rate at which moral depreciation transfers value to output.
29 US Bureau of Economic Analysis 2013.
30 Note that this is different from tracking the prices paid *over time* for a particular car, which would also be subject to general price inflation.
31 US Bureau of Economic Analysis 2011, p. M–5.
32 Marx 1981, p. 213.

Marx distinguishes this depreciation from devaluation and revaluation, which he describes in the following way:

> Revaluation and devaluation, for their part, are self-explanatory. We simply mean that the capital present increases or decreases in value as the result of certain general economic conditions (since what is involved here is not the particular fate of one single private capital), i.e. that the value of the capital advanced to production rises or falls independently of its valorization by the surplus labour it employs.[33]

In the national accounts, revaluation and devaluation are treated in much the same way. If, for example, the price of buying a new car of a particular type increases by 5%, then the stock of cars of this type will have its current value inflated by 5% after subtracting depreciation. This is also called a 'holding gain'.

Marx does not devote much discussion to devaluation and revaluation in *Capital*, because these phenomena 'assume for their full development the credit system and competition on the world market' (which he has not introduced at this stage of the manuscript).[34] But he acknowledges their importance for the rate of profit, because:

> they make it appear as if it is not only the rate of profit but also its mass (which is in fact identical with the mass of surplus-value) that can increase and decrease independently of movements of surplus-value, whether of its mass or its rate.[35]

The problem he seems to be raising is that revaluation and devaluation appear to exert an influence on the mass of profits:

> Since the rate of profit is equal to the proportionate excess in the value of the product over the value of the total capital advanced, an increase in the rate of profit that arose from a devaluation of the capital advanced would involve a loss in capital value, while a decline in the profit rate that arose from a rise in value of the capital advanced could well involve a gain.[36]

---

33   Marx 1981, p. 205.
34   Ibid.
35   Ibid.
36   Marx 1981, p. 208.

If, for example, a company's assets increase in value due to revaluation, this is a form of profit; conversely, devaluation is a loss. But neither revaluation nor devaluation affects the mass of surplus value produced. Kliman draws the reasonable conclusion that Marx's aggregate equality refers to an equality between the sum of surplus value and the sum of profits *from production*, i.e. excluding revaluation and devaluation.[37] (However, as will be argued in Chapter 4, once we introduce unproductive expenditures of surplus value, taxation and credit, this equality needs to be further modified.)

This argument that revaluation and devaluation can change capital values might also seem to contradict Marx's argument that 'the sum of the values in circulation can clearly not be augmented by any change in their distribution'.[38] But revaluation is not a part of circulation. As Marx argues, '[t]he value of a commodity is expressed in its price *before it enters into circulation*, and it is therefore a pre-condition of circulation, not its result'.[39] Prices are offered *prior* to exchange; exchange is what happens when a buyer takes up a seller's offer, and the commodity and money change hands. So there is no inconsistency if we say that: 1) the act of *exchange* cannot alter the sum of values in circulation, and 2) movements in prices *can* alter the total value that is embodied in already produced commodities (for example, when capital is devalued due to moral depreciation or crises).

In the national accounts, holding gains and losses are excluded from all measures of profit. But this is not the case for company accounts. In particular, companies are *not* entitled to write down the value of their assets without charging this against profits.[40] So we must recognise that there is the possibility for a divergence between some measures of total profit and total surplus value. We will return to this issue further below and in the next chapter.

5   The MELT and Revaluation

In order to measure the effects of revaluation and devaluation in value terms, and to do the analysis generally, we need a method of adjusting for inflation. That is, we need a way to measure the Monetary Expression of Labour

---

37   Kliman 2010, p. 74.
38   Marx 1981, p. 265.
39   Marx 1981, p. 260, emphasis added.
40   The treatment of gains due to revaluation is different: if they reverse previous losses due to devaluation, they are counted towards profit, but if they do not, then are accounted for separately as a 'revaluation surplus'. Horngren 2013, p. 477.

Time (MELT). The most common approach is based on the New Interpreta-tion, which is to define the MELT as the 'net product' (output less constant capital inputs consumed) divided by a measure of the labour time performed to produce it. This treats each period as a self-contained entity, unaffected by results from the previous period (as well as not being compatible with all of Marx's aggregate equalities). In contrast, a temporal measure of the MELT should measure the monetary expression of both the direct and indirect SNLT that gross output embodies, with inputs valued at the prices prevailing when production commences.

Within the limits prescribed by national accounting statistics, the best way to allow for this is to calculate the MELT by dividing gross output (measured in current dollars) by the sum of productive labour expended during the year (measured in worker years) and depreciation valued at input prices after divid-ing by last year's MELT (which also gives a result in worker years).[41] Unlike the New Interpretation definition, this means the value of fixed capital at the start of the year (i.e. at 'input prices') determines the value it transfers to output.

With the MELT and depreciation defined, we can isolate the effect of revalu-ation on fixed assets. This is just the growth in the value of fixed assets after subtracting investment net of depreciation and adjusting for MELT inflation. In most cases this will be negative – i.e. there will be devaluation – as the forces of production develop and it takes less socially necessary labour time to pro-duce each unit of fixed capital. But the approach makes no assumptions about whether revaluation will be positive or negative, or how far it could go.

In principle, a crisis could devalue the elements of constant capital all the way down to near zero if prices fell far enough. But this does not mean that the dynamics of devaluation and revaluation are inexplicable. For example, suppose there is a crisis that causes a massive devaluation of capital. Once production recommences, prices of fixed assets are likely to remain low until capacity utilisation reaches more normal levels; since, during this time, newly produced fixed assets will have to compete with idle assets that have already been produced. However, as this slack is taken up and full capacity utilisation approaches (which could be many years later), prices for fixed assets are also likely to move to near their prices of production. If they do not, then capital-ists producing fixed assets will continue to make below average rates of profit, and investment in increasing output in this sector will be very low. If prices for

---

41 This means the initial MELT needs to be estimated. We can do this using the New Inter-
    pretation definition. The small error this creates will rapidly diminish over subsequent
    years.

fixed assets *do* return to near prices of production, or above, the prices of existing fixed assets will also rise to near or above these prices of production (after accounting for moral and ordinary depreciation), hence pushing the value of capital advanced back up to more 'normal' levels.

This explains why devaluation does not mean that the rate of profit is unlikely to decline over the long term, as the forces of production develop. If devaluation due to crises tended to be permanent, then Marx's law would predict only a tendency for the rate of profit to fall between the recovery in the rate of profit after a crisis and the next major crisis: i.e. it would predict only a cyclical movement. There would be no basis for predicting a long-term decline in the rate of profit as the means of production developed, because it would be possible that the devaluation after each crisis could be severe enough to allow the rate of profit to stay at the same average level (or higher) across each cycle. But since there are good reasons to suppose that such devaluations would not be permanent, there is likely to be a tendency for the rate of profit to move cyclically *and* to decline over the long term.

However, we need to distinguish this from the effects of the *destruction* of the material elements of capital. Unlike devaluation, this cannot be reversed by price changes. Value cannot be recovered once its embodiment in use values is destroyed. The destruction of the material elements of capital therefore tends to set back the decline in the rate of profit until this is reversed by new investments.

This approach also suggests a new measure of the rate of profit. Above, we argued that surplus value is unaffected by revaluation or devaluation, but that profits *are* (if we define profits more broadly than just profits from production). For some purposes (though not for testing Marx's law) it may be relevant to measure the rate of profit as the ratio of surplus value *plus revaluation* to the capital stock. We would expect this to be much more volatile than the ratio of surplus value to the capital stock, and generally also to be lower (since devaluation is more common than positive revaluation). The counterexample to the Okishio Theorem in the Appendix includes a measure of the rate of profit that does this, and shows that it also has a (faster) tendency to fall with cost-reducing technical change.

6   The Rate of Profit, the Rate of Accumulation and the Rate of Growth

So far, we have considered the interpretative virtues of a measure of the rate of profit using fixed assets at input cost: i.e. why this fits better with the LTFRP as

Marx formulates it. However, testing Marx's law is not an end in itself. Marx's law is only useful insofar as it helps to explain phenomena in which we are interested.

The most important reason to test Marx's law is to see if the falling rate of profit can explain economic crises. But another, related reason to measure the rate of profit is to see if it can explain movements in other measures of economic performance.

Marx suggests one such relationship when he comments that the falling rate of profit leads to a falling rate of expansion of the stock of capital:

> As the capitalist mode of production develops, so the rate of profit falls, while the mass of profit rises together with the increasing mass of capital applied. Once the rate is given, the absolute amount by which capital grows depends on its existing magnitude. But if this magnitude is given, the proportion in which it grows, i.e. its rate of growth, depends on the profit rate.[42]

The rate of growth of the stock of capital is also called the 'rate of accumulation'. It is connected with the profit rate because any net investment in capital advanced must be funded from surplus value; so if the ratio of surplus value to capital advanced is larger, then, if the share of surplus value spent on investment is constant, the rate of accumulation will increase. So there are good *a priori* reasons to expect that as the rate of profit declines, so will the rate of accumulation.

There is, in turn, a connection between the rate of accumulation and the rate of growth of real net output. Broadly speaking, there are two ways to increase real net output. One is to increase the output produced by each existing physical unit of fixed capital, by, for example, raising the ratio of workers employed to fixed capital, or increasing the intensity or skill of their work: i.e. to raise the capacity utilisation rate. The other is to accumulate more fixed capital, i.e. to increase capacity (including buying fixed capital that requires less SNLT per unit of output).

The capacity utilisation rate can be influenced by many different factors: a fall in capacity utilisation does not necessarily indicate 'over-production' or 'over-accumulation', though of course capacity utilisation falls sharply at moments of crisis. But if capacity utilisation tends to be trendless, then the growth rate of output will tend to be proportional to the rate of accumulation

---

42   Marx 1981, p. 356.

and, potentially, the rate of profit. If this turns out to be the case, it would show how the development of the forces of production under capitalism creates its own limits, not only in terms of crises brought about by the falling rate of profit, but also through a slowing growth rate over the long term.

7   Conclusion

We now have definitions of value and the rate of profit that are consistent with Marx's hypothesis of a downward spiral in the rate of profit and his approach generally. We also now have the basis for measuring the effect on the rate of profit due to devaluation and revaluation, and two additional hypotheses to test concerning the relationship between the rate of profit, the rate of accumulation, and the rate of growth. But to test these we will need a method for measuring the numerator of the rate of profit. This chapter has shown that not all definitions of profit fit with Marx's axiom that the sum of profit is equal to the sum of surplus value. Chapter 4 will discuss how this is modified further when we introduce unproductive expenditures of surplus value, taxes, and the financial system. But first, the next chapter continues the task of quantifying the influences on the rate of profit.

8   Appendix: A Counter-Example to the Okishio Theorem Using
         Current Cost Measures of the Rate of Profit

As discussed in the last chapter, the Okishio Theorem defines the rate of profit such that input prices and output prices are equal. The counterexamples to the Okishio Theorem given by others do not include fixed capital, which means there is no difference between valuing the capital stock at historical cost or at input prices.[43] So we need a counter-example that satisfies the conditions of the Okishio Theorem (a constant real wage and cost-reducing technical change) and includes fixed capital.

To keep the example as simple as possible, we will assume an economy that produces only two commodities: new machines and old machines. Initially the whole capital stock is made up of old machines, three quarters of which are used to produce new machines, and one quarter of which is used to produce more of the older style machines. The difference between a newer and

---

43   Kliman 1996; Kliman 2007, pp. 120–1.

an older style machine is their productivity: newer machines are slightly more than twice as productive than older machines (i.e. each machine produces over twice the physical output). Both types of machine take a tenth of a worker to operate (i.e. one worker can 'mind' ten machines, and we will make the simplifying assumption that it is possible to hire fractions of a worker – alternatively we could just scale up the example by 10 times or 100 times, etc.). As new machines come into service, we assume three quarters produce new machines, and one quarter produces older style machines. This means that over time new machines account for growing shares of the capital stock and output, so there is rising physical productivity per worker (i.e. rising technical composition of capital).

The simplest way to satisfy the condition of a constant real wage is to assume workers are paid nothing. This is obviously not a realistic assumption, but since we are giving a counterexample to a theorem which makes a general claim (cost-reducing technical change cannot lead to a falling rate of profit) any counterexample, however unrealistic, refutes the theorem. It would no doubt be possible to get the same result with a more realistic assumption, but this would make the example more difficult for readers to follow and verify.

Because workers are paid nothing and there is no circulating capital, the cost price of machines is made up entirely of the depreciation costs of the fixed capital used to produce them. We are assuming a depreciation rate of ten percent per year, and that the physical productivity of the machines declines at the same rate (this also keeps the example simpler). There are six different cost prices involved in the example, the cost prices of producing: old machines using old machines; old machines using new machines; new machines using old machines; new machines using new machines; and the average cost prices of producing both new machines and old machines. These all measure costs at input (i.e. actual) prices. All six cost prices are tracked to show that: 1) as capitalists switch from using old machines to using new machines they reduce their costs per unit; and 2) the average cost prices of producing both old and new machines decline over time.[44] To keep all prices comparable we are assuming a constant MELT of $2 per worker year.

---

44   The reader might ask why the capitalists do not all switch to producing the newer style, more productive machines once they become available. One explanation we could give is that it takes time to train workers to use the newer style machines. If we instead assumed that production of older style machines stopped immediately we would no longer be able to use prices of production to value the old machines, and would have to make our own assumptions about the prices old machines sell for over time. But strictly speaking we do

Because we are assuming new machines produce both new machines and old machines at lower cost prices than old machines, capitalists who own new machines will make higher rates of profit than capitalists who own old machines (whatever we assume about the price at which new and old machines sell). But we will assume that average rates of profit across the two branches (the old machine producing branch and the new machine producing branch) are equal. Since both types of machine are capable of producing both types of output, this assumption makes intuitive sense: if there were a difference in the average rates of profit across branches, some capitalists would switch from producing one type of output to producing the other. So the prices for which older and newer style machines sell are calculated as the average cost price for that branch plus the average rate of profit multiplied by the capital stock for that branch at input prices, divided by the quantity of output.

The average rate of profit for determining these prices is the one we favour generally, and values both inputs and the capital stock at input prices. For the purposes of the counter-example we are free to make any assumption about output prices we like, as long as we calculate the MELT correctly (i.e. such that the sum of values is equal to the sum of prices and the sum of profits is equal to the sum of surplus value). Consistent with temporalism (and the unidirectional movement of time) one year's output prices are the next year's input prices. Since prices decline over time as productivity per worker rises, each year the pre-existing capital stock is devalued (apart from the first year, where we only have old machines).

The results calculate four other measures of the rate of profit for comparison, which are all graphed in Figure 1 below. One subtracts devaluation from the numerator (i.e. it is not just a measure of 'cash profits' or 'profits from production', but also takes into account 'capital write-downs'), and this measure falls fastest. The next values the capital stock at output prices on the denominator (as mentioned above, this is not a measure of the actual rate of profit, but might be relevant for investment decisions which depend on estimating the likely future rate of return). It also falls, though not as quickly as the previous two measures, because it uses the value of the capital stock after devaluation on the denominator. The average rate of profit at historical cost is also calculated, and it falls the second fastest of the measures.

The only rate of profit that increases (very slowly) is the one that mismeasures total profit, by valuing input costs at output prices. Note that, in

---

not need to give an explanation, we are free to construct the counter-example however we like as long as it meets the conditions assumed by the theorem.

this case, total profit is not equal to total surplus value. The Okishio Theorem appears to be valid because it uses a definition of the rate of profit like this. This is in no sense an actual measure of the rate of profit: to calculate it in effect we have to retroactively change the price paid for inputs at the beginning of the year, without changing the revenue capitalists made from selling those inputs.

This rate of profit would only be an actual rate of profit if we changed the example to compare one equilibrium state with another, which is not what Marx's law is intended to do. To put the issue another way: it is one thing to say that investors might look at the ratio of actual profits to assets valued at their end of the year prices to determine their investment decisions (though, in this case, they would get a better estimate of likely to future profits by valuing assets at start of year prices). This kind of hypothetical measure of the rate of profit might at least have a function (though not for testing Marx's law). But it is quite another to say that investors should go back and recalculate the profits a company made *as if* the cost of their inputs were determined by today's prices. *Even if* this were a good way of determining what the company's costs are likely to be in future, it would be a very poor way of estimating its profits, since it does not take into account the fact that the prices paid for its outputs are also falling. And it is certainly not justified to insist that Marx's law be ruled illegitimate, *a priori*, on the basis that he should have used this flawed, hypothetical measure of the rate of profit and no other.

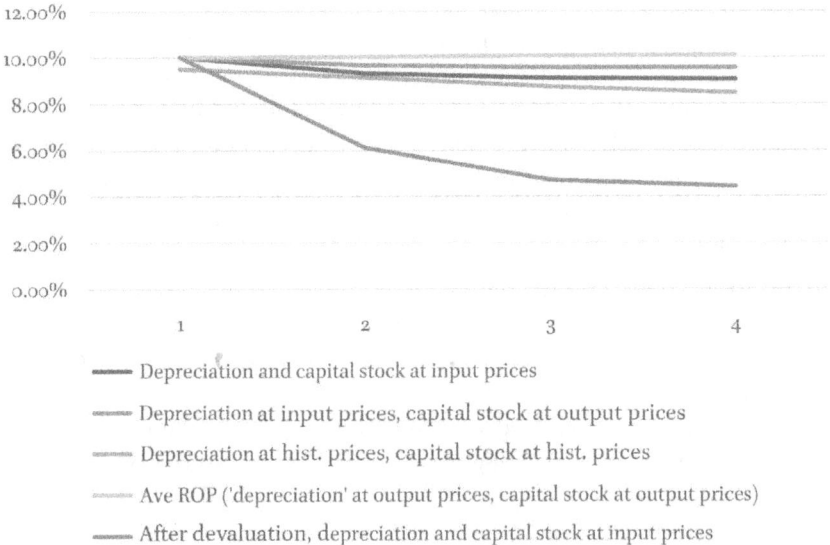

FIGURE 1   Measures of the average rate of profit in the counterexample to the Okishio Theorem

TABLE 1   A counter-example to the Okishio Theorem

			Year			
			1	**2**	**3**	**4**
Quantity of capital stock (start of year)	used to produce old machines	by old machines	25.0	23.8	22.8	22.0
		by new machines	0.0	1.9	3.8	5.7
	used to produce new machines	by old machines	75.0	71.3	68.3	66.0
		by new machines	0.0	5.6	11.3	17.0
Number of worker years	spent to produce old machines	using old machines	2.5	2.4	2.3	2.2
		using new machines	0.0	0.2	0.4	0.6
	spent to produce new machines	using old machines	7.5	7.1	6.8	6.6
		using new machines	0.0	0.6	1.1	1.7
	total		10.0	10.3	10.6	11.1
Value of capital stock (start of year) at input prices	used to produce old machines	by old machines	$50	$48	$44	$40
		by new machines		$8	$14	$21
		sub total	$50	$55	$58	$61
	used to produce new machines	by old machines	$150	$143	$132	$121
		by new machines		$23	$43	$62
		sub total	$150	$165	$175	$183
	total		$200	$220	$233	$244
Depreciation at input prices	expended producing old machines	by old machines	$5.0	$4.8	$4.4	$4.0
		by new machines	$–	$0.8	$1.4	$2.1
		total	$5.0	$5.5	$5.8	$6.1
	expended producing new machines	by old machines	$15.0	$14.3	$13.2	$12.1
		by new machines	$–	$2.3	$4.3	$6.2
		total	$15.0	$16.5	$17.5	$18.3

TABLE 1   A counter-example to the Okishio Theorem (*cont.*)

			Year			
			1	2	3	4
Quantity of output	of old machines	produced by old machines	5.0	4.8	4.6	4.4
		produced by new machines	0.0	0.8	1.5	2.3
		total	*5.0*	*5.5*	*6.1*	*6.7*
	of new machines	produced by old machines	7.5	7.1	6.8	6.6
		produced by new machines	0.0	1.1	2.3	3.4
		total	*7.5*	*8.3*	*9.1*	*10.0*
Cost prices (depreciation at input prices / quantity of output)	per old machine	produced by old machines	$1.00	$1.00	$0.96	$0.92
		produced by new machines		$0.99	$0.95	$0.91
		average	*$1.00*	*$1.00*	*$0.96*	*$0.91*
	per new machine	produced by old machines	$2.00	$2.00	$1.93	$1.83
		produced by new machines		$1.98	$1.90	$1.81
		average	*$2.00*	*$2.00*	*$1.92*	*$1.83*
Ave ROP (depreciation and capital stock at input prices)			10.00%	9.32%	9.08%	9.05%
Prices of production (cost price + average ROP * capital stock at input prices / quantity of output)	per old machine	produced by old machines	$2.00	$1.93	$1.84	$1.75
		produced by new machines		$1.91	$1.82	$1.73
		average / output price	*$2.00*	*$1.93*	*$1.83*	*$1.74*
	per new machine	produced by old machines	$4.00	$3.86	$3.68	$3.49
		produced by new machines		$3.82	$3.64	$3.45
		average / output price	*$4.00*	*$3.86*	*$3.67*	*$3.48*
Revaluation of capital stock			$–	-$7.08	-$10.24	-$11.32

TABLE 1   A counter-example to the Okishio Theorem (*cont.*)

	Year			
	1	2	3	4
Ave ROP (after devaluation, depreciation and capital stock at input prices)	10.00%	6.10%	4.70%	4.42%
Total capital stock (start of year) valued at output prices	$200	$212	$222	$232
Ave ROP (depreciation at input prices, capital stock at output prices)	10.00%	9.66%	9.55%	9.54%
Depreciation at historical prices	$21.0	$22.5	$23.7	$24.6
Total profit with depreciation valued at historical prices	$19.0	$20.0	$20.9	$22.0
Total capital stock (start of year) valued at historical prices	$200	$219	$239	$260
Ave ROP (depreciation at hist. prices, capital stock at hist. prices)	9.50%	9.13%	8.73%	8.46%
Total 'depreciation' valued at output prices	$20.00	$21.21	$22.20	$23.18
Total 'profit' with depreciation valued at output prices	$20.00	$21.29	$22.34	$23.38
Ave ROP ('depreciation' at output prices, capital stock at output prices)	10.00%	10.03%	10.06%	10.08%

Turnover Time and the Organic Composition of Capital

One of Marx's major advances over classical political economy is his explanation of *why* the rate of profit tends to fall. This centres on his argument that, as capital accumulates, its 'organic composition' tends to increase. However, this concept of the organic composition of capital is widely misunderstood, and, as a result, so is Marx's explanation. This is largely due to a related failure to integrate it into Marx's understanding of the turnover time of circulating capital.

This chapter will show how these problems can be overcome, both in theory and in a way that can be operationalised using the national accounts; making it possible to quantitatively decompose the rate of profit in way that captures more of the richness of Marx's analysis than existing approaches.

1 Decomposing the Rate of Profit: Existing Approaches

Marx gives a precise definition of the organic composition of capital (OCC) in *Capital* I:

> The composition of capital is to be understood in a twofold sense. As value, it is determined by the proportion in which it is divided into constant capital, or the value of the means of production, and variable capital, or the value of labour-power, the sum total of wages. As material, as it functions in the process of production, all capital is divided into means of production and living labour-power. This latter composition is determined by the relation between the mass of the means of production employed on the one hand, and the mass of labour necessary for their employment on the other. I call the former the value-composition, the latter the technical composition of capital [TCC]. There is a close correlation between the two. To express this, I call the value-composition of capital, in so far as it mirrors the changes in the latter, the organic composition of capital. Wherever I refer to the composition of capital, without further qualification, its organic composition is always understood.[1]

---

1 Marx 1976, p. 762.

© KONINKLIJKE BRILL NV, LEIDEN, 2021 | DOI:10.1163/9789004398320_004

In other words, the change in the OCC is the change in the value composition of capital (VCC) insofar as this reflects changes in purely 'technical' or
'volumetric' factors: i.e. holding fixed the unit values of the elements of constant and variable capital.

Nevertheless, the OCC is commonly confused with the VCC, or some similar measure. The most common approach to analysing movements in the rate
of profit is to separate out 'distributional influences' from 'technical influences'.
For example, the rate of profit can be decomposed into the product of the profit
to output ratio, and the ratio of output to the capital stock:

$$ROP = \frac{profit}{output} \times \frac{output}{capital\,stock}.$$

Movements in the second ratio are then supposed to reflect movements in the
OCC, or at least to be a reasonable approximation for this. 'Marx's' LTFRP then
becomes the claim that the rate of profit falls, and it falls primarily due to a
falling output to capital ratio.

Gillman's early empirical study of the rate of profit, for example, calculates
the OCC as the ratio of constant capital to wages (though he argues that this
applies only to constant and variable capital *turned over* – see below).[2] Another
important early study, by Mage, defines the OCC as the ratio of the stock of constant capital to new value added, which he defines as $c / (v + s)$.[3] Similarly, Weisskopf uses the ratio of output to profit as a proxy for the influence of changes in
the rate of surplus value (ROSV), and the ratio of output to the capital stock as
a proxy for the influence of changes in the OCC.[4] More recently, Kliman takes
a similar approach to decomposing changes in the rate of profit (though he is
careful *not* to confuse this with measuring the OCC), as do Mohun, Basu and
Vasudevan.[5]

Early in *Capital* III, Marx does do something similar. He examines the effect
of changes in the rate of surplus value (s/v) and the ratio of variable capital to
total capital advanced (v/C) on the rate of profit (s/C). But in doing so, he tells
us he is ignoring the influence of the rate of turnover of variable capital; which,
as we will explore in this chapter, must be understood if we are to measure the
VCC and the OCC accurately.[6]

---

2 Gillman 1957, p. 16.
3 Mage 1963, pp. 68–74.
4 Weisskopf 1979, pp. 342–3.
5 Basu and Vasudevan 2012, pp. 72–3; Mohun 2006, pp. 347–8; Kliman 2011, pp. 128–33.
6 Marx 1981, p. 142.

Marx also has a detailed argument about *why* v/C tends to fall over time, which can only be understood if we understand the differences between the VCC, the TCC and the OCC. First, for Marx, it is almost true by definition that the development of the forces of production under capitalism will result in a growing TCC and hence a growing OCC:

> Apart from natural conditions, such as the fertility of the soil, etc., and apart from the skill of independent and isolated producers ... the level of the social productivity of labour is expressed in the relative extent of the means of production that one worker, during a given time, with the same degree of intensity of labour-power, turns into products ... This change in the technical composition of capital, this growth in the mass of the means of production, as compared with the mass of the labour-power that vivifies them, is reflected in its value-composition by the increase of the constant constituent of capital at the expense of its variable constituent.[7]

It is less certain (though still likely) that the rising TCC, and hence the rising OCC, will express itself in a rising *value* composition. The chief counter-tendency to this process is the cheapening of constant capital (new and existing). As Marx puts it:

> the same development that raises the mass of constant capital in comparison with variable reduces the value of its elements, as a result of the higher productivity of labour, and hence prevents the value of the constant capital, even though this grows steadily, from growing in the same degree as its material volume, i.e. the material volume of the means of production that are set in motion by the same amount of labour-power.[8]

Fine and Harris recognise the importance of Marx's distinction between the OCC and the VCC. They return to Marx's definition of the OCC quoted above, and point out that this makes it clear that the OCC cannot be the ratio of c to v at current prices. Instead, Marx implies that the OCC is the ratio of constant to variable capital at their 'old values': i.e. holding the unit values of the elements of constant and variable capital constant.[9] In this way, the OCC is equivalent to the VCC insofar as it 'mirrors changes' in the technical composition of cap-

---

7   Marx 1976, p. 773.

8   Marx 1981, pp. 342–3.

9   Fine and Harris 1979, p. 59.

ital. Under this approach it also becomes possible to identify the cheapening of constant capital as a distinct counter-tendency to the rising OCC.

There is also the related problem of whether the OCC refers to flow magnitudes or to stocks. Gillman defines the OCC as the ratio of constant capital turned over to variable capital turned over: i.e. he defines it purely in terms of flows. The problem with this approach is that it is not clear exactly how this definition of the OCC relates to the rate of profit, since the rate of profit is the ratio of surplus value to the *stock* of capital, as Marx makes clear.[10] Gillman's definition of the OCC leads him to calculate two separate measures of the rate of profit, one on a stock basis and one on a flow basis.

Mage draws attention to this problem, and instead defines the OCC as the ratio of a stock to a yearly flow.[11] This aspect of his definition has become widely accepted, and makes it unnecessary to calculate the turnover time to calculate the OCC. Defined in this way, the OCC is no longer a measure of the composition of *capital* tied up at a point in time, but the ratio of capital to an annual flow. If this definition is an accurate interpretation, then it is not clear why Marx devotes considerable space to discussing the turnover time of variable capital, or why he and Engels thought that its tendency to get shorter acted as a counteracting tendency to the falling annual rate of profit.

Below we will set out an alternative approach.

2   The Stock of Variable Capital

Let us consider the VCC first. As Marx explains in the definition given above, this is the ratio of constant capital, c, to variable capital, v. As we have seen, Marxists are used to thinking of variable capital as a synonym for annual wages, and hence think of the VCC as the ratio of a stock to a flow.

This chapter proposes that the VCC is better conceived of as the ratio of one portion of the stock of capital advanced to another. But what is the *stock* of variable capital, and how might we measure it? One possibility is to estimate it indirectly, by first measuring the number of turnovers of variable capital that take place during a period, and dividing this by wages. But I have not found anywhere where Marx or Engels gives an actual method for measuring turnover time or the stock of variable capital. Nor are any of the methods proposed in the secondary literature ideal (they are reviewed at the end of the chapter).

---

10   Marx 1981, pp. 136–7.
11   Mage 1963, pp. 69–70.

Indeed, arguably Marx never fully integrates his extensive analysis of turn-over time in *Capital* II into his analysis of the rate of profit in Volume 3. As mentioned, early in Volume 3 he explicitly assumes away the effect of changing turnover times on the annual rate of profit.[12] He says he will take this up in a later chapter, but as it turned out, it was left to Engels to write a chapter on the subject which he inserted into Volume 3 as Chapter 4.

As far as they go, Engels' observations in this chapter are sound. He points out that there are two main ways of increasing the rate at which variable capital turns over and hence increasing the rate of profit: shortening production time by increasing the productivity of labour (which, however, also often involves an increase in the OCC); or shortening circulation time, e.g. through faster transportation.[13]

However, I do not think he gives a clear method for calculating the stock of variable capital advanced. He begins by observing, correctly, that 'the capitalist himself does not know in most cases how much variable capital he employs in his business', and points out, again correctly, that we cannot calculate the amount of variable capital tied up in a business based on wages data alone.[14] He then tries to set out a method for calculating the number of turnovers of variable capital, based on an example from a spinning mill Marx gives in *Capital* I. However, in this example, Engels explains '[t]he circulating capital was not given; we shall take it to be £2,500'.[15] Once Engels has *assumed* we know the value of the circulating capital tied up at a point in time, it is possible to calculate the turnover time of circulating capital, based on the weekly expenses Marx sets out in the original example. Engels may have made this assumption because, as we will see, the value of circulating capital is generally equal to inventories, which accountants do measure. But Engels does not actually *say* that the two are equal, and, in any case, this needs to be demonstrated, and not merely asserted. So the overall effect seems to be to re-state the original problem in a different form, not to solve it.

To solve it ourselves, we need to conceptualise the circuit though which variable capital passes. Suppose a capitalist starts a new business producing widgets. Before production can begin, she has to obtain some money capital (M) to pay her initial expenses, including wages. When the wages bill is due – say, at the end of every week – she pays the workers out of this stock of money capital, and has to ensure that there is enough available at the end of every week to cover this expense.

---

12   Marx 1981, p. 142.
13   Marx 1981, pp. 163–4.
14   Marx 1981, p. 167.
15   Marx 1981, p. 168.

Suppose our capitalists' wages bill is $20,000 per year, suppose each batch of widgets takes 2 weeks to produce, and suppose it takes a further 4 weeks to ship to each batch its buyers, whose payment is received at the beginning of the next week. In that case, by the end of the 6th week, our capitalist will have paid out $120,000 in wages, but not yet received any income from selling widgets. In other words, she has had to *advance* $120,000 of variable capital. This is tabulated in Table 2.

If our capitalist has no access to credit, and cannot obtain any extra money as production proceeds, she will have to obtain the whole of this $120,000 before production starts. This is the assumption Marx works with in *Capital* II:

> Take capital A of £500, for instance. It is advanced for five weeks, but each week only £100 of it successively enters the labour process. In the first week, one fifth of it is applied [£100]; four fifths [£400] is advanced without being applied, although since it must be on hand for the labour process for the four following weeks it must certainly be advanced.[16]

That is, Marx argues the capitalist must keep enough capital on hand to cover the entire wages bill from the start of the production period until the end of the circulation period.

Notice that, if this is the case, then the stock of variable capital advanced is not necessarily equal to the wages cost of unsold and unfinished commodities. In our example, at the end of the first week, the wages cost of the stock of widgets will be $20,000, but the stock of variable capital would be $120,000. Only by the end of the 6th week would the two be equal, and even then, this would only be true until payment for the widgets is received at the beginning of the next week. If we use this conception of variable capital advanced, then to measure it precisely, we would need to know the wages bill and the combined length of the production and circulation periods for each industry, and multiply the two together.

In practice, however, the capitalist does not have to keep the entire $120,000 tied up in her stock of capital from the beginning of the production period. If she has access to credit, she only needs to obtain as much money as is necessary to pay her wages bill when it falls due. For example, suppose she did in fact start with $120,000 set aside to pay wages. In the first week, all she has to do is to ensure she can pay $20,000 by Friday. She can lend out the rest of her $120,000 at interest, which may then be lent to another capitalist for some

---

16   Marx 1981, p. 374.

other purpose, such as paying *their* wages bill. If she has a bank account, and leaves the $120,000 deposited there, the banker will perform this function for her. This raises the question of exactly what such a bank account *is*, and what portion of its value, if any, remains tied up in the overall stock of capital. We will address this question in chapters 5 and 6 on finance.

But in this chapter, we will restrict our attention to the capital that must unavoidably be advanced for the wages bill to be paid on time. We will call *this* the stock of variable capital. In effect, we are relaxing Marx's assumption that there are no credit relations. This means that, in the first 6 weeks, the stock of variable capital advanced will not be $120,000 from the beginning of the first week, but will grow from zero to $20,000 at the end of week one, and then grow by a further $20,000 for each of the next 5 weeks. At the end of every week, this will be equal to the wages cost of the inventory of widgets which are unfinished, unsold, or for which payment is yet to be received. And if the workers were paid for their work continuously, rather than having to advance their labour power to the capitalist over the course of every pay period, then the stock of variable capital and the wages cost component of inventories would be equal throughout (as discussed further below).

By the end of the 6th week, the workers will have produced three fortnights' worth of widgets, with batches finished at the end of week 2, week 4 and week 6. At this stage, the first batch has reached its destination, but payment has not yet been received, and the other two batches have not yet completed their circulation period. So the wages cost of the finished widgets for which payment has not yet been received is 3 × 2 × $20,000 = $120,000: again, equal to the stock of variable capital.

What about the workers' consumption? If we assume the workers spend all of their wages at a steady rate throughout the week, and that workers manage to cover these same costs in their first week of work out of their savings (before they have been paid anything), then, throughout these first 6 weeks, the value of their accumulated consumption will be equal to the wages cost of inventories. That is, the wages cost component of inventories will reflect the accumulated value of the labour power that was expended to produce them. In the next chapter, we will see that this is not always the case: that there can be a difference between the price of labour power (the wage) and its value.

But now let us continue with the example. At the start of the 7th week, our capitalist sells her first consignment of widgets, the ones her workers finished producing at the end of the 2nd week. Suppose she sells these above their cost price. This means she recovers the full cost of the wages paid to workers in the first two weeks – $40,000, equivalent to the variable capital the widgets embody – plus the constant capital component of the widgets' cost price and a profit. So, temporarily, the stock of variable capital falls to $80,000, before rising back up to $100,000 when the wages bill is due at the end of the week. That is, $40,000 is temporarily 'released' from the stock of variable capital when the widgets are sold; then, when the next wages bill is due at the end of the week, another $20,000 is tied back up. As before, this is equivalent to the wages cost of unsold and unfinished widgets, which is now $7 - 2 = 5$ weeks' worth, i.e. $100,000.

In the 8th week, no widgets are sold and another $20,000 is paid out in wages. So the stock of variable capital advanced rises back up to $120,000, i.e. the remaining $20,000 of the $40,000 that was released at the start of last week is tied back up, and the wages cost of the stock of unsold and unfinished widgets rises by $20,000. In the 9th week, more widgets are sold, and variable capital advanced falls back to $80,000 and then reaches $100,000 by the end of the week; then, by the end of week 10, it rises back up to $120,000, and continues to alternate in this way – $120,000 at the end of even numbered weeks, $100,000 at the end of odd numbered weeks. This pattern continues while the production period, circulation period and wages stay constant, and the widgets are not sold at a loss.

Expressed more generally, the stock of variable capital, v, expands by the difference between the wages bill, w, and the wages cost component of the total price of final commodities sold during the period, which we will call 'vr' (for 'variable capital realised'). This is before we take into account the effects of devaluation, which we will introduce soon.

But now suppose, due to a technical improvement, from the 20th week onwards it takes 3 weeks instead of 4 for each new consignment of widgets to reach its destination and be sold. This means the widgets shipped in the 20th week will now reach their destination in the 23rd week, and payment will be received at the beginning of the 24th. So, by the end of the 24th week, instead of increasing to $120,000, the stock of variable capital advanced will fall to $80,000. Then, in the 25th week, no widgets will be sold, and variable capital advanced will increase to $100,000. Widgets will be sold again in week 26, and variable capital advanced will fall back down to $80,000; and this pattern will continue. In this case, $20,000 of variable capital has been released permanently, corresponding to the one week's worth of widgets that no longer need to be tied up in the circulation process (and the one weeks' worth of workers' consumption that no longer has to be covered by wage payments in advance of receiving payment for output). This is *not* profit: it is the 'release' of part of the original amount of variable capital that the capitalist advanced.

Now suppose, at the start of week 27, it becomes possible to produce twice as many widgets in the same SNLT and using the same equipment and cost

TABLE 2   Turnover of variable capital

Week (t)	Wages paid at the end of each week ($w_{t-1,t}$)	Wages cost component of income ($vr_{t-1,t}$)	Wages cost component of unsold and unfinished widgets at end of week (v_t)
1	$20,000	$0	$20,000
2	$20,000	$0	$40,000
3	$20,000	$0	$60,000
4	$20,000	$0	$80,000
5	$20,000	$0	$100,000
6	$20,000	$0	$120,000
7	$20,000	$40,000	$100,000
8	$20,000	$0	$120,000
9	$20,000	$40,000	$100,000
10	$20,000	$0	$120,000
...	...	...	...
20	$20,000	$0	$120,000
21	$20,000	$40,000	$100,000
22	$20,000	$0	$120,000
23	$20,000	$40,000	$100,000
24	$20,000	$40,000	$80,000
25	$20,000	$0	$100,000
26	$20,000	$40,000	$80,000
27	$20,000	$0	$50,000 (inc. −$50,000 revaluation)

of inputs. That is, the value of each widget halves, and the quantity of output doubles. Suppose this also causes the price of widgets to fall by half. This means the current price of inventories will also fall by half. Similarly, in replacement cost terms, the wages cost component of inventories will also fall by half, from $100,000 at historical cost to $50,000 at replacement cost. For the capitalist, this is a loss of $50,000, which is deducted from their stock of variable capital, and from their profits (as a devaluation). Notice this is quite different from a *release* of variable capital, which transforms part of the value of inventories into cash. But its effect on the stock of variable capital is the same, and we need to account for by incorporating it into our expression for the change in the stock of variable capital advanced. We can do this calculating growth in the stock of variable capital as the difference between wages and the wages cost component of final commodities sold, and adding the initial stock of variable capital multiplied by the ratio of the revaluation of inventories to the initial stock of inventories. As in all cases we need to adjust all these magnitudes for MELT-inflation.

To apply this method in practice we need to make two estimates: 1) an estimate of the stock of variable capital initially (since to calculate the stock of variable capital based on an equation for its growth we need to know its initial level); and 2) an estimate of the wages cost of final commodities sold (since the national accounts do not track this directly). The most straightforward way to estimate (1) is to multiply the initial stock of inventories by the wages cost of output for the preceding year (i.e. the ratio of wages to output). Similarly, we can estimate (2) by multiplying total sales of final commodities for the year by the ratio of wages to output for that year.[17]

We can also use the estimates of vr and v to estimate the number of turnovers of variable capital that take place during the period, which we will call nv. This is just the ratio of vr to v: i.e. the ratio of the total value of variable capital turned over to the initial stock of variable capital.

In Chapter 7 we will check this against the ratio of sales of final commodities to inventories, which is a simpler way of estimating nv. Effectively this simpler method assumes $v = (w/y) \times inv$ every year, and not just in the first year. The two approximations should give similar results.

Now that we can estimate the *stock* of variable capital we can estimate the VCC as the ratio of one stock to another. First, we define the stock of constant capital (c) as what is left over after subtracting variable capital from the total stock of capital (i.e. inventories plus fixed capital). Constant capital therefore incorporates the stock of fixed capital, and the depreciation and profit components of the total price of inventories. The VCC is then just the ratio of c to v.

Note that our measure of turnover time also allows us to apply Marx's neglected distinction between the 'real' rate of surplus value and the annual rate of surplus value.[18] The real rate of surplus value is just the familiar ratio of surplus value produced over a year to wages paid over a year, s/w. The *annual* rate of surplus value, however, is the ratio of surplus value produced over the year to the *stock* of variable capital at the start: i.e. s/v.

---

17   This simplifies to give the following expression for the stock of variable capital at the end of the year:

$$v_{t+1} \approx v_t + w_{t,t+1} - \frac{w_{t,t+1}}{y_{t,t+1}} \times ys_{t,t+1} + Rinv_{t,t+1} \times \frac{v_t}{inv_t} = (1 + \frac{Rinv_{t,t+1}}{inv_t})v_t + (1 - \frac{ys_{t,t+1}}{y_{t,t+1}})w_{t,t+1}$$

where: v = the stock of variable capital, w = total wages, y = output, ys = (final) output sold, $Rinv$ = revaluation of inventories (see previous chapter), and inv = the stock of inventories.

18   Marx 1978b, pp. 369–383.

3   The OCC

With the stock of variable capital, turnover time and the VCC defined, we are in a position to define the OCC. As mentioned, for Marx this is the 'value-composition of capital, in so far as it mirrors the changes in the [TCC].'[19] The TCC 'is determined by the relation between the mass of the means of production employed on the one hand, and the mass of labour necessary for their employment on the other'.[20]

But to speak of *the* TCC is somewhat misleading. In a single branch which uses a single input, we could measure *the* TCC as the ratio of inputs to hours worked. For the spinning industry, for example, we could measure how many kilograms of raw cotton each spinning worker can turn into yarn per hour (setting aside the depreciation of the machines). But in other industries, there are other, qualitatively different TCCs – e.g. the ratio of iron ore to labour hours in the steel industry. Even within an industry there is generally more than one TCC – e.g. in the steel industry we could also measure the ratio of coal to labour hours. In other words, it is only possible to measure technical compositions of capital in the plural, using a measure with different units for each type of input.

Fortunately, this does not pose problems for measuring the OCC. Following Fine and Harris, and Marx's own definition given above, I take Marx to mean that the OCC measures what would have happened to the VCC over time if only the TCCs had changed – i.e. if unit prices had remained constant while the quantities of constant capital and hours worked per turnover had changed.[21]

National accounts can be used to approximate this, since standard measures of inflation rely on tracking changes in volume indexes at fixed prices. Since the OCC measures what would have happened to the VCC over a period of time, to calculate its value at any point in time we have to specify an initial reference point. This is i in the expression below.

$$OCC_t = \frac{(F_i + inv_i) \times \frac{QC_t}{QC_i} - v_i \times \frac{L_{t,t+1}/nv_{t,t+1}}{L_{i,i+1}/nv_{i,i+1}}}{v_i \times \frac{L_{t,t+1}/nv_{t,t+1}}{L_{i,i+1}/nv_{i,i+1}}}.$$

Here, QC is a volumetric index for the stock of fixed assets and inventories. The national accounts report these indexes separately, but to avoid unnecessary complications later, we need a single index. We can construct this in the following way, where QF is the volumetric index for fixed assets, and $Qinv$ is the index for inventories:

---

19   Marx 1976, p. 762.
20   Marx 1981, p. 762.
21   Fine and Harris 1979, p. 59.

$$QC_t = \frac{F_i \times \frac{Qf_t}{Qf_i} + inv_i \times \frac{Qinv_t}{Qinv_i}}{F_i + inv_i} \times 100.$$

In the definition above, note that the OCC at time t is defined in terms of the value added by living labour over a single turnover for the *following* period: i.e. for the period $t, t + 1$. This is because Marx specifies that the TCC is the mass of labour necessary for the employment of the existing means of production. Since the means of production must first be produced and *then* the labour power necessary for their employment obtained, we have defined the OCC in terms of employment in the following period rather than the preceding period.

One final aspect of this definition is worth noting. The OCC is *not only* what the VCC would be if there were no devaluation or revaluation. The OCC is *also* influenced by the ROSV, because the ROSV affects the size of the stock of variable capital. This will be important for the decomposition below.

4   Conclusion

Now we have explored the relationships between inflation, capital advanced, revaluation, the turnover time of variable capital, the VCC, the OCC, the real and the annual rates of surplus value, and, of course, the rate of profit. But to actually measure any of these, we need methods for measuring output and surplus value using the national accounts. This is what we will set out in the next chapter.

5   Appendix: Decomposing Changes in the Rate of Profit

Now that we can measure the OCC, we have the basis for quantifying its influence on the rate of profit. This appendix shows how we can identify, separately, the influences on the rate of profit of changes in the OCC, turnover time, the rate of surplus value, the devaluation of the existing capital stock and the cheapening of new elements of the capital stock. Unlike the standard decomposition, this will allow us to test directly whether the rising OCC (if it rises) is the main influence on the falling rate of profit (if it falls). Readers can choose whether to go through the working in this section or take its results 'on faith'.

Neither Marx nor Engels gives us a formula for separating out the effect of the OCC on the ROP, but in his chapter on turnover time, Engels makes a relevant observation. He argues the formula $p' = s'v/C$ [the rate of profit] is strictly correct only for a single turnover period of the variable capital, while for the annual turnover the simple rate of surplus-value s' has to be replaced by $s'n$, the annual rate of surplus-value, n standing for the number of turnovers that the variable capital makes in the course of a year.[22]

This suggests a decomposition based on three terms, not two: i.e. separating the influence of the ROSV, the VCC and turnover time. Our expression for the rate of profit:

$$ROP_{t,t+1} = \frac{s_{t,t+1}}{F_t + inv_t}$$

can also be expressed in the more familiar form:

$$ROP_{t,t+1} = \frac{s_{t,t+1}}{c_t + v_t}$$

since we now know $c + v = F + inv$.

If we divide through by our estimate of v_t, this becomes:

$$ROP_{t,t+1} = \frac{s_{t,t+1}/v_t}{\frac{c_t}{v_t} + 1} = \frac{s_{t,t+1}/v_t}{VCC_t + 1}.$$

Now, since

$$v_t = \frac{vr_{t,t+1}}{nv_{t,t+1}};$$

$$ROP_{t,t+1} = \frac{s_{t,t+1} \times \frac{nv_{t,t+1}}{vr_{t,t+1}}}{VCC_t + 1}.$$

Substituting in our expression for the estimate of vr:

$$ROP_{t,t+1} = \frac{s_{t,t+1} \times nv_{t,t+1} \times \frac{y_{t,t+1}}{w_{t,t+1}} \times \frac{1}{ys_{t,t+1}}}{VCC_t + 1} = \frac{\frac{s_{t,t+1}}{w_{t,t+1}} \times nv_{t,t+1} \times \frac{y_{t,t+1}}{ys_{t,t+1}}}{VCC_t + 1}.$$

---

22 Marx 1981, p. 142. It is also worth observing that in Volume 2 Marx comments that confusion surrounding the distinction between the annual rate of surplus value and the rate of surplus value 'led to the complete destruction of the Ricardian school', suggesting he thought this distinction was rather important. Marx 1978b, p. 373.

We also know that the ratio of s to w is the rate of surplus value; i.e.

$$ROSV_{t,t+1} \equiv \frac{s_{t,t+1}}{w_{t,t+1}}.\ 23$$

Therefore

$$ROP_{t,t+1} = \frac{ROSV_{t,t+1} \times \left(nv_{t,t+1} \times \frac{y_{t,t+1}}{ys_{t,t+1}}\right)}{VCC_t + 1}.$$

This breaks up the expression for the rate of profit into three component parts: the rate of surplus value, the VCC, and the number of turnovers of variable capital multiplied by the ratio of output to sales (y to ys, which will drop out further below).

Next, we want to separate the influence of the OCC from the effect of other changes in the VCC. So we will rearrange the expression as follows:

$$ROP_{t,t+1} = \frac{ROSV_{t,t+1} \times nv_{t,t+1} \times \frac{y_{t,t+1}}{ys_{t,t+1}}}{\frac{VCC_t+1}{OCC_t+1} \times (OCC_t + 1)}.$$

As an approximation, we could use these four terms as the basis for our decomposition of the rate of profit. But the ratio $(VCC + 1)\,/\,(OCC + 1)$ in fact incorporates several different influences. The difference between the change in constant capital in purely volumetric terms and the actual change in constant capital is the effect of changes in the prices of the elements of constant capital. However, for the variable capital component the relationship between the OCC and the VCC is more complicated. The purely volumetric influence is the effect of changes in the total SNLT performed by productive workers. But the stock of variable capital is also influenced by the ROSV, the turnover time of variable capital, and any devaluation or revaluation of the existing stock of inventories. We want to separate out all these influences. First, we can re-arrange the expression in the following way:

$$\frac{VCC_t + 1}{OCC_t + 1} = \left(\frac{C_t - v_t}{v_t} + 1\right) \Big/ \left(\frac{C_i \times \frac{QC_t}{QC_i} - v_i \times \frac{L_{t,t+1}/nv_{t,t+1}}{L_{i,i+1}/nv_{i,i+1}}}{v_i \times \frac{L_{t,t+1}/nv_{t,t+1}}{L_{i,i+1}/nv_{i,i+1}}} + 1\right)$$

$$= \frac{C_t}{v_t} \times \frac{v_i \times \frac{L_{t,t+1}/nv_{t,t+1}}{L_{i,i+1}/nv_{i,i+1}}}{C_i \times \frac{QC_t}{QC_i}} = \frac{C_t}{C_i \times \frac{QC_t}{QC_i}} \times \frac{L_{t,t+1}/nv_{t,t+1}}{L_{i,i+1}/nv_{i,i+1}} \times \frac{v_i}{v_t}.$$

23 Though this definition is modified in the next chapter.

The first ratio here is the ratio of the stock of capital advanced after the effect of price changes to the stock of capital advanced excluding them. So this is a measure of the combined effect of devaluation and revaluation on the existing stock of capital advanced at time i, and the effect of the cheapening of capital on newly produced capital advanced since time i. We will set this aside to separate out the effects of the rate of surplus value and changes in turnover time on the ratio of the stock of variable capital to living labour employed, i.e. on:

$$\frac{L_{t,t+1}}{L_{i,i+1}} \times \frac{v_i}{v_t} \times \frac{nv_{i,i+1}}{nv_{t,t+1}}.$$

First, since

$$v_t = \frac{vr_{t,t+1}}{nv_{t,t+1}};$$

$$\frac{L_{t,t+1}}{L_{i,i+1}} \times \frac{v_i}{v_t} \times \frac{nv_{i,i+1}}{nv_{t,t+1}} = \frac{L_{t,t+1}}{L_{i,i+1}} \times \frac{vr_{i,i+1}}{nv_{i,i+1}} \times \frac{nv_{t,t+1}}{vr_{t,t+1}} \times \frac{nv_{i,i+1}}{nv_{t,t+1}} = \frac{L_{t,t+1}}{L_{i,i+1}} \times \frac{vr_{i,i+1}}{vr_{t,t+1}}.$$

We are also using this approximation for vr:

$$vr_{t,t+1} = \frac{w_{t,t+1}}{y_{t,t+1}} \times ys_{t,t+1};$$

so

$$\frac{L_{t,t+1}}{L_{i,i+1}} \times \frac{vr_{i,i+1}}{vr_{t,t+1}} = \frac{L_{t,t+1}}{L_{i,i+1}} \times \frac{\frac{w_{i,i+1}}{y_{i,i+1}} \times ys_{i,i+1}}{\frac{w_{t,t+1}}{y_{t,t+1}} \times ys_{t,t+1}} = \frac{w_{i,i+1}/L_{i,i+1}}{\frac{y_{i,i+1}}{ys_{i,i+1}}} \bigg/ \frac{w_{t,t+1}/L_{t,t+1}}{\frac{y_{t,t+1}}{ys_{t,t+1}}}.$$

That is, our expression is equal to the ratio of the initial wage rate to the ratio of output to sales, divided by the same ratio for the current period.

The wage rate is determined by the rate of surplus value, since:

$$ROSV_{t,t+1} = \frac{s_{t,t+1}}{w_{t,t+1}} = \frac{L_{t,t+1} - w_{t,t+1}}{w_{t,t+1}} = \frac{L_{t,t+1}}{w_{t,t+1}} - 1$$

$$\frac{w_{t,t+1}}{L_{t,t+1}} = \frac{1}{ROSV_{t,t+1} + 1}.$$

As the next chapter will discuss, here we are implicitly assuming that the wage is equal to the total cost of the commodities consumed by producers. In the next chapter we will relax this assumption, which will change our definition of the ROSV. But for the moment, we can now say:

$$\frac{L_{t,t+1}}{L_{i,i+1}} \times \frac{vr_{i,i+1}}{vr_{t,t+1}} = \frac{\frac{y_{t,t+1}}{ys_{t,t+1}} \times (ROSV_{t,t+1} + 1)}{\frac{y_{i,i+1}}{ys_{i,i+1}} \times (ROSV_{i,i+1} + 1)}.$$

Hence $(VCC + 1) / (OCC + 1)$ can be expressed as the product of the ratios of: capital advanced at current prices to capital advanced at initial prices; the current number of turnovers to the initial number of turnovers, after multiplying by the ratio of output to sales; and the ratio of the current rate of surplus value plus one to the initial rate of surplus value plus one, i.e.

$$\frac{VCC_t + 1}{OCC_t + 1} = \frac{C_t}{C_i \times \frac{QC_t}{QC_i}} \times \frac{\frac{y_{t,t+1}}{ys_{t,t+1}}}{\frac{y_{i,i+1}}{ys_{i,i+1}}} \times \frac{ROSV_{t,t+1} + 1}{ROSV_{i,i+1} + 1}.$$

Now, applying this to the rate of profit:

$$ROP_{t,t+1} = \frac{ROSV_{t,t+1} \times nv_{t,t+1} \times \frac{y_{t,t+1}}{ys_{t,t+1}}}{\frac{VCC_t+1}{OCC_t+1} \times (OCC_t + 1)}$$

$$ROP_{t,t+1} = ROSV_{t,t+1} \times nv_{t,t+1} \times \frac{y_{t,t+1}}{ys_{t,t+1}} \times \frac{C_i \times \frac{QC_t}{QC_i}}{C_t} \times \frac{\frac{y_{i,i+1}}{ys_{i,i+1}}}{\frac{y_{t,t+1}}{ys_{t,t+1}}} \times$$

$$\frac{ROSV_{i,i+1} + 1}{ROSV_{t,t+1} + 1} \times \frac{1}{OCC_t + 1} = \frac{ROSV_{t,t+1}}{ROSV_{t,t+1} + 1} \times nv_{t,t+1} \times \frac{C_i \times \frac{QC_t}{QC_i}}{C_t} \times \frac{y_{i,i+1}}{ys_{i,i+1}} \times$$

$$(ROSV_{i,i+1} + 1) \times \frac{1}{OCC_t + 1}.$$

Between any two periods, the average exponential growth rate of the rate of profit is the difference between the natural logarithm of the rate of profit in each period. We can use this to decompose changes in the rate of profit between any period $t, t + 1$ and a later period $f, f + 1$ in the following way:

$$\log(ROP_{f,f+1}) - \log(ROP_{t,t+1}) = \log\left(\frac{ROSV_{f,f+1}}{ROSV_{f,f+1} + 1} \Big/ \frac{ROSV_{t,t+1}}{ROSV_{t,t+1} + 1}\right) +$$

$$\log\left(\frac{nv_{f,f+1}}{nv_{t,t+1}}\right) + \log\left(\frac{C_i \times \frac{QC_f}{QC_i}}{C_f} \Big/ \frac{C_i \times \frac{QC_t}{QC_i}}{C_t}\right) + \log\left(\frac{y_{i,i+1}}{ys_{i,i+1}} \times \frac{ys_{i,i+1}}{y_{i,i+1}} \times\right.$$

$$\left.\frac{ROSV_{i,i+1} + 1}{ROSV_{i,i+1} + 1}\right) + \log\left(\frac{OCC_f + 1}{OCC_t + 1}\right) = \log\left(\frac{ROSV_{f,f+1}}{ROSV_{f,f+1} + 1} \Big/ \frac{ROSV_{t,t+1}}{ROSV_{t,t+1} + 1}\right) +$$

$$\log\left(\frac{nv_{f,f+1}}{nv_{t,t+1}}\right) - \log\left(\frac{C_f}{QC_f} \Big/ \frac{C_t}{QC_t}\right) + \log\left(\frac{OCC_t + 1}{OCC_f + 1}\right).$$

Notice here that this measure no longer depends on choosing an arbitrary initial point in time i.

This allows us to neatly separate out the influence on the rate of profit of the rate of surplus value, the turnover time of variable capital, the effect of (inflation-adjusted) changes in the prices of the material elements of capital advanced, and the effect of changes in the OCC. In the expression above, these correspond to each of the four logarithms in order.

Note that, in each case, this is not 'what the rate of profit would have been in the year beginning at time f if the OCC were the only factor that changed since the initial year', but rather 'the influence which changes in the OCC have had since the initial year given other factors also changed'. If we were using the first type of measure, the negative influence of the OCC could never exceed the initial level of the rate of profit, since no matter how much the OCC rises, it can never make surplus value and hence the rate of profit negative. But since we are using the second type of measure, it is possible for the cumulative negative influence of the OCC to exceed the initial level of the rate of profit. The advantage of this approach is that, each year, the sum of the four influences is equal to the change in the rate of profit.

Also note that the third term, the effect of changes in prices on the stock of capital advanced, just subtracts the log of the ratio of the average price of capital advanced at times f and t (i.e. the ratio of the total values of the stocks divided by their volumes), since:

$$\frac{C_f}{QC_f} \bigg/ \frac{C_t}{QC_t} = \frac{PC_f}{PC_t}$$

where PC is an index of the average price level of constant capital.

Thus this incorporates the effect of both revaluation (i.e. the effect of price changes on the already existing stock) and the effect of price changes on the newly produced stock. We will now separate these out. Recall from the last chapter that:

$$RF_{t,t+1} \equiv F_t - F_{t+1} - i_{t,t+1} + d_{t,t+1}$$

where RF is revaluation of fixed assets. This can be generalised to apply to any two points in time t and f:

$$RF_{t,f} \equiv F_f - F_f - i_{t,f} + d_{t,f}.$$

A similar relationship is true for the revaluation of inventories:

$$Rinv_{t,f} \equiv inv_f - inv_t + ys_{t,f} - y_{t,f}.$$

So now we can measure total revaluation, R:

$$R_{t,f} \equiv RF_{t,f} + Rinv_{t,f}.$$

Returning to the expression for the ratio of the average prices of capital advanced between two points in time, we can separate out the influence of revaluation on the pre-existing stock of capital advanced from its influence on the value of the newly produced stock:

$$\frac{C_f}{QC_f} \bigg/ \frac{C_t}{QC_t} = \frac{C_f}{QC_f} \times \frac{C_f - R_{t,f}}{C_f - R_{t,f}} \bigg/ \frac{C_t}{QC_t} = \frac{C_f}{C_f - R_{t,f}} \times \frac{C_f - R_{t,f}}{QC_f} \bigg/ \frac{C_t}{QC_t} =$$
$$\frac{C_f}{C_f - R_{t,f}} \times \frac{C_f - R_{t,f}}{C_t \times \frac{QC_f}{QC_t}}.$$

So

$$-\log\left(\frac{C_f}{QC_f} \bigg/ \frac{C_t}{QC_t}\right) = -\log\left(\frac{C_f}{C_f - R_{t,f}} \times \frac{C_f - R_{t,f}}{C_t \times \frac{QC_f}{QC_t}}\right) = -\log\left(\frac{C_f}{C_f - R_{t,f}}\right) -$$
$$\log\left(\frac{C_f - R_{t,f}}{C_t \times \frac{QC_f}{QC_t}}\right).$$

Here, the first term is the log of the ratio of the final stock of C to what the stock of C would have been if there had been no revaluation over the previous year. This (multiplied by minus one) is the effect of revaluation on the rate of profit. The second is the log of the ratio of C excluding revaluation to the initial stock of C multiplied by its volumetric increase (in other words, what C would have been if the initial stock and the quantity of investment in inventories and fixed capital was valued at initial prices). This is the effect on the rate of profit of the cheapening (or otherwise) of the elements of capital advanced on the value of its newly produced material elements. Finally, we can incorporate this into the decomposition of the rate of profit:

$$\log(ROP_{f,f+1}) - \log(ROP_{t,t+1}) = \log\left(\frac{ROSV_{f,f+1}}{ROSV_{f,f+1} + 1} \bigg/ \frac{ROSV_{t,t+1}}{ROSV_{t,t+1} + 1}\right) +$$
$$\log\left(\frac{nv_{f,f+1}}{nv_{t,t+1}}\right) - \log\left(\frac{C_f}{C_f - R_{t,f}}\right) - \log\left(\frac{C_f - R_{t,f}}{C_t \times \frac{QC_f}{QC_t}}\right) + \log\left(\frac{OCC_t + 1}{OCC_f + 1}\right).$$

CHAPTER 4

Surplus Value, Profit and Output

So far we have been assuming that measuring the numerator of the rate of profit is not a problem, as long as we refrain from valuing inputs at output prices. But there are still major practical issues we need to discuss and resolve before we can translate the national accounts into measures of total profit we can use to test Marx's law. We also need to specify Marx's value theory in a precise enough way that concepts like surplus value, profit and output can be measured empirically without making too many approximations or conflating Marx's concepts with the ones used in the national accounts. Without going through this process thoroughly we leave the work open to the charge that the measures used to test Marx's hypotheses have been 'backwards engineered' to get a desired result, rather than being consistent with first principles.

For this reason most of this chapter is concerned with explaining and justifying why the national accounts have been used in a particular way to calculate Marx's aggregates, pointing out where we have had to use approximations, and the extent to which these might affect the results. Readers less interested in this detailed work could skip this chapter, though the work on productive and unproductive labour and the value of labour power may be of more general theoretical interest. The distinction between profits from production and surplus value less unproductive expenditures also gets taken up later in the book when reporting on results for various measures of the rate of profit and specifying the relationship between rates of profit and financial rates of return.

The main theme of the chapter is that the relationship between surplus value and profit is not straightforward, even at the aggregate level. It starts by looking at Marx's distinction between productive and unproductive labour, and how this influences the relationship between profit and surplus value. It then shows how this relationship is further mystified by borrowing and saving: specifically, how government borrowing can create additional after-tax profit from production, without any change in the production or expenditure of surplus value; and how differences between wages and workers' consumption also mean that surplus value can differ from profits from production (both before- and after-tax). Finally it shows how we can measure output, surplus value, unproductive expenditures of surplus value and profits from production before- and after-tax, using the national accounts, after taking these complications into account.

1   The Forms of Appearance of Surplus Value

Debates concerning the transformation problem understandably emphasise Marx's premise that, across the economy as a whole, the sum of surplus value is equal to the sum of profits. This is also the basis on which Marx develops the LTFRP. But as the notebooks for *Capital* III progress, Marx starts to show how this surplus value gets split up into different forms: specifically, interest, rent, and profits retained by enterprises.[1] The relationship between surplus value and total profit is also complicated by the fact that a large portion of surplus value is spent by the state in various ways, and by businesses on paying managers and other unproductive employees, which does not necessarily count for them as 'profit'. Moreover, the surplus value produced by workers in any given country is not necessarily equal to the surplus value appropriated in that country. All of this not only obscures the fact that workers' surplus labour is the source of profit, it means calculating the numerator of the rate of profit in a way that has some grounding in Marx's value theory is more difficult than just taking GDP and subtracting depreciation and wages.

How, then, are we to conceive of and measure surplus value using national accounts? If we start with the assumption Marx generally makes in *Capital*, that productive workers spend all of the wages they receive in a year on commodities, then surplus value can be looked at in two equivalent ways. On the income side, surplus value is equal to the total income capitalists receive for selling commodities after subtracting wages paid to productive workers and the productive consumption of constant capital.[2] On the expenditure side, surplus value is the total price paid for all newly produced commodities after subtracting productively consumed constant capital, less productive workers' total *expenditure*.[3] This means surplus value covers large chunk of expenditures, including: the personal consumption of anyone who is not a productive worker, government spending on commodities including wages (except for the wages of productive government workers), and all net investment, including investment in employing additional labour power (whether productive or unproductive).

The first step towards estimating this in practice, and from there to measuring numerators of the rate of profit, is to clarify what Marx means by unproductive labour.

---

1   Marx 1981, pp. 459–953.
2   Marx 1976, pp. 320–1.
3   Marx 1978b, pp. 586–7.

2   Unproductive Labour

Like Marx's theory of value, his distinction between productive and unproductive labour is seen by contemporary mainstream economists as a quaint concern, peculiar to Marx and the classical political economists. In fact no economic analysis is possible unless we distinguish productive from unproductive activities; the question is where to draw the line and how the line drawn by Marx relates to the line drawn by the national accounts.[4]

Marx's position emerges from a critique of Adam Smith. He argues Smith characteristically jumbles together two conceptions of productive labour, one correct and one incorrect. Smith's correct conception, as interpreted by Marx, is the following:

> [Smith] defined productive labour as labour *which is exchanged directly with capital*; that is, an exchange through which the means of production required for labour, and value in general – money or commodities – are first transformed into capital and labour into wage labour in its scientific meaning. Thereby also what is *unproductive labour* is absolutely defined. It is labour which is not exchanged against capital, but *directly* against revenue, that is, against wages or profit, including of course the various categories of those who share in the profit of the capitalist, as interest and rent ... These definitions are therefore not derived from the material processes of labour – neither from the nature of its product nor from the work performed as concrete labour – but from the definite social forms, the social relations of production, within which these processes are realised.
>
> An actor, for example, or even a clown, according to this definition is a productive worker, if he works in the employ of a capitalist (an *entrepreneur*) to whom he returns more labour than he receives from him in the form of wages; while a jobbing tailor who comes to the capitalist's house and patches his trousers for him, producing a mere use value for him, is an unproductive worker. The labour of the former is exchanged against capital, that of the latter against revenue. The former produces a surplus value; in the latter, revenue is consumed.[5]

Note that here Marx is investigating the question of which labour is productive *under the capitalist mode of production*. With this qualification, he endorses

---

4   Shaikh and Tonak 1994, pp. 32–4.
5   Marx 1951, pp. 153–4, emphasis in original.

Smith's argument that this is labour that directly augments capital. This is Marx's theoretical starting point. But on its own, this is not a criterion for distinguishing productive from unproductive labour, because it begs the question of which labour augments the stock of capital across the economy as a whole. As we will explore, this is not as simple as identifying which workers allow their employers to appropriate a profit, because some labour appropriates profit for one capitalist at the expense of others.

From his correct starting point, Marx discusses how Smith goes on to draw the further, incorrect conclusion that productive labour must 'fix itself' in 'vendible commodities': i.e. that it must be embodied in a physical object. Labour which produces services would therefore necessarily be unproductive.[6] Against this position, Marx gives the following example:

> The cook in the hotel produces a commodity for the person who has bought her labour as a capitalist, the hotel proprietor. The consumer of the lamb cutlet has to pay for her labour, and this replaces for the hotel proprietor (apart from profit) the fund out of which he continues to pay the cook. But if on the other hand I buy the labour of a cook so that she may cook meat etc. for me, not to make a profit out of it as labour in general but to enjoy it, to use it as that particular concrete labour, then her labour is unproductive; although this labour fixes itself in a material product and could just as well (in its result) be a vendible commodity as it in fact is for the proprietor of the hotel.
>
> The great difference remains however: the cook does not replace for me (the private person) the fund out of which I pay her. For I buy her labour not as a value-creating element, but merely for the sake of its use value.[7]

This may sound as though Marx is saying that all workers employed by capitalists to make a profit are productive, and all other labour is unproductive. But in fact the situation is more complicated. First, Marx allows for the possibility that workers who own their own means of production produce surplus value, and 'exploit themselves':

> [I]n the capitalist mode of production the independent peasant or handicraftsman is sundered into two persons. As owner of the means of production he is capitalist, as worker he is his own wage worker. As capitalist,

---

6   Marx 1951, pp. 159–60.
7   Marx 1951, pp. 162–3.

he therefore pays himself his wages and draws his profit from his capital; that is to say, he exploits himself as wage worker and pays himself, with the surplus value, the tribute that labour owes to capital.[8]

Note that this is only true under capitalism. In pre-capitalist societies, some independent peasants and artisans may produce commodities for exchange, but there is no reason for them to treat one part of their income from doing so as wages, and the rest as profit. This only makes sense where they have the alternative to work for a wage.

Second, Marx argues that some workers who are employed by capitalists do not augment surplus value. Instead, they help their employer to appropriate surplus value produced elsewhere. This includes workers employed in the retail and financial sectors, and follows from Marx's argument that productive labour must *produce* commodities.[9] The retail sector is concerned with the *realisation* of the value which commodities embody, but does not enhance their use value, and therefore does not add to their value either. An exception here is work necessary to transport commodities to their point of sale, which Marx counts as part of the socially necessary labour time involved in producing them, because it enhances the use value of the commodity for its consumer (by changing its location to make it accessible).[10] The financial sector is unproductive because, like the retail sector, it does not directly enhance commodities' use values. Both sectors nevertheless perform important functions for capital, and can *indirectly* increase the average rate of profit. For example, if the retail sector succeeds in selling commodities more quickly, this reduces the turnover time of variable capital; or, if it increases sales relative to its costs, this reduces the surplus value it consumes unproductively relative to total sales. Similarly, if it performs its function for capital effectively, the financial sector can help to direct credit towards capitalists most likely to use it profitability, or to other borrowers from whom it is most likely to extract the highest repayments.

Third, Marx argues supervisory labour that 'merely arises from the antagonistic contradiction between capital and labour', rather than being necessary for co-ordinating production, is also funded out of capitalists' revenue, rather than directly augmenting their capital. Again, the more effective the supervisor, the more surplus value they will tend to extract from their workforce, so supervisory labour has an *indirect* effect on the rate of profit. But because this work is

8   Marx 1951, p. 192.
9   Marx 1981, pp. 438–9; Marx 1951, p. 185.
10   Marx 1978b, pp. 225–9.

not a necessary step in the process of augmenting use values, supervisors do not produce surplus value insofar as they perform this function.[11]

Marx also argues that some labour which produces value does not produce *surplus* value. Workers who produce commodities which are sold at below their cost price are a drain on capital: it costs more to reproduce their labour power than the value the capitalist obtains from purchasing it.[12] Marx sometimes refers to this as simply 'unproductive labour', but it is only 'unproductive' in the sense that it does not produce *surplus* value, not in the sense that it produces *zero* value. As Marx explains early in *Capital* I:

> If we now compare the process of creating value with the process of valorization, we see that the latter is nothing but the continuation of the former beyond a definite point. If the process is not carried out beyond the point where the value paid by the capitalist for the labour-power is replaced by an exact equivalent, it is simply a process of creating value; but if it is continued beyond that point, it becomes a process of valorization.[13]

This is important because a significant number of workers in the government and not-for-profit sectors produce commodities which are sold below their cost price. Universities, for example, are generally government-owned or not-for-profit institutions, and usually rely on government funding or private philanthropy to cover some of their costs. But in most cases their employees produce commodities – degrees – which the institution sells to students who pay fees. Rather than saying the teaching staff produce *zero* value, it is more consistent to say that they produce value equivalent to the fees they allow the university to extract from their students: or, equivalently, that the surplus value teaching staff consume in net terms is reduced by the fees they extract.[14]

There is also the question of how the value of capital advanced for unproductive purposes is reproduced. In *Capital* Marx considers this question in some detail, at least insofar as it applies to commercial and finance capital. First, unlike productive constant capital, the constant capital invested in the

---

11   Marx 1963, p. 505.
12   Assuming away the complications introduced by the transformation of values into prices, and differences between the price and value of labour power.
13   Marx 1976, p. 302.
14   However, this does not mean we should include outlays in these sectors in the denominator of the rate of profit. Except for profit-making government-owned enterprises, these outlays do not function as capital, because they do not function as self-expanding value.

equipment, buildings and raw materials used for unproductive purposes does *not* transfer its value to output. Yet its cost must be recovered somehow. Exactly how this cost is recovered depends on the unproductive expenditure in question. First consider commercial capital:

> This part of the constant capital advanced would have the same constricting effect on the profit rate as does all constant capital directly invested in production. In as much as the industrial capitalist hands over the commercial side of his business to the merchant, he does not need to advance this portion of capital. Instead of him, it is the merchant who advances it. Yet this is really only an advance in name, in as much as the merchant neither produces nor reproduces the constant capital that he uses (his material expenses). The production of these appears as a separate business of certain industrial capitalists, or at least a part of their business, so that these play the same role as those supplying constant capital to the producers of means of subsistence. The merchant thus receives firstly the replacement for this constant capital, and secondly the profit on it. *On both counts*, the profit of the industrial capitalist is reduced.[15]

The phrase 'on both counts' here is crucial. If the profit of the industrial capitalist were only reduced by the size of the profit made by the commercial capitalist, then there would be no change in total profit, or total profits from production. But Marx is saying that the industrial capitalist's profit is also reduced by the cost of replacing the merchant's constant capital. He goes on to explain that one of the functions of the merchant is to reduce these costs by assuming these functions for more than one industrial capitalist:

> But because of the concentration and economy that results from the division of labour, this reduction is less than it would be if he had to advance this capital himself. The reduction in the profit rate is less, because the capital advanced in this way is less.[16]

The same applies to the capital advanced for paying commercial workers, which Marx examines by supposing this capital is advanced by the industrial capitalist:

---

15   Marx 1981, pp. 410–11, emphasis added.
16   Marx 1981, p. 411.

The expenditure on [commercial workers' wages], even though incurred in the form of wages, is distinct from the variable capital laid out on the purchase of productive labour. It increases the outlays of the industrial capitalist, the mass of capital he has to advance, without directly increasing the surplus-value. For this is an outlay for labour employed simply in realizing values already created. Just like other outlays of the same kind, this too reduces the rate of profit, because the capital advanced grows, but not the surplus-value. The surplus-value s remains constant, but the capital advanced C still grows from C to ΔC, so that the profit rate s / C is replaced by the smaller profit rate $s / (C + \Delta C)$.[17]

Notice here Marx continues to measure the numerator of the rate of profit as 's', even after introducing the unproductive workers. But if the function of selling commodities is performed directly by the industrial capitalist, it is clear that the capitalist must pay for the commercial workers' wages out of the total price the capitalist receives for selling their commodities, and, if prices are equal to values, out of the total surplus value produced by their productive workers. Although the total surplus value remains constant, *less of it appears as profit for the capitalist*. The same applies to the costs the industrial capitalist pays for purchasing unproductive supervisory labour power, and administrative labour power.

As Marx puts it elsewhere, the wage of a worker in the commercial sector 'derives from' commercial profit:

> even though the income the circulation agent receives may appear to him as a simple wage, as payment for the work he has performed, and even though, where it does not take this form, the size of his profit may still be only equivalent to the wage of a better-paid worker, this income still derives solely from the commercial profit. This results from the fact that his labour is not value-creating labour.[18]

Mage takes Marx's decision to continue to use 's' on the numerator of the rate of profit to mean that the wages of unproductive workers are in fact *constant* capital, because they increase capital advanced without changing the numerator of the rate of profit. If that were true, then, like ordinary productive capital, the wages of unproductive workers would have to transfer their value to output. But

---

17   Marx 1981, p. 413.
18   Marx 1981, p. 404.

in fact workers never *transfer* the value of their labour power to the commodities they produce; they create a wholly new value, throughout the working day, part of which produces a value equivalent to the value of their labour power, and part of which is surplus value (as discussed further below). Moreover, this is true only for productive workers, not for unproductive workers.

The same arguments apply to the costs of reproducing the labour power and other commodities used as inputs in all unproductive sectors: they must, at some stage, be funded 'out of' surplus value. As Gillman argues, this means we must now distinguish between two measures of the average rate of profit: s / C, the ratio of surplus-value to capital advanced, and $(s - u) / C$, where u stands for certain unproductive expenditures on both wages and constant capital.[19]

However, this still does not answer the question of exactly which unproductive expenditures of surplus value we should subtract. If we subtract *all* unproductive expenditures of surplus value from the numerator, including capitalists' personal consumption (which is certainly unproductive), then we are left with a measure of the ratio of net investment to capital advanced: i.e. a measure of the rate of accumulation, not the rate of profit.

In this chapter, we will devote most of the discussion to how to measure surplus value after deducting all unproductive expenditures *except* capitalists' personal consumption. The 'rate of profit' with this measure of $(s - u)$ on the numerator is a measure of the 'maximum' rate of accumulation.

Sometimes it is argued that $(s - u) / C$ is the measure that matters for capitalists' decision making, whereas s / C is the better measure of the maximum potential rate of profit, or maximum possible rate of accumulation. Mohun, for example, argues 'trends in productive labour and the means of production with which it works determine what is potentially available for profits'.[20] But it is not clear in what sense the cost of paying unproductive wage earners is 'potentially' available for profits, since these employees generally perform necessary functions for capital. As we have seen, they include, for example, most supervisory labour and the entire unproductive machinery of the capitalist state, which will not be eliminated this side of the revolution. As Marx argues:

> The capitalist mode of production, while it enforces economy in each individual business, also begets, by its anarchic system of competition, the most outrageous squandering of labour-power and of the social

---

19   Gillman 1957, pp. 81–106.
20   Mohun 2009, p. 1024.

means of production, not to mention the creation of a vast number of functions at present indispensable, but in themselves superfluous.[21]

Similarly, from the point of view of accumulation, it does not make sense to say that the 'maximum' rate of accumulation includes surplus value spent on u.

On the other hand, as we will explore further, $(s-u)/C$ is *not* a relevant measure of the 'rate of profit' for capitalists' investment decisions. This is because not all unproductive expenditures of surplus value are deductions from *profits from production*. Precisely which expenditures *are* deductions from profits from production depends on the measure we use. For most purposes, we will want to define profits from production in before-interest terms. This means that expenses incurred in the financial sector, including wages, are *not* deducted from profits from production. Similarly, if we measure profits from production on a before-tax basis, then wages paid to unproductive government workers and other unproductive state expenditures are not deducted. If we measure profits from production on an after-tax basis, then unproductive state expenditures have an *indirect* influence, insofar as they have an effect on company taxes and pre-tax wages of business employees.

We will explain how to define and measure profits from production on a before- and after-tax basis towards the end of the chapter. For many purposes these are the most important measures of the rate of profit, because they are close approximations of rates of return which actually *appear* to (some) capitalists. This is also ultimately what Marx's law sets out to explain. However, measuring the rate of profit with $(s-u)$ on the numerator is important both for explaining movements in the rate of accumulation and for understanding the relationship between the production and consumption of value and profits from production.

But first, in order to decompose movements in $(s-u)/C$, we need to estimate the size of $s-u$ relative to s; meaning we have to measure s itself. To do this, we need a method for distinguishing productive from unproductive workers that we can apply to the national accounts. The national accounts are not well set-out to do this, and the different proxies that Marxists employ can lead to significantly different results.[22] However, since we are measuring the rate of profit as $(s-u)/C$ and not s/C, our measure of the rate of profit will not be affected by the way in which we distinguish between productive and unproductive labour. Whether we classify them as productive or unproduct-

---

21   Marx 1976, p. 667.
22   Mohun 2014.

ive expenditures, all depreciation and the value of all employees' labour power need to be subtracted from total output to calculate $s - u$. Our choice of approximation for the distinction between productive and unproductive labour will only affect s, not $s - u$, and therefore will mainly affect the extent to which we attribute changes in the rate of profit to changes in the rate of surplus value or to changes in the ratio of $s - u$ to s.[23]

Because it will not change our most important results, we could afford to use a fairly approximate distinction between productive and unproductive labour. The US national accounts provide data by industry stretching back to 1929, but unfortunately there are three breaks in the series when different industry classifications are introduced. We will use the approximation that all non-supervisory employees in the following sectors are unproductive: wholesale trade; retail trade; finance, insurance and real estate; and government, excluding employees of government enterprises. Fortunately all but one of these categories exists for all years from 1929, and the breaks in the series do not make a great deal of difference to the data.[24] Estimating the ratio of supervisory to non-supervisory workers in productive sectors is not straightforward: we have used figures reported in a study by Mohun.[25] The major deficiency of this approach is that it does not attempt to distinguish productive from unproductive employees in the 'services' sector. It is likely that the share of unproductive employees in this category has grown over time, so this is likely to mean we will underestimate the growth in unproductive employees.[26]

---

23   It will also have a small effect on the other elements of the decomposition, because it affects the proportion of capital advanced that we classify as 'v'.

24   The exception is that before 1948 there is no standalone 'retail trade' category, only 'retail trade and automobile services'. I have checked that this and other differences in the classification systems do not make large differences to the results by comparing results for the years in which the classification systems overlap.

25   His study reports results for the ratio of supervisory workers' wages in productive sectors as a proportion of all wages (call this psw / w), and productive workers' wages as a proportion of all wages (call this pw / w), for 1964, 1979 and 2000. This means we can calculate non-supervisory workers' wages in productive sectors as a proportion of all wages paid in productive sectors as $(pw / w) / (psw / w + pw / w) = pw / (psw + w)$. Between these years we have assumed the ratio follows a straight line. Prior to 1964 we use the 1964 figure (i.e. we assume the ratio was constant), and after 2000 we use the average decline per year in the ratio between 1979 and 2000 to extend the series forward. This means the ratio starts at 73% and declines to 57% by 2015. The same approach was applied to calculating the ratio of full-time equivalent non-supervisory employees to total FTE employees in productive sectors, and these ratios were also applied to distinguishing supervisory from non-supervisory petty-bourgeois in productive sectors. Mohun 2014.

26   Another problem with this definition is that it does not account properly for the circulating constant capital consumed by unproductive sectors. For example, the retail sector has

3   Measuring Surplus Value after Unproductive Expenditures

Before showing how we can use this to measure surplus value, we will start by discussing the more important task of developing an appropriate measure of $s - u$. Intuitively, this seems as though it should be equivalent to something like total profit made by businesses after tax. Similarly, intuitively it seems as though s should be equal to total profit before tax, plus wages and depreciation in unproductive sectors.

This intuition is reflected in the range of measures Marxists use to measure the numerator of the rate of profit. The broadest definition of the numerator that is regularly used is gross domestic product less depreciation of fixed assets and compensation of employees (excluding measures which try to incorporate expenditures on wages and depreciation in unproductive sectors). Then there is a list of other expenses recorded in the US NIPAs which may or may not be treated as deductions from this 'broad profit': taxes on production less subsidies, net proprietors' income (i.e. income for owners of small businesses), net interest payments (i.e. interest payments paid by domestic businesses), net rental income of persons (which is rent paid on dwellings and land owned by people, including an imputation for the rent that the national accounts treat owner occupiers as 'paying to themselves'), current surplus of government enterprises, and taxes on corporate profits. If we deduct all of these, we arrive at what the national accounts call 'corporate profits after tax', which is really corporate profits from production after taxes and interest, with 'production' defined in a way that incorporates transfers for some financial payments (as discussed further below).[27]

There is a problem with treating any of these measures as a proxy for $(s - u) / C$, which an empirical issue helps to illustrate. From around 1983 until the Great

---

expenses for inputs such as heating and electricity. For the owners of the utilities which supply these inputs the labour power and constant capital consumed to produce them is consumed productively, since it enlarges their capital if they sell their output above cost price. But since this heating and electricity is part of the cost of *realising* the value of the commodities it is used to help sell, without enhancing their use values, for the capitalist class as a whole the cost of these commodities is a component of both surplus value (s) and its unproductive expenditure (u). Ideally we would classify the labour power used to produce these inputs as unproductive, along with the labour power used to produce the inputs needed to produce these inputs, and the labour power used to produce the inputs for these inputs for these inputs, etc. But again, the consequences of not doing this are not dire: it affects our decomposition of changes in the rate of profit, but not the rate of profit itself.

27   For results from measuring the rate of profit using nearly all these alternatives (and others) see Basu and Vasudevan 2012.

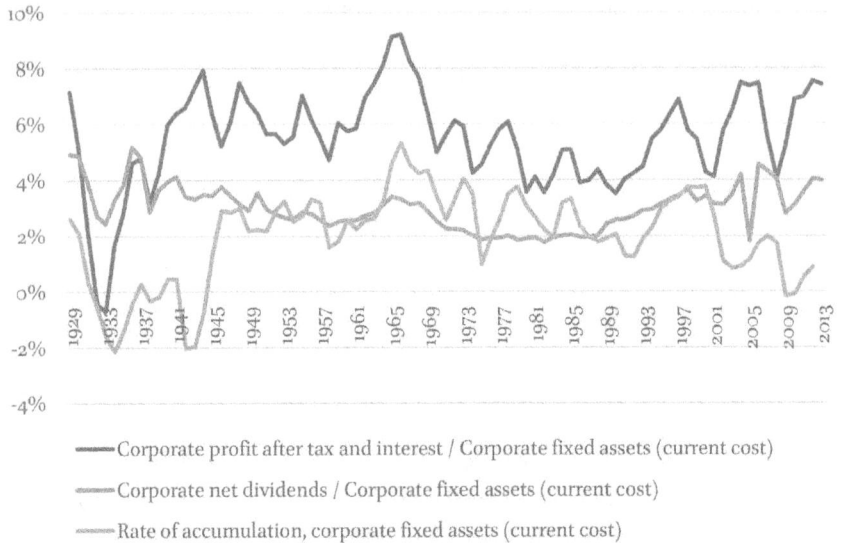

FIGURE 2   A 'rate of profit' compared with dividends and accumulation divided by fixed
assets at current cost

Recession dividend payments by US corporations increased sharply relative to
their fixed assets. This is graphed in Figure 2 below. It also includes the 'rate of
profit' defined as the ratio of 'corporate profits after tax' to fixed assets, and the
ratio of corporate net investment to corporate fixed assets, which is a measure
of the rate of capital accumulation.

Although there is clearly a downward trend in the rate of accumulation from
the mid-1960s onwards, the downward trends in dividends and profits relative to fixed assets are interrupted in the mid-1980s. From that period onwards,
there is a large increase in dividends relative to fixed assets, along with a much
smaller increase in the 'corporate profits after tax' measure of the rate of profit.

Based on evidence such as this, some have drawn the conclusion that corporate managers developed a preference for boosting dividends instead of rein-
vesting their profits. Duménil and Lévy, for example, explain this as a result of
changing incentives faced by corporate managers, whose remuneration is now
more closely tied to movements in their company's share price.[28]

But there is another, less intuitive possibility. The divergence between the
rate of accumulation and the after-tax 'rate of profit' may be due to an increase
in government borrowing. To see how, consider the following scenario. Suppose

28   Duménil and Lévy 2011, p. 152.

the government decides to fund a corporate tax cut by increasing the deficit, and leaving government spending unchanged. Suppose revenue from corporate tax falls by $10 billion as a result, and government borrowing increases by the same amount. Assume banks (domestic or foreign) fund this deficit by purchasing $10 billion of extra Treasury bonds. Now suppose, as a simplification, that corporations' investment decisions are completely unaffected by changes in the way a given level of government spending is financed, and that the earnings that they retain are entirely determined by how much they are planning to invest. This implies that the extra $10 billion in after tax profit that they make as a result of the tax cut will be spent entirely on paying dividends. Also suppose that the recipients of these extra dividends leave them as deposits in their bank accounts, rather than spending them. In that case, banks will have an extra $10 billion in funds available: i.e. just enough to cover the value of the new Treasury bonds.

So under these simplified assumptions, a corporate tax cut funded by increased borrowing brings about an equivalent increase in dividend payments, which in turn 'creates' the loanable funds required to finance the increased deficit. Both the income and wealth of shareholders increases by the size of the corporate tax cut, the after-tax profit share of income increases, but shareholders' consumption, and everyone else's, remain unchanged. Most importantly, the after-tax profit rate increases (though before-tax it is constant).

This scenario may or may not help to explain the divergence between the 'after-tax rate of profit' and the rate of accumulation in the US since the 1980s. The more important point here is the effect the increase in the deficit has on the after-tax rate of profit. In this example, there is no change in either the socially necessary labour time performed by productive workers, productive workers' consumption (or their wages), or unproductive expenditures of surplus value (u). So there is no change in $(s - u) / C$, even though the after-tax rate of profit increases. This is one way in which we can be misled if we treat an after-tax measure of profit as a proxy for $s - u$.

What about a pre-tax measure of the rate of profit? It differs from both s / C and $(s - u) / C$. Total pre-tax profit from production is not equal to s because, as we have seen, s includes the costs of wages and other inputs used up by unproductive sectors (and, as we will see below, includes the difference between the price and the value of labour power). On the other hand, $s - u$ is not equal to total pre-tax profit because pre-tax profit does not subtract the costs incurred by the state on reproducing the labour power of the workers it employs and on the cost of other inputs.

Another way of putting the problem is that once we introduce government borrowing, it is no longer simply a question of the *division* of surplus value into

after-tax profit, the value of labour power and other inputs used by unproductive businesses, and unproductive government expenditures of surplus value.
Government borrowing makes it possible for some of the after-tax profit which
companies appropriate to be lent on to the government to cover its expenditures. In this way, compared to a situation in which unproductive government
expenditures of surplus value are funded by taxes, government borrowing can
'create' after-tax profit, further obscuring the fact that workers' surplus labour
is the source of profit. If we do not account for this, and treat after-tax profit
as though it measures $s - u$, we implicitly adopt the fetishistic assumption that
government borrowing itself can create surplus value.

4   The Value of Labour Power

Workers' saving and borrowing introduce similar complications. In *Capital*,
Marx generally operates with the assumption that the wages bill is equal to the
value of the commodities that productive workers purchase and consume in
order to reproduce their labour power. As mentioned earlier, under this simplifying assumption, surplus value can be looked at in two ways. On the income
side, it is equal to total output net of productive depreciation less the wages
paid to productive workers.[29] On the expenditure side, it is net output less productive workers' total expenditure.[30]

But in reality productive workers' income is not necessarily equal to their
expenditure. Just as the state's expenditure need not be equal to its income,
wage earners too can save or dis-save, including when considered as a group.
This means it cannot be true that surplus value is equal to both new value added
less productive workers' wages *and* new value added less productive workers'
consumption. We have to choose one or the other.

In Chapter 6 of *Capital*, Volume 1, 'The Sale and Purchase of Labour-Power',
Marx provides us the concepts we need to resolve this issue. He points out that
the existence of a class of people willing and able to sell their labour power does
not materialise out of thin air. It depends on certain historical, i.e. *temporal*,
antecedents: first, that this class has been stripped of access to the means of
production, so that they cannot themselves produce use values to sell or consume; but second, that they *do* have access to the means of subsistence with
which to reproduce their capacity to work. The production and reproduction

29   Marx 1976, pp. 320–1.
30   Marx 1978b, pp. 586–7.

of this labour power must have occurred *before* it is purchased by the capitalist, as well as for the duration of the employment contract:

> Nobody – not even a practitioner of *Zukunftsmusik* [music of the future] – can live on the products of the future, or on use-values whose production has not yet been completed; just as on the first day of his appearance on the world's stage, man must still consume every day, before and while he produces.[31]

For the capitalist, how this comes about is mostly a matter of indifference, just as the process of production is a matter of indifference for the purchaser of any other commodity; the capitalist's main interest is in the quality and the *price* of the labour power he is purchasing:

> Why this free worker confronts him in the sphere of circulation is a question which does not interest the owner of money, for he finds the labour-market in existence as a particular branch of the commodity-market.[32]

Nevertheless, like all other commodities, labour power must be produced before it can be sold, and it this process of *production* which endows it with value:

> The value of labour-power is determined, as in the case of every other commodity, by the labour-time necessary for the production, and con-sequently also the reproduction, of this specific article. In so far as it has value, it represents no more than a definite quantity of the average social labour objectified in it.[33]

Moreover:

> Its value, like that of every other commodity, *is already determined before it enters into circulation*, for a definite quantity of social labour has been spent on the production of the labour-power.[34]

---

31   Marx 1976, p. 272.
32   Marx 1976, p. 273.
33   Marx 1976, p. 274.
34   Marx 1976, p. 277, emphasis added.

It follows that the value of labour power is *not* necessarily equal to its price, the wage. Before the worker enters the 'very Eden of the innate rights of man' she encounters in the sphere of circulation, she must first possess a hide to bring to market. The value of the means of subsistence she consumes to make this possible is determined by the total price she pays for *those* commodities, not the price the capitalist pays to buy the labour power those commodities are used to produce.

Marx also argues the commodities needed to produce and reproduce labour power are not restricted to those necessary for a bare subsistence, but include commodities purchased to replace '[t]he labour-power withdrawn from the market by wear and tear, and by death' with labour power supplied by the next generation of workers. This includes the costs of their education, healthcare, etc., insofar as these are purchased as commodities. The value of labour power also famously includes a 'historical and moral element' determined by 'the level of civilization attained by a country' and 'the conditions in which, and consequently on the habits and expectations with which, the class of free workers has been formed'; which is also, as Marx argues elsewhere, a result of struggle.[35]

Marx then seems to sweep all these complexities aside when he declares '[n]evertheless, in a given country at a given period, the average amount of the means of subsistence necessary for the worker is a known *datum*'.[36] But since Marx's value theory is temporal, this is not a simplification: it is *true*. The total price paid for the commodities a worker has consumed before she sells her labour power to a capitalist is a known *datum* because these commodities were bought in the past, before the new wage is negotiated. Just as the revaluation of constant capital cannot retroactively change the value of the means of production and raw materials purchased by the capitalist, a change in the wage cannot retroactively change the value of the commodities bought by the worker to reproduce her labour power. The most important determinant of the value of labour power in one period is therefore the price that was *previously* agreed for it, since this is what determines how much income workers have to spend on their consumption.

However, where wages are high enough to allow for it, during most periods productive workers will, as a group, spend less than their total wages on buying commodities. First, a portion of the wage is extracted from them in the form of 'secondary' exploitation: e.g. interest payments, rent above the depreciation of their dwelling or income taxes (as discussed further below). Second,

---

35   Marx 1985, p. 104; Marx 1976, p. 275.
36   Ibid.

workers need to save money not just to cover large expenses (e.g. cars and houses) they will incur in future during their working lives (which should roughly balance out across workers as a whole over most periods, and are often bought by going into debt), but also for retirement. Like the reproduction of unproductive workers' labour power and the labour power of people unable to work due to unemployment or disability, the cost of reproducing the labour power of retired workers is a deduction from *surplus* value. Workers' access to this surplus value after they retire is determined by the amount of money they have saved from their wages during their working lives (and by their access to other income such as state pensions). That is, it is determined by the extent to which they have kept down the cost of reproducing their labour power while they were working, and the extent to which they have won wages that keep the price of their labour power above this value. Therefore the 'normal' state of affairs, at least in advanced capitalist economies, is that workers are paid a wage at least a little above the value of their labour power.

This can also be a result of rising wages. Even if total saving by the productive working class is zero, if wages rise by enough to allow workers to purchase a larger proportion of the total value they produce, this implies workers are winning wages above the value of their labour power. On the other hand, if real wages *fall* by enough, then the price of labour power can fall below its value, forcing workers to spend savings, go into debt, or cut back consumption (and in doing so reduce the value of the labour power they will sell in future). Marx mentions this possibility, and Grossman rightly argues it becomes particularly important at moments of crisis when wages fall dramatically.[37] Interpretations which define the value of labour power as being equal to its price, such as the New Interpretation, cannot allow for this important aspect of Marx's system. Finally, even if real wages remain constant, the production of relative surplus value through reductions in the labour time that is socially necessary to produce means of subsistence can also allow capitalists to pay a price for labour power below its current value.

Another reason to take this approach is that an income-based definition of surplus value runs into an important problem. Consider a hypothetical economy consisting of productive workers hired by capitalists, with no fixed capital and strictly alternating periods of production and circulation. Suppose the total value of commodities produced is y, productive workers are paid total wages of w, but in order to reproduce their labour power for the next period, at

---

37 Marx 1976, pp. 276–7; Lapides 1994, pp. 256–65.

the end the period workers buy commodities with a total price of $r < w$. Finally, assume the portion of output not bought by workers is spent on new investment.

Under these assumptions, profits from production will be $y - w$. But investment will be the larger sum of $y - r$. In practice the credit system makes this possible: by investing their savings or leaving them in the bank workers make them available for spending on investment. If we simply define total 'surplus value' to be equal to profits from production, then we also have to say that net investment can be larger than surplus value, which robs the concept of an important part of its intended meaning.

One implication of instead defining surplus value as net output less productive workers' *consumption* is that, when the price of labour power is above its value, the difference between the two is surplus value. That is, a portion of surplus value is paid to workers as wages. Conversely, if the price of labour power is below its value, then capitalists extract a sum greater than surplus value from workers (and usually degrade the quality of their labour power in the process by preventing workers from reproducing it to the same standard). This means we have to distinguish the rate of surplus value from the rate of *primary exploitation*.

The rate at which productive workers are subjected to primary exploitation is determined by the *price* paid for their labour power. That is, the rate of primary exploitation (ROPE) is defined as the ratio of net output after productive workers' wages to productive workers' *wages*.[38] This is what we had previously called the 'rate of surplus value'. The actual rate of surplus value, ROSV, is the ratio of net output less productive workers' consumption (r) to productive workers' consumption (r itself if defined further below).

We can also measure the rate of *total* exploitation, for which the numerator is net output after subtracting both productive workers' wages and the value extracted from them through secondary exploitation. Secondary exploitation incorporates productive workers' spending on rent and mortgage interest above the value of the depreciation of their houses, interest on paid on other loans and other transfers, and income taxes and payments for social insurance.

---

38   Because they do not produce value, strictly speaking unproductive workers are not exploited. They are, as Carchedi puts it, 'economically oppressed', insofar as their wages are less than the value they would have produced had their labour power been expended productively. Carchedi 1991, p. 31.

5   Measuring Output

Measuring surplus value in the way described above also depends on having
an appropriate measure of output. For reasons we will consider GDP does not
quite fit this requirement, so we need to make some adjustments to it. Readers
who are less interested in the details of how this was done or how the numerator of the rate of profit was calculated more generally, are advised to skip this
section or the rest of this chapter.

For Marx, to count towards new value produced, goods and services must
be produced for sale by the expenditure of labour power; i.e. they must be produced commodities.[39] The value they embody is the new value added to them
by living labour ('net output') plus the value this labour transfers to them by
productively consuming existing commodities. We want to alter the national
accounts' definition of gross domestic product to give us a measure of net output which fits this definition.

On the expenditure side, the national accounts define GDP using the iden-
tity $C + I + G + X - M$, where 'C' is personal consumption (which we will call
'PCE', to avoid confusing it with capital advanced), I is gross private investment,
G is government spending on 'consumption' and gross investment, and $X - M$
is exports minus imports. As the national accounts define them, each of these
terms includes items which are not payments for newly produced commodities, and which we therefore want to exclude from net output. Below we will
discuss each in turn. Appendix A gives the full, line-by-line definition we are
using for output based on this discussion.

5.1   *Personal Consumption Expenditure*
Most PCE is money spent by individuals on newly produced commodities,
which we want to include in our measure of output. But PCE also includes
spending on housing rent, gambling, 'financial services' (which includes bank
fees and the interest rate 'spread' between the rate at which banks lend money
and the interest rate they pay depositors, multiplied by total personal deposits)
and insurance. Gambling, financial services and insurance are not payments
for produced use values, and we therefore need to exclude them from the total
price of newly produced output.

Housing rent is a more complicated case. PCE includes an allowance for the
cost of renting dwellings and the land they occupy, whether the dwelling is
actually rented out or is occupied by its owner. From a Marxist perspective, in

---

39   Marx 1951, p. 154.

neither case is this part of the total price of output. To see why, it is helpful to consider the rent paid for land and the rent paid for dwellings separately. Rent paid for the unimproved value of land is payment for the use of a non-produced commodity: i.e. a commodity with zero value. So it is clearly a transfer payment, and not a part of output. However, the rent paid for dwellings *is* a payment for the use of a commodity with value. This value is produced when the dwelling is *built*, and realised when the dwelling is sold. In the national accounts, this is *already counted* as part of gross investment. So when the dwelling is later rented by a tenant, they are paying to use an *already produced* commodity, the value of which was already counted towards output when it was produced. By counting dwelling rent towards PCE, the national accounts effectively count part of the value of the house twice: once when it is produced and sold, and then again when it is rented. So we want to exclude both dwelling rent and land rent from our measure of net output.

However, adjusting PCE in this way creates a new complication. The national accounts treat the inputs consumed in order to 'produce' the non- and non-new commodities that are part of PCE as 'intermediate inputs': i.e. as components of the prices of final commodities. So if we subtract the entire value of PCE on financial services, housing rent, gambling and insurance, we are also subtracting the total price of the commodities consumed by the banks, landlords, etc. to 'produce' this component of PCE. But, from a Marxist perspective, these inputs are a part of *final* output (and, specifically, a part of unproductive expenditures on surplus value). Therefore we want to add the total price paid for these commodities back in to our measure of output.

We can do this by taking the ratio of intermediate inputs to gross output for the industries in question and multiplying this by each of the components of PCE we are excluding. Unfortunately gross output and intermediate inputs by industry is only published from 1987 onwards, so we will assume that before 1987 this ratio is unchanged. This is far from ideal, but because this is a component of unproductive expenditures of surplus value, this estimate only influences our measures of output and surplus value, and not our measure of $s - u$.

5.2   *Private Investment*

Next we need to adjust the measure of gross private investment used to calculate GDP. The US national accounts now include an estimate of investment in 'intellectual property' through research and development, along with investment in structures and equipment. From a Marxist perspective the labour involved in producing 'intellectual property' is not productive, for a range of reasons we will consider. First, a great deal of what is counted as research and development cannot be sold as a commodity; it is just knowledge that is pro-duced and retained 'in house' that largely exists within the brains of those who produce it. Of the research and development that is produced in a saleable format, there are broadly three cases. First, a business might pay employees to do research and development in order to produce a patent it can sell to another business. These patents sound as though they might be a newly produced com-modity (i.e. a use value produced for exchange). But a patent *itself* is just a legal instrument. Its only purpose is to give its owner a monopoly over the use of the process to which it refers. It does not have any use value beyond this. Know-ledge of the design or process *itself* has a concrete use value, but the sale of a patent *as such* is just a transfer of the *right to use* this knowledge.

The knowledge *itself* can only be commodified indirectly. One possibility is that research and development may produce knowledge that can then be 'sold' in the form of education or training. For example, researchers at a company or university might develop a new industrial process of some kind, and then charge fees to attend a course to learn how to implement it. But in this case the price of the *education*, which is the commodity in this case, is already accoun-ted for as part of PCE if it is bought by an individual. Only if it is bought by a government or business are we potentially erroneously excluding this from our measure of output by excluding all investment in 'intellectual assets', and even in this case there is no reason for the price charged for the education to be the same as the cost of the investment.[40] The third case is if the research and development leads to the publication of, for example, a book or some computer software. In this case, the money spent on the final commodity – i.e. the books or the computer software – has already been accounted for.

If none of these are the case, and the knowledge is made freely available, then it is not a commodity. Therefore in nearly all cases we should not treat investment in intellectual property as part of output. We will use the approx-imation that this is true in all cases.

5.3   *Government Consumption and Investment*

The national accounts treat all government spending on 'consumption' and investment as part of GDP. What they mean by 'consumption' is not restricted to spending on ordinary commodities. It also includes spending on compensa-tion for government employees and depreciation of government-owned fixed

---

40   There is a separate question of whether the research and development itself in this case is productive labour or an unproductive expenditure of surplus value, which is related to the question of whether 'intellectual property' is part of capital advanced, which is discussed below.

assets, after subtracting sales to other sectors and own account investment (so that own-account investment can be re-classified as investment). In this way, government employees who do not produce commodities are counted as producing output. So, for example, wages paid to soldiers in the US military are all counted towards GDP.

From a Marxist perspective the labour of any employee who does not produce commodities is not productive labour, so this imputation is not legitimate. Similarly, fixed assets that are not used to produce commodities do not transfer their value to output, including those owned by the government sector. The only component of government 'consumption' that we do need to include is the unproductive government sector's purchases of 'intermediate inputs'; since, as for other unproductive sectors, this now represents consumption of final commodities. The national accounts list this as a separate line item, but this covers intermediate inputs bought by the whole government sector, and not just the unproductive government sector. So to roughly account for the intermediate inputs used by the government sector to produce commodities, we will multiply total government intermediate inputs by gross government output (according to the national accounts' definition) less government sales to other sectors divided by gross government output.

Government sales to other sectors are already counted towards output elsewhere. For example, if a government enterprise produces a commodity bought for personal consumption, this is counted towards PCE. So there is no need to 'add back in' government sales to other sectors.

Government investment also needs to be modified slightly. In their measure of government investment the NIPAs include 'own account' investment; that is, fixed assets produced by the government sector for use by the government sector. In most cases these fixed assets will be produced directly for use, and not for exchange, and therefore are not commodities, so we will exclude government own account investment from our measure of output. The rest of government investment, excluding investment in intellectual assets, is part of final output.

5.4   Net Exports

Finally we need to exclude net exports of items that the NIPAs count as commodities but which in fact are not. From 1967 onwards there is data for 'royalties and license fees' (and for previous years we can back-cast using more aggregated data). We will count 'royalties and license fees' as entirely transfer payments which need to be subtracted from output. We also want to subtract net exports of financial services and insurance, which is more complicated given the available data; but from 1986 onwards the data with which to do this is available (this is also around the time when these payments start to become a significant size), and for previous years we can make estimates (as explained in the Appendix in Chapter 3). We also need to 'add back in' an estimate of the intermediate inputs used to produce these non-commodities, as we did for PCE on financial services and insurance.

This completes our redefinition of output. Chapter 7 compares the results it produces with GDP over time. This measure of output is also important for testing the hypothesis that the rate of profit and the rate of growth of output have similar trends. However, the main reason to construct this measure is to allow us to measure surplus value. In order to do that, we need to subtract productive depreciation and the value of productive labour power from output.

5.5   *Productive Depreciation*

We will count productive depreciation as the capital consumption adjustment used in the NIPAs for the industries we are defining as 'productive' (excluding the NIPAs' allowance for depreciation on intellectual property), adjusted to fit the temporal definition of depreciation given in Chapter 2. We will also include an allowance for productive depreciation in the government and non-profit sectors. As mentioned, the categories used to define 'productive' industries change a little over time, and are listed comprehensively in Appendix A, but in 1929 they are: agriculture, forestry and fisheries; mining; contract construction; manufacturing; transportation and public facilities; and services.

Because we are using a fairly approximate distinction between productive and unproductive industries the results this gives will also be fairly approximate. However, all depreciation we classify as 'unproductive' will be counted as an unproductive expenditure of surplus value. So, as will be shown below, any over- or under-estimate of d caused by our approximate definition of productive and unproductive industries will create an equal under- or over-estimate of u. This means our estimate of $s - u$ will not be affected by this type of error.

6   Differences between the Total Price and Total Value of Output

As it has been defined, y is a measure of the total *price* of output only. International trade means that this can be different from its total value. This is the aggregate effect, at the national level, of transfers between capitals as a result of differences between prices and values.

In principle, if it made sense to calculate a MELT that applied at the world level, and if we could calculate it, we could use this to calculate the difference between total price and total value at the national level. But we do not have an adequate theory that would allow us to do this, even assuming the necessary data were available.[41]

This means that if we take y as our starting point for calculating s, as we will below, we are not, strictly speaking, calculating the surplus value produced in the US. We are calculating surplus value produced by US workers plus the difference between the total price and the total value of US output; i.e. we are calculating the surplus value 'available' to the US capitalist class (before accounting for financial transfers) after accounting for so-called 'unequal exchange'.

What does this mean for our analysis? As mentioned in Chapter 1, in *Capital* Marx was not discussing movements in a world average rate of profit, but in a national average rate of profit. This is why when Marx discusses the tendency of the rate of profit to fall, he includes the effects of international trade as a potential counter-tendency – which would not make sense if he was considering movements in the average rate of profit at the world level.[42] The main problem this introduces for our analysis is that we cannot separate out the effect on the rate of profit of international trade from the effect of changes in the rate of surplus value. What we will measure as the effect of changes in the 'rate of surplus value' in fact incorporates both these influences together. When conducting the analysis we need to bear this limitation in mind.

---

41   The method used to calculate the MELT outlined here, for example, does not allow for the existence of more than one currency. Simply using current exchange rates to convert world output into a single currency would create problems: for example, how do we deal with currencies which are kept 'artificially' high or low by currency trading restrictions? The total price of a country's output might be very large if its currency is kept very high in this way. Also, many commodities are not or cannot be traded internationally (e.g. certain services), so the labour time that is socially necessary for their production is determined at a national level, or potentially even more locally than this. The problem of skill differences also becomes quantitatively more significant when looking at the world scale rather than the national scale, and we would need a way of taking this into account. It seems likely that assuming the existence of a world MELT applying to all production is the wrong starting point, and that instead we should calculate a MELT that applies only to commodities traded across currency zones, and explain the interaction between this MELT and the MELT within each currency zone. Note also that the total value of internationally traded commodities produced in a single country is determined by the SNLT determined at the *world* level, not the national level. So in industries where workers in a given country use more advanced techniques than average, each hour of labour time worked will produce commodities worth more than one hour of average socially necessary labour time. This is probably the main reason for inequality between workers in different nations. Any attempt to calculate the MELT on the world and national levels would need to account for this.

42   Marx 1981, pp. 344–7.

This issue also introduces a problem for our terminology. Sometimes 'total surplus value less the difference between total price and total value' is thought to be equivalent to 'total profit', but we have shown that unproductive expenditures of surplus value complicate this issue. For the analysis in this work, we need a shorthand way of referring to the former without confusing it with the latter. On the other hand, we generally will not need to distinguish between 'total surplus value less the difference between total price and total value' and the actual surplus value produced, since we cannot measure the latter in any case. So, to distinguish it from total profit, we will just use the names 'surplus value' or 'total surplus value' to refer to 'total surplus value produced by workers in the US less the difference between total price and total value'.

7 Surplus Value after Unproductive Expenditures

This means that 'surplus value', s, can be defined as $y - d - r$, where r is the total cost of the commodities bought to reproduce the labour power that is expended productively; i.e. its value.

To estimate r, we need to estimate the total value of commodities consumed by productive workers and petty-bourgeois producers engaged in productive labour. The national accounts do not allow us to estimate r straightforwardly, because they do not break consumption down by class categories. But they do compare personal income with personal consumption expenditure for the population as a whole. We will use this to calculate the average propensity to consume personal income, and then multiply this by an estimate of productive workers' wages, to get an estimate of productive workers' consumption.

This estimate is not ideal. In nearly all cases we would expect workers' average propensity to consume to be higher than the general average, because workers have lower incomes. One alternative would be to assume that *all* workers' income is spent on consumption: i.e. to assume that the price and value of labour power are equal. But since wages make up the majority of personal income, the general propensity to consume is likely to be closer to workers' propensity to consume than the propensity to consume of other classes, and to be closer to workers' average propensity to consume than the assumption that this propensity is 100 %. More importantly, in trend terms, assuming a 100 % propensity to consume for workers would fail to register any changes as a result of changes in taxes on workers' incomes, secondary exploitation from rent, tax and interest, or changes in the proportion of income that workers set aside as savings.

Fortunately, as we will see towards the end of the chapter, we do not need to use this estimate of the average propensity to consume to measure the rate of profit on production; it only affects the decomposition of changes in it. It does, however, affect our measure of the rate of profit in terms of $s - u$.

To calculate the average propensity to consume, we first have to strip out some imputations included in personal income and consumption expenditures as they are defined in the national accounts. To do this, we will start with the adjusted measure of personal consumption expenditure we used to calculate output: i.e. PCE as measured in the national accounts less PCE on housing, gambling and financial services and insurance. However, unlike gambling, financial services and insurance, the real and imputed rent paid for housing is not exclusively a transfer payment (or imputed transfer payment). Like the sale of newly produced commodities, the sale of access to a dwelling includes a portion which covers the cost of producing the commodity (the depreciation of the dwelling) plus profit appropriated by the landlord. Unlike newly produced commodities, none of this dwelling rent embodies newly produced value (as mentioned above). Yet clearly the cost of housing is part of the cost of reproducing labour power. How then are we to account for it?

Marx explains:

> Some of the means of subsistence, such as food and fuel, are consumed every day, and must therefore be replaced every day. Others, such as clothes and furniture, last for longer periods and need to be replaced only at longer intervals. Articles of one kind must be bought or paid for every day, others every week, others every quarter and so on. But in whatever way the sum total of these outlays may be spread over the year, they must be covered by the average income, taking one day with another. If the total of the commodities required every day for the production of labour-power = A, and of those required every week = B, and of those required every quarter = C, and so on, the daily average of these commodities $= \frac{365A + 52B + 4C + \dots}{365}$.[43]

It is perhaps strange that Marx does not mention housing here, but it does not seem fundamentally different from the case of other commodities. If we extend this approach to include housing, then the value of the housing necessary to reproduce workers' labour power is the depreciation of the housing stock they occupy. This applies to all workers, whether the dwelling is rented, mortgaged

---

43   Marx 1976, p. 276.

or owned outright. For workers who rent their dwelling or are paying off a mortgage, the costs they incur as a result contribute towards their secondary exploitation, insofar as they exceed the depreciation of the dwelling.

This gives us the basis for calculating the propensity to consume, which is defined in Appendix A, and hence also a method for estimating r and s.

Our analysis of the turnover and stock of variable capital, on the other hand, still needs to be made in terms of wages rather than the value of labour power, since it is wages that capitalists must pay to workers, and forms their variable capital. Appendix B shows that defining surplus value and the rate of surplus value in terms of the *value* of labour power nevertheless does not alter our method for decomposing the rate of profit, just the magnitude of one of its elements.

Next, we want to measure unproductive expenditures of surplus value, u. This is surplus value spent on purposes other than: net private investment and personal consumption not devoted to reproducing the labour power of employees or self-employed people. Defined positively, u is: surplus value spent by unproductive workers and the unproductive self-employed on reproducing their labour power; the depreciation of non-residential fixed assets used by unproductive businesses (since *residential* depreciation is either part of the value of productive or unproductive labour power or non-workers' consumption); all commodities (excluding labour power, which is already counted above) bought by the government sector (whether for consumption or investment) excluding commodities the sector consumes productively; constant circulating capital consumed by unproductive businesses; and the total cost of the commodities bought with government social benefits. We assume this last amount is equal to the social benefits the government pays: i.e. that this income is consumed at an average propensity of 100%. We make this assumption because this income is overwhelmingly paid to people with little choice but to spend it over a short length of time (it includes social security, unemployment insurance, veterans' benefits, Medicare and Medicaid).

With both s and u defined we can calculate $s - u$. The workings for doing this are included in Appendix A, and give the following result:

$s - u$ = Gross private investment in equipment and structures + Net exports excluding financial services, insurance, royalties and license fees + Adjusted PCE – Total non-residential business depreciation of equipment and structures – Productive non-profit and co-op depreciation – Government social benefits $- p \times$ (All employees' compensation + All proprietors' 'wages').

Our measure of $s - u$ therefore does not depend on any of the more approximate distinctions we have made between productive and unproductive labour.

To get a 'feel' for what $s - u$ refers to we can break it down into three components. First, a portion of $s - u$ is what we will call, as a shorthand, 'non-workers' consumption', plus investment in the private housing stock not including the housing component of the value of labour power:

> Gross private residential investment + Adjusted PCE – Government social benefits – p × (All employees' compensation + All proprietors' 'wages').

We can think of this as 'luxuries' or 'capitalists' consumption'.

Second, there is net non-residential private investment:

> Gross private non-residential investment in equipment and structures – Total non-residential business depreciation of equipment and structures – Productive non-profit and co-op depreciation.

We can think of this as 'net investment' or 'accumulation'.

This leaves the third component, which is net exports excluding financial services, insurance, royalties and license fees. This is the difference between value produced in the US and value spent in the US, assuming zero unequal exchange. The difference accumulates (or, if net exports are negative, disaccumulates) in the form of net financial assets (though financial assets also accumulate and disaccumulate for other reasons, as we will explore in the next two chapters).

For some purposes we will also want to calculate $s - u$ excluding investment and personal consumption funded out of 'profits' made by the self-employed. This is the surplus value after unproductive expenditures that is 'available' to the corporate sector, which we will call $(s - u - ep)$, where 'ep' is 'expenditure by proprietors' (i.e. proprietors' personal consumption and net investment). This is defined in Appendix A.

8   Profits from Production

Finally we will return to the issue of measuring profits from production. The measures of profit used in the NIPAs are described as measures of 'profits from production' because they do not include profits from capital gains. But they *do* include profits made by businesses from 'output' we excluded earlier: 'output' from 'financial services', insurance, gambling, rental payments for real estate above the depreciated value of dwellings, and net exports of other private services, royalties and license fees. These *are* indeed profits (and they are also forms of appearance of surplus value, and are included in our measure of surplus value above) but they are business profits from *transfers* between individuals and businesses of *already realised value*, and not profits *from production*.

This distinction is important because these two types of profit have different implications for investment decisions. For capitalists considering whether to invest their capital in producing commodities, the rate of return that interests them includes, in the numerator, the total price they would receive for the commodities they would expect to produce, less their costs. These costs include the *price* they pay for labour power, not its value. A portion of that price is then appropriated by *other* capitalists and the state in the form of, for example, interest paid to banks, rent paid to landlords or income taxes. But for these workers' employers (or potential employers) it generally makes no difference whether their workers have to 'spend' income in this way, and certainly is not incorporated into their investment decisions or the rate of return they receive.

Investments in commercial capital also depend exclusively on profits from production. Specifically, their profits depend on selling the commodities they buy at a higher price than they pay for them from the productive capitalist, after subtracting their costs for wages, depreciation and other inputs.[44]

For both commercial and productive capital, the largest component of the *denominator* of the rate of return that interests them is fixed assets plus inventories; i.e. the *produced* component of capital that was Marx's main focus. For productive capital this includes the whole of the variable component of their capital, the whole value of their productive constant capital, and potentially also capital tied up in the unrecovered costs of paying unproductive employees (e.g. managers and accountants, whose wages still contribute to the cost price of commodities and hence to the cost price of inventories, even though they add no *value* to these commodities) and unproductive constant capital (e.g. office space for the unproductive employees). For commercial capital, their fixed assets and inventories exclusively embody the value of their constant capital. This capital is productive for them (i.e. they need it to generate profits), but is unproductive in the sense that it is not used to enhance the use value of commodities, and therefore does not transfer its value to output.

However, fixed assets and inventories are not the whole of the capital which must be invested to make it possible to employ workers to produce or sell com-

---

44   Marx 1981, pp. 394–416.

modities. The capitalist must also buy or rent the land needed for this purpose, pay any necessary taxes or bribes, put money in the businesses' bank accounts and cash registers, buy (other) financial assets or borrow money, and meet other sundry expenses. All of this is capital, some of which contributes to the balance sheet (which includes the businesses' stock of 'goodwill'), and some of which the accountant will 'expense' immediately.

For the purposes of calculating the average rate of profit from production, we will ignore these components of capital. Since these components of capital are not *produced* (except for the labour power of unproductive employees of commercial capital), their cost is determined quite differently from the cost of the produced components of capital advanced. They are 'fictitious' components of capital, which is a concept we will explore further in the next two chapters. Here we need to note that it is only the rate of return *as capitalists measure it* which has a direct influence on their investment decisions. The ratio of profits from production to *produced* commercial and productive capital is therefore only a proxy for the average rate of return on investments in commercial and productive capital as capitalists measure it. However, it is a useful proxy because its dynamics can be described and measured without having to deal with the complications that non-produced capital introduces.

On the other hand, for finance capital and for landlords, non-produced capital is an especially large component of their capital, and the relationship between their profits, surplus value and profits from production is highly mediated. The ratio of their profits to their produced capital is therefore not a good approximation for their average rate of return, and the relationship between the average rate of profit on production and their rates of return involves complications which we cannot consider in detail without exploring the concept of fictitious capital further. For example, for capital advanced as finance, the entire capital is the current exchange value of their holdings of shares or bonds, or the principal on a loan. A financial *institution* (e.g. a bank) depends in an even more mediated fashion on the production of value, since its profits depend on the effectiveness with which it performs its function as a financial intermediary, and its capital is overwhelmingly fictitious. Financial *profits* either derive from profits from production or value extracted through secondary exploitation, or can be fictitious.

We will explore these issues to some extent in the next two chapters, but one important point here is that it does not make sense to count financial profits towards profits from production. If financial profits are extracted in the form of interest or dividends from commercial or productive capitalists then they are already a part of profits from production, if they are extracted from individuals then they are the result of a process that is *secondary* to the direct exploitation of workers in production, and if they are fictitious they are the result of an expansion of the stock of financial assets.

For a landlord, their rate of return is determined in a similarly mediated fashion. The largest component of their capital is usually land, and the part of the exchange value of land which corresponds to its unimproved value does not embody the expenditure of human labour, and is therefore non-produced capital. If they rent to individual people, the landlord's revenue depends on extracting money from already realised value paid in the form of wages, profits paid to individuals in their various forms, or savings, in the same way as financial profit extracted from individuals. If they rent to a productive or commercial business, then the situation is similar to that for interest and dividends paid by these businesses. Again, this is discussed further in the next two chapters, but the important point here is that it does not make sense to account explicitly for landlords' profit or capital as part of calculating the average rate of profit on production.

It is not surprising that studies of the rate of profit based on the corporate sector as a whole, including financial institutions, sometimes find results which appear to be inconsistent with Marx's LTFRP. By including the profits made by corporations on 'personal consumption expenditure' on financial services, insurance, gambling, and dwelling rent, and 'net exports' of financial services, insurance, patents and licenses, these studies are including profit in the numerator of the rate of profit that is not profit from production. As mentioned above, they are also poor starting points for explaining the rate of accumulation, because although for this purpose we *do* want to include profits appropriated through secondary exploitation, we *also* need to account for the effects of saving and borrowing by workers and the state.

Within the framework we have developed so far, measuring profits from production is relatively straightforward. Our measure of total output already excludes the 'output' recorded in the national accounts from non-commodities (financial services, insurance, etc.). To measure total profits from production in the business sector, we will start with this measure of output, after subtracting the total price of the commodities produced by the government and non-profit sectors. Then we subtract the cost of the productive and unproductive labour power and constant capital used to produce and realise profits from production. This includes the cost of wages paid to managers to discipline this labour, and the wages of other unproductive workers hired in the commercial and productive sectors, since these are all costs businesses must pay to produce and realise this profit. This gives us profits from production before tax, interest and rent, π:

$$\pi \equiv by - nfd - nfw$$

where: by = output produced by businesses; nfd is depreciation of non-residential fixed assets owned by businesses excluding the finance, insurance and real estate sectors ('non-financial depreciation'); and nfw is the total wages paid to employees of these businesses and the 'wages' proprietors' of these businesses 'pay themselves'.

As before, we can also measure this excluding non-corporate businesses, by subtracting all of proprietors' income in these sectors (and not just their 'wages'). It is also important to measure profits from production on an after-tax basis, since taxes are relevant for investment decisions. After-tax profits will also be important for assessing the fictitious component of financial profits in Chapter 6. To do this, we need to subtract taxes on production less subsidies, and taxes on corporate income. This creates four measures of profits on production, which are defined in Appendix A.

The denominators for these measures of the rate of profit are the same as those we will use for the rate of profit defined in terms of $(s - u)$. For the measures which include non-corporate business, this is non-residential fixed assets plus inventories at pre-production prices for all businesses excluding financial corporations. For the measures which apply to corporate businesses only, this is corporate non-residential fixed assets excluding financial corporations plus corporate inventories, again at pre-production prices. These estimates are not ideal because the category 'financial corporations' is not exactly the same as 'all businesses outside the productive and commercial sectors', but it seems unlikely that the difference in the stock of fixed assets owned by these two categories of business would have a significant effect on the results.

9   Conclusion

This concludes the three chapters devoted to measuring and decomposing changes in rates of profit. These chapters have constructed an interpretation of Marx's value theory as it applies to the rate of profit that has aimed to stay as close as possible to Marx's original text. The next chapter considers Marx's less developed but still very valuable work in *Capital* on finance, so that, in Chapter 6, we can construct a theory of average financial rates of return.

10 Appendix A: Accounting Definitions

10.1 *Abbreviations for Sources*

NIPA National Income and Product Accounts[45]
FA Fixed Assets Accounts[46]
VA / GO GDP-by-industry accounts (including estimates of value added and gross output by industry).[47]

10.2 *Output (y)*

Output ($\$_{t-1}, y_{t-1,t}$) ≡ Gross Domestic Product (NIPA 1.1.5 line 1) – PCE (NIPA 2.4.5 line 1) + Adjusted PCE – Net exports of financial services and insurance – Exports of royalties and license fees (NIPA 4.2.5 line 21)[48] + Imports of royalties and license fees (NIPA 4.2.5 line 45)[49] – Gross private domestic investment in intellectual property products (NIPA 1.1.5 line 12) – Gross government investment in intellectual property (FA 7.5 sheet A line 16, sheet B line 18) – Government consumption expenditures (NIPA 3.10.5 line 1) + Intermediate goods and services purchased by government for unproductive purposes – Government own-account investment (NIPA 3.10.5 line 10) + Intermediate inputs consumed in producing: PCE on finance and insurance, PCE on gambling, PCE on real estate and net exports of other private services
where:

Adjusted PCE ≡ PCE (NIPA 2.4.5 line 1) – PCE on Housing (NIPA 2.4.5 line 50) – PCE on Gambling (NIPA 2.4.5 line 79) – PCE on Financial services and insurance (NIPA 2.4.5 line 86).

Net exports of financial services and insurance ≡ Payments less receipts of financial services (US International Services detailed statistics tables 5a to 5c) + Payments less receipts of net insurance (US International Services detailed statistics tables 5a to 5c).[50]

---

45 US Bureau of Economic Analysis 2015b.
46 US Bureau of Economic Analysis 2015a.
47 US Bureau of Economic Analysis 2014.
48 Before 1967 this is estimated using Exports of Services [NIPA 1.1.5, line 24] * Imports of Royalties and license fees, 1967 [NIPA 4.2.5, line 21] / Exports of Services, 1967 [NIPA 1.1.5, line 24].
49 Before 1967 this is estimated using Imports of Services [NIPA 1.1.5, line 27] * Imports of Royalties and license fees, 1967 [NIPA 4.2.5, line 45] / Imports of Services, 1967 [NIPA 1.1.5, line 27].
50 Between 1986 and 1997 there is no data for financial services exported and imported

Intermediate goods and services purchased by government for unproductive purposes ≡ Government intermediate goods and services purchased (NIPA 3.10.5 line 6) * [Gross output of general government (NIPA 3.10.5 line 2) – Government sales to other sectors (NIPA 3.10.5 line 11)] / Gross output of general government (NIPA 3.10.5 line 2).

Intermediate inputs consumed in producing: PCE on finance and insurance, PCE on gambling, PCE on real estate and net exports of other private services ≡

[PCE on Financial services and insurance (NIPA 2.4.5 line 86) + Net exports of financial services and insurance (NIPA 4.2.5 line 22)] * Intermediate inputs for Finance and insurance (VA/GO 1987–92 line 798; VA/GO 97–12 line 850) / Gross output for Finance and insurance (VA/GO 1987–92 line 519; VA/GO 97–12 line 553)

+ PCE on Gambling (NIPA 2.4.5 line 79) * Intermediate inputs for Gambling (VA/GO 1987–92 line 824; VA/GO 97–12 line 877) / Gross output for Gambling (VA/GO 1987–92 line 545; VA/GO 97–12 line 580)

+ Intermediate goods and services consumed producing housing sector output (NIPA 7.4.5 line 6).

Business output (by) ≡ Output (y) – Receipts from sales of goods and services by non-profit institutions (NIPA 2.3.5 line 24) – General government sales to other sectors (NIPA 3.10.5 line 11) – Compensation of employees of government enterprises (from NIPA 6.2) – Surplus of government enterprises (NIPA 1.10 line 20).

10.3   *Productive Private Industries*
The measures of productive depreciation (d), socially necessary labour time (L), and the value and price of productive labour power (r and w) depend on distinguishing productive industries from unproductive industries. For this purpose the private industries listed below were defined as productive. Some

---

through affiliated corporations. This was estimating by assuming the ratio of affiliated net exports of other private services to unaffiliated other private services was equal to the ratio of affiliated financial services to unaffiliated financial services. Before 1986 there is no data for trade in financial services or insurance. We have estimated them assuming a constant ratio of net exports of financial services and insurance to 'other private services' for all years until and including 1986. Before 1967 there is no data for trade in 'other private services', so we have assumed constant ratios of exports and imports of 'other private services' to exports of all services. Until around 1997 net exports of financial services and insurance are negligibly small (less than 0.05% of output according to our estimates).

government employees are also classified as productive, and the method for estimating this is explained in each case.

A difficulty with the data is that the system of industry classifications changes three times between 1929 and 2013. We need to 'smooth over' the breaks this would otherwise introduce into the series. The NIPA facilitate this by always including at least one year in which the classification systems 'cross over'. The longest stretch over which there are no discontinuities is between 1948 and 2000, so for these years we have used results for compensation of employees, FTE employment and number of self-employed from the NIPA figures directly. (The change in classifications in 1987–88 has no effect on our results, given the definitions of productive sectors we are using.) Prior to 1948 there is a very slight break introduced, and to smooth this over we calculate each year's level by multiplying the previous year's level by the ratio of this year's level to last year's level according to the NIPA's raw data. The latest classification system, introduced from 1998 to 2001, introduces more substantial changes. We have used to same approach to smoothing the series for years from 2001 onwards, except going forwards rather than backwards in time. As mentioned elsewhere, any exercise is trying to distinguish productive from unproductive labour using national accounting definitions is bound to involve approximations, but the strength of the approach is that these only affect the measures of the rates of profit insofar as they affect the measures of inflation used to adjust them (and to put this issue further in context, many studies make no adjustment for inflation in calculating the rate of profit *at all*: i.e. they just divide profits measured at prices over the course of the year by the stock of fixed assets measured at end or start of year prices).

1929–2000: Agriculture, forestry and fisheries; Mining; Construction (called 'Contract construction' from 1929–48); Manufacturing; Transportation and public facilities; Services excluding Legal services; Rest of World.

2001–13: Agriculture, forestry, fishing and hunting; Mining; Utilities; Construction; Manufacturing; Transportation and warehousing; Information; Professional, scientific and technical services excluding Legal services; Management of companies and enterprises; Administrative and waste services; Professional, scientific, and technical services; Administrative and waste management services; Education services; Healthcare and social assistance; Arts, entertainment and recreation; Accommodation and food services; Other services, except government.

10.4   *Depreciation* (d)

Productive depreciation in SNLT $\equiv d_{t-1,t} \equiv \$_{t-1,t}d_{t-1,t}$ * [Price index for non-residential private fixed investment for last year (i.e. t-2, t-1; NIPA 1.1.4 line 9) / Price index for non-residential private fixed investment for this year (i.e. t-1, t; NIPA 1.1.4 line 9)] * $n_{t-1,t} / n_{t-2,t-1}$.

Productive depreciation at current prices $(\$_{t-1,t}d_{t-1,t}) \equiv$ Current cost productive depreciation plus 'depreciation' of intellectual assets for non-corporate business (NIPA 6.22, sheets A to D) + Current cost productive depreciation plus 'depreciation' of intellectual assets for corporate business (NIPA 6.13, sheets A to D) – Current cost 'depreciation' of relevant intellectual assets + Current cost productive depreciation for government + Current cost productive depreciation for non-profit institutions and co-operatives.

Where:

Depreciation attributed to relevant intellectual assets $\equiv$ Current cost depreciation of private non-residential intellectual property products (FA 4.4 line 4) – [Current cost depreciation of private non-residential intellectual property products (FA 4.4) for: Financial corporations (line 36) + Non-profit institutions (line 68) + Households (line 72) + Tax-exempt cooperatives (line 76)].

Current cost productive depreciation for government $\equiv$ Sales to other sectors (NIPA 3.10.5 line 11) * [Consumption of general government fixed capital (NIPA 3.10.5 line 5) – Current cost depreciation of residential fixed assets for government (FA 5.4 line 8)} / Gross output of general government (NIPA 3.10.5 line 2)

Current cost productive depreciation for non-profit institutions and co-operatives $\equiv$ Receipts from sales of goods and services by non-profit institutions (NIPA 2.3.5 line 24) / Gross output of non-profit institutions (NIPA 2.3.5 line 23)[51] * [Current cost depreciation of non-residential equipment and structures for non-profit institutions (FA 4.4 line 66 + 67) + Current cost depreciation of non-residential equipment and structures for tax exempt co-operatives (FA 4.4 line 74 + 75)].

Non-financial business depreciation (*nfd*) $\equiv$ TSSI depreciation for corporations excluding finance, insurance and real estate + TSSI depreciation for non-corporate businesses excluding finance, insurance and real estate

where

---

51   Before 1959, this ratio is assumed to be equal to its level in 1959.

TSSI depreciation for corporations excluding finance, insurance and real estate ≡ [Consumption of fixed capital for corporations excluding finance, insurance and real estate (NIPA 6.22 sheet A line 1 – 52, sheets B and C line 1 – 50, sheet D line 1 – 51 – 57; note this includes 'depreciation' of intellectual assets) – 'Depreciation' of intellectual assets for non-financial corporations (NIPA 4.4 line 50)] × [Price index for non-residential private investment$_{t-2,t-1}$ (NIPA 1.1.4 line 9, previous year) / Price index for non-residential private investment$_{t-1,t}$ (NIPA 1.1.4 line 9)] × $n_{t-2,t-1}$ / $n_{t-1,t}$.

TSSI depreciation for non-corporate businesses excluding finance, insurance and real estate ≡ [Consumption of fixed capital for non-corporate business excluding finance, insurance and real estate (NIPA 6.13 sheets A to C line 1 – 16, sheet D line 1 – 15; note this includes 'depreciation' of intellectual assets) – 'Depreciation' of intellectual assets for non-corporate business (NIPA 4.4 line 60 + 64)] × [Price index for non-residential private investment$_{t-2,t-1}$ (NIPA 1.1.4 line 9, previous year) / Price index for non-residential private investment$_{t-1,t}$ (NIPA 1.1.4 line 9)] × $n_{t-2,t-1}$ / $n_{t-1,t}$.

10.5 *Net Output* $(y - d)$

Using this approach we can measure net output in one of three ways. The first and most important is the value added by living labour, L:

$$\$_{t-1,t}L_{t-1,t} = \$_{t-1,t}y_{t-1,t} - d_{t-1,t} \times n_{t-1,t}.$$

The measure of depreciation used here is the value transferred by fixed assets; and it is equivalent to gross output less the labour time that was socially necessary to reproduce the depreciated portion of fixed assets at the start of the period.

The second is cost of reproducing the depreciated portion of the stock of fixed assets in *physical* terms, at *output* prices. This is net output as measured in the national accounts (except here adjusted for the distinction between productive and unproductive labour):

$$\$_{t-1,t}y_{t-1,t} - \$_{t-1,t}d_{t-1,t}.$$

This will usually be higher than the first measure, as technological change tends to make it cheaper, in MELT adjusted terms, to replace a given physical stock of fixed assets over time.

Notice that, unlike other magnitudes, it is not true generally that $\$_{t-1,t}d_{t-1,t} = d_{t-1,t} \times n_{t-1,t}$. The same would true of other inputs if we were using a more consistently temporal measure of the MELT, rather than the approximation used here.

The third measure of net output subtracts the value required to maintain the stock of fixed at a constant value, after accounting for both depreciation *and* revaluation. This is:

$$\$_{t-1,t}y - (d_{t-1,t} - RF_{t-1,t}) \times n_{t-1,t}.$$

Since devaluation is more common than revaluation, this will usually be the smallest of the three measures.

This also implies three corresponding measures of investment net of depreciation. Different measures will be appropriate for different purposes.

10.6   *Wages of Producers* (w)

To calculate the total 'wages' paid to producers we need to include the 'wages' that productive self-employed people 'pay themselves'. We will mostly assume this is equal to the average wage paid to a productive worker. However, until around 1940 this gives the result that productive self-employed people pay themselves total 'wages' which are higher than their total income (i.e. higher than 'proprietors' income' in the NIPA for productive sectors). This is probably because in these years the category 'proprietors' includes large numbers of small farmers earning low incomes. So in cases where proprietors' average income is lower than the average wage we will assume proprietors' total 'wage' is equal to their income. The definition is:

$w \equiv w \, (workers) + w \, (self\text{-}employed)$

where

$\$w \, (workers) \equiv$ Wages paid to workers in productive private industries (as defined above, NIPA 6.2, sheets A to D) + Government employees (NIPA 6.2, sheets A to D) * Government sales to other sectors (NIPA 3.10.5 line 11) / Gross output of general government (NIPA 3.10.5 line 2)

$\$w \, (self\text{-}employed) \equiv$ the smaller of:

non-farm proprietors' income for productive industries (NIPA 6.12, sheets A to D) + farm proprietors' income (NIPA 2.1 line 10);

and

$\frac{\$w(workers)}{L(workers)} \times L(self-employed).$

Wages of non-financial business employees and proprietors $(nfw) \equiv$ Compensation of employees of businesses excluding finance, insurance and real estate (NIPA 6.2, sheet A line 1 – 54, sheet B line 1 – 52, sheet C line 1 – 52, sheet D line 1 – 57 – 62)

10.7   *Propensity for Producers to Spend Their Income on Consumption* (p)

$p \equiv$ [Adjusted PCE (defined in the Appendix in Chapter 3) + Depreciation of residential fixed assets (FA 5.4 line 1, adjusted into a temporal measure) – Government social benefits to persons (NIPA 2.1 line 17)] / [Personal income (NIPA 2.1 line 7) – Imputed rental income of persons with capital consumption adjustment (NIPA 7.12 line 53) – Proprietors' net income from housing (NIPA 7.4.5 line 20) – Government social benefits to persons (NIPA 2.1 line 17) + Contributions for government social insurance (NIPA 2.1 line 25)].

In the numerator this replaces PCE on housing rent with the depreciation of the housing stock (consistent with the argument made in the chapter). The denominator, income, is personal income less 'rental income of persons' and proprietors' net income from the housing sector (since the NIPAs count both towards 'personal income', when in reality they are transfers between individuals, and not new income). Finally, we also want to exclude income from consumption financed by government social benefits, since below we will separately account for consumption financed this way, on the assumption that all this income is spent on commodities. 'Personal income' as defined in the national accounts only includes social benefits *net* of contributions to social insurance; so on the denominator we need to subtract net social benefits. On the numerator, however, in order to subtract the full value of the commodities we assume are consumed out of social benefits, we need to subtract gross social benefits.

10.8   *Value of Reproducing Productive Labour Power* (r)

$\equiv p \times w$.

10.9   *Surplus Value* (s)

$s \equiv y - d - r =$ Gross Domestic Product (NIPA 1.1.5 line 1) – PCE (NIPA 2.4.5 line 1) + Adjusted PCE – Net exports of financial services and insurance – Exports of Royalties and license fees (NIPA 4.2.5 line 21)[52] + Imports of Royalties and license fees (NIPA 4.2.5 line 45)[53] – Gross private domestic investment in intellectual property products (NIPA 1.1.5 line 12) – Gross government investment in intellectual property (FA 7.5 sheet A line 16, sheet B line 18) – Government

---

52   Before 1967 this is estimated using Exports of Services [NIPA 1.1.5, line 24] * Imports of Royalties and license fees, 1967 [NIPA 4.2.5, line 21] / Exports of Services, 1967 [NIPA 1.1.5, line 24].

53   Before 1967 this is estimated using Imports of Services [NIPA 1.1.5, line 27] * Imports of Royalties and license fees, 1967 [NIPA 4.2.5, line 45] / Imports of Services, 1967 [NIPA 1.1.5, line 27].

consumption expenditures (NIPA 3.10.5 line 1) + Intermediate goods and services purchased by government for unproductive purposes – Government own-account investment (NIPA 3.10.5 line 10) + Intermediate inputs consumed in producing: PCE on finance and insurance, PCE on gambling, PCE on real estate and net exports of other private services – $d - p \times w$.

10.10   Unproductive Expenditures of Surplus Value (u)

$u \equiv$ Intermediate goods and services purchased by government for unproductive purposes + Intermediate inputs consumed in producing: PCE on finance and insurance, PCE on gambling, PCE on real estate and net exports of other private services + Value of purchases of unproductive labour power + Government social benefits to persons (NIPA 2.1 line 17) + Unproductive non-residential business depreciation of equipment and structures + Government gross investment excluding own account investment – Productive depreciation for government + Value of unproductive proprietors' labour power.

Here, we need to include the intermediate inputs consumed unproductively on producing PCE on finance and insurance, gambling, real estate and net exports of other private services and royalties, etc. because we have (correctly) excluded them from personal consumption expenditure, and classified them instead as u. Other unproductive industries such as the retail sector also consume commodities unproductively – e.g. the electricity consumed by shops. But unlike the intermediate inputs used to 'produce' financial services, etc. the intermediate inputs used by the retail sector are accounted for as part of the cost of the final commodities that we have *not* excluded from personal consumption expenditure. So if we included them again here we would be counting their consumption twice. This means we are effectively incorrectly classifying the value of these commodities as productively consumed constant capital rather than as unproductive expenditure of surplus value. This leads to an equal underestimate of both s and u, and therefore has no effect on $s - u$.

The elements not defined in the definition above are:

Value of purchases of unproductive labour power $\equiv p \times$ [Compensation of employees (NIPA 2.1 line 2) – $\$w$ (*workers*)]

Unproductive non-residential business depreciation$_{t-1,t}$ $\equiv$ [Depreciation of non-residential business equipment and structures$_{t-1,t}$ (FA 4.4 line 2 + line 3 – line 66 – line 67 – line 70 – line 71 – line 74 – line 75) – Productive business depreciation] $\times$ [Price index for non-residential private investment$_{t-2,t-1}$ (NIPA 1.1.4 line 9, previous year) / Price index for non-residential private investment$_{t-1,t}$ (NIPA 1.1.4 line 9)] $\times n_{t-2,t-1} / n_{t-1,t}$.

Government gross investment excluding own account investment ≡ Government consumption expenditures and gross investment (NIPA 1.1.5 line 22) – Government consumption expenditures (NIPA 3.10.5 line 1) – Government own-account investment (NIPA 3.10.5 line 10)

Value of unproductive proprietors' labour power ≡ $p \times [\$w\ (self-employed) - \$w\ (self-employed)]$

where $\$w\ (self-employed)$ ≡ the smaller of:

Proprietors' net income (NIPA 2.1 line 9);

and

Self-employed persons (NIPA 6.7, sheets A to D line 1) × Compensation of employees (NIPA 2.1 line 2) / Full-time equivalent employees (NIPA 6.5, sheets A to D line 1).

10.11 *Surplus Value Less Unproductive Expenditures* (s – u)

$s - u$ = GDP – PCE + Adjusted PCE – Net exports of financial services, insurance, royalties and license fees – Gross domestic investment in intellectual property products – Government consumption expenditures + Intermediate goods and services purchased by government for unproductive purposes – Government own-account investment + Intermediate inputs consumed in producing: PCE on finance and insurance, PCE on gambling, PCE on real estate and net exports of other private services – $d - p \times w$ – [Intermediate goods and services purchased by government for unproductive purposes + Intermediate inputs consumed in producing: PCE on finance and insurance, PCE on gambling, PCE on real estate and net exports of financial services and insurance + Value of purchases of unproductive labour power + Government social benefits to persons + Unproductive non-residential business depreciation of equipment and structures + Government gross investment excluding own account investment – Productive depreciation for government + Value of unproductive proprietors' labour power]

= GDP – PCE + Adjusted PCE – Net exports of other private services, royalties and license fees – Gross domestic investment in intellectual property products – Government consumption expenditures – Government own-account investment – $d - p \times w$ – [Government social benefits to persons + Unproductive non-residential business depreciation of equipment and structures + Government gross investment excluding own account investment – Productive depreciation for government].

Now, since GDP = PCE + Gross private investment + net exports + government consumption + gross government investment;

$s - u$ = Gross private investment in equipment and structures + Net exports excluding other private services, royalties and license fees + Adjusted PCE – d –

$p \times w$ – [Government social benefits to persons + Unproductive non-residential business depreciation of equipment and structures – Productive depreciation for government].

Further, since

d = Productive business depreciation + Productive depreciation for government + Productive depreciation for non-profits and co-ops;

$s - u$ = Gross private investment in equipment and structures + Net exports excluding financial services, insurance, royalties and license fees + Adjusted PCE – $p \times w$ – [Government social benefits to persons + Unproductive non-residential business depreciation – Productive depreciation for government + Productive business depreciation + Productive depreciation for government + Productive depreciation for non-profits and co-ops];

and, since all productive depreciation is non-residential, Unproductive non-residential business depreciation of equipment and structures + Productive business depreciation = Non-residential business depreciation;

$s - u$ = Gross private investment in equipment and structures + Net exports excluding financial services, insurance, royalties and license fees + Adjusted PCE – $p \times w$ – Government social benefits to persons – Non-residential business depreciation of equipment and structures – Productive depreciation for non-profits and co-ops.

10.12   Surplus Value 'Available' to the Corporate Sector (s – u – ep)

$s - u - ep \equiv s - u$ – Proprietors' consumption and net investment = Gross private investment in equipment and structures + Net exports excluding financial services, insurance royalties and license fees + Adjusted PCE – $p \times$ [w (*workers*) + Proprietors' income (NIPA 2.1 line 9)] – Government social benefits to persons – Non-residential business depreciation – Productive depreciation for non-profits and co-ops – {Gross investment in non-corporate business non-residential equipment and structures (FA 4.7 lines 58 + 59 + 62 + 63) – Current cost depreciation of non-corporate business non-residential equipment and structures (FA 4.4 lines 58 + 59 + 62 + 63) × [Price index for non-residential private investment$_{t-2,t-1}$ (NIPA 1.1.4 line 9, previous year) / Price index for non-residential private investment$_{t-1,t}$ (NIPA 1.1.4 line 9)] × $n_{t-2,t-1}$ / $n_{t-1,t}$ + Gross investment in non-corporate business residential fixed assets (FA 5.7 line 5) – Current cost depreciation of non-corporate business residential fixed assets (FA 5.4 line 5) × [Price index for residential private investment$_{t-2,t-1}$ (NIPA 1.1.4 line 13, previous year) / Price index for residential private investment$_{t-1,t}$ (NIPA 1.1.4 line 13)] × $n_{t-2,t-1}$ / $n_{t-1,t}$}.

10.13   Pre-tax Profits from Production for All Businesses (π)

π ≡ Output of businesses (*by*) – Compensation of employees of private industries (NIPA 6.2, sheets A to D, line 3) + Compensation of employees of finance, insurance and real estate (NIPA 6.2, sheet A line 54, sheet B line 52, sheet C line 52, sheet D lines 57 + 62) – TSSI depreciation for businesses excluding finance, insurance and real estate – $w (*self-employed*) + $w (*self-employed in finance, insurance and real estate*)

where

Output of businesses (*by*) ≡ *y* – Receipts from sales of goods and services by non-profit institutions (NIPA 2.3.5 line 24) – Government sales to other sectors (NIPA 3.10.5 line 11) – Output of government enterprises;[54] and

TSSI depreciation for businesses excluding finance, insurance and real estate ≡ TSSI consumption of fixed capital for corporations excluding finance, insurance and real estate + TSSI consumption of fixed capital for non-corporate businesses excluding finance, insurance and real estate.[55]

$w (*self-employed in finance, insurance and real estate*) ≡ the smaller of: Nonfarm proprietors' net income excluding finance, insurance and real

---

54   Before 1959 sales by non-profit institutions are not recorded, so we estimate them by assuming that the ratio of non-profit sales to the current cost depreciation of their fixed assets remains the same until 1959, since we can get the depreciation for the years before 1959 and this is an estimate that does not have any significant effect on the results. Specifically,

Non-profit sales before 1959 ≡ Non-profit sales in 1959 (NIPA 3.10.5 line 11) / [Current-cost depreciation of private non-residential fixed assets for non-profit institutions and tax-exempt co-operatives in 1959 (FA 4.4 lines 66 + 67 + 74 + 75)] * Current-cost depreciation of private non-residential fixed assets for non-profit institutions and tax-exempt co-operatives in the current year (FA 4.4 lines 66 + 67 + 74 + 75).

55   Where: TSSI consumption of fixed capital for corporations excluding finance, insurance and real estate ≡ [Corporate capital consumption allowances (NIPA 6.22, sheets A to D line 1) – Corporate capital consumption allowances (NIPA 6.22, sheet A line 52, sheet B line 50, sheet C line 50, sheet D lines 51 + 57)] * [Price index for non-residential private fixed investment for last year (i.e. t-2, t-1; NIPA 1.1.4 line 9) / Price index for non-residential private fixed investment for this year (i.e. t-1, t; NIPA 1.1.4 line 9) * $n_{t-1,t} / n_{t-2,t-1}$; and Consumption of fixed capital for non-corporate businesses excluding finance, insurance and real estate ≡ [Non-corporate capital consumption allowances (NIPA 6.13, sheets A to D, line 1) – Non-corporate capital consumption allowances for finance, insurance and real estate (NIPA 6.13, sheet A line 16, sheet B line 16, sheet C line 16, sheet D line 15)] * [Price index for non-residential private fixed investment for last year (i.e. t-2, t-1; NIPA 1.1.4 line 9) / Price index for non-residential private fixed investment for this year (i.e. t-1, t; NIPA 1.1.4 line 9) * $n_{t-1,t} / n_{t-2,t-1}$.

estate (NIPA 6.12 sheets A to C, lines 1 – 14, sheet D lines 1 – 13) + Farm proprietors' net income (NIPA 2.1 line 10);

and

Self-employed persons excluding finance, insurance and real estate (NIPA 6.7, sheets A to C lines 1 – 14, sheet D lines 1 – 13) × Compensation of employees (NIPA 2.1 line 2) / Full-time equivalent employees (NIPA 6.5, sheets A to D line 1).

10.14   *Pre-tax Profits from Production for Corporations* ($\pi - \pi p$)

$\pi - \pi p \equiv$ Output of businesses – Compensation of employees of private industries (NIPA 6.2, sheets A to D, line 3) + Compensation of employees of finance, insurance and real estate (NIPA 6.2, sheet A line 54, sheet B line 52, sheet C line 52, sheet D lines 57 + 62) – TSSI consumption of fixed capital for corporations excluding finance, insurance and real estate – Nonfarm proprietors' net income excluding finance, insurance and real estate (NIPA 6.12 sheets A to C, lines 1 – 14, sheet D lines 1 – 13) – Farm proprietors' net income (NIPA 2.1 line 10) – Non-corporate capital consumption allowances (NIPA 6.13, sheets A to D, line 1) + Non-corporate capital consumption allowances for finance, insurance and real estate (NIPA 6.13, sheet A line 16, sheet B line 16, sheet C line 16, sheet D line 15).

10.15   *After-Tax Profits from Production for All Businesses* ($\pi - g$)

Here $g \equiv$ Taxes on production less subsidies on production, excluding financial corporations + Taxes on non-financial corporate income (NIPA 1.14 line 28), where:

Taxes on production less subsidies on production, excluding financial corporations $\equiv$ Taxes on production and imports (NIPA 1.10 line 7) – Subsidies (NIPA 1.10 line 8) – Taxes on production and imports less subsidies for corporate business (NIPA 1.14 line 7) + Taxes on production and imports less subsidies for non-financial corporate business (NIPA 1.14 line 23).

10.16   *After-Tax Profits from Production for Corporations* ($\pi - \pi p - g + g p$)

Here $(g - gp) \equiv$ Taxes on production and imports less subsidies for non-financial corporate business (NIPA 1.14 line 23) + Taxes on non-financial corporate income (NIPA 1.14 line 28).

10.17   *Constant and Variable Capital Advanced for All Non-financial Businesses* (C)

$C_t \equiv F_t + inv_t$

where:

F_t ≡ Current cost non-residential business equipment and structures excluding financial corporations in year t (FA 4.1 lines 8 + 9 − 34 − 35 − 66 − 67 − 70 − 71 − 74 − 75) * [Price index for non-residential private fixed investment for last year (i.e. for year t-1, t; NIPA 1.1.4 line 9) / Average price index for non-residential private fixed investment for the previous quarter and the following quarter (i.e. the average of the price level for quarters t-0.25, t and t, t+0.25; NIPA 1.1.4 line 9)] * $n_{t,t+1} / n_{t-1,t}$;[56] and

inv$_t$ ≡ Average current cost business inventories for the last quarter of the preceding year and the first quarter of the next year (NIPA 5.8.5 sheets A and B line 1) * [Price index for durable goods for last year (i.e. t-1, t; NIPA 1.1.4 line 4) / Average price index for durable goods for the previous quarter and the following quarter (i.e. t-0.25, t and t, t+0.25; NIPA 1.1.4 line 4)] * $n_{t-1,t} / n_{t-2,t-1}$.

10.18   Constant and Variable Capital Advanced for Corporate Non-financial Businesses (C – Cp)

$C_t - Cp_t \equiv F_t - Fp_t + inv_t - invp_t$
where:

$F_t - Fp_t$ ≡ Current cost non-residential non-financial corporate equipment and structures in year t (FA 4.1 lines 38 + 39) * [Price index for non-residential private fixed investment for last year (i.e. for year t-1, t; NIPA 1.1.4 line 9) / Average price index for non-residential private fixed investment for the previous quarter and the following quarter (i.e. the average of the price level for quarters t-0.25, t and t, t+0.25; NIPA 1.1.4 line 9)] * $n_{t,t+1} / n_{t-1,t}$;[57] and

inv$_t$ – invp$_t$ ≡ Estimated average current cost corporate inventories for the last quarter of the preceding year and the first quarter of the next year[58] * [Price index for durable goods for last year (i.e. t-1, t; NIPA 1.1.4

---

56 As for depreciation, for the years prior to 1948 we divided by the average price level for the preceding and following *years* instead of quarters.

57 As for depreciation, for the years prior to 1948 we divided by the average price level for the preceding and following *years* instead of quarters.

58 This is estimated as: Non-farm corporate inventories + Farm corporate inventories where: Farm corporate inventories ≡ [FA 4.1 lines 22 + 23] * [NIPA 5.8.5 line 2] / [FA 4.1 lines 6 + 7]; and Non-farm corporate inventories ≡ [FA 4.1 lines 18 + 19 − 22 − 23] * [NIPA 5.8.5 line 3] / [Current cost non-residential non-farm business equipment and structures (FA 4.1 lines 8 + 9 − 13 − 14 − 66 − 67 − 70 − 71 − 74 − 75) − FA]. This is assumes that, after separating farms from non-farms, inventories are divided between corporate and non-corporate business in proportion to their fixed assets.

line 4) / Average price index for durable goods for the previous quarter and the following quarter (i.e. t-0.25, t and t, t+0.25; NIPA 1.1.4 line 4)] * $n_{t-1,t}/n_{t-2,t-1}$.

11   Appendix B: Decomposing Changes in the Rate of Profit from Production

To decompose changes in the rate of profit from production, we will start by replacing $(s-u)/s$ with two separate ratios: the effect on profits from production of the ratio of price of labour power to its value, and the effect of the ratio of taxes net of subsidies to before-tax (and before-subsidy) profits from production. That is,

$$\frac{\partial/}{s} = \frac{by - nfd - nfr}{y - d - r} \times \frac{by - nfd - nfw}{by - nfd - nfr}$$

where nfr the value of the labour power of employees and proprietors of non-financial businesses.

The first ratio is the ratio of what before-tax profit from production to surplus value would be if labour power was sold at its value. Since relatively few commodities are produced by the US government and non-profit sectors, the main influence on this ratio should be unproductive expenditures by non-financial businesses. The second is the ratio of the latter to actual before-tax profits from production: i.e. the effect of the difference between the price and value of labour power on this measure of the rate of profit.

Next, we incorporate the combined effect of taxes and subsidies to give us the decomposition of the after-tax measure of profits from production:

$$\frac{\partial/ - g}{s} = \frac{by - nfd - nfr}{y - d - r} \times \frac{by - nfd - nfw}{by - nfd - nfr} \times \frac{\partial/ - g}{by - nfd - nfw}$$

The last ratio in this expression is the effect of taxes on after-tax profits from production.

We can use these expressions to perform full decompositions on both the before- and after-tax measures of the rate of profit from production, as set out in Appendix A below.

12 Appendix C: Decomposing Rates of Profit When the Value of Labour Power Is Not Equal to Its Price

The definitions of turnover time, variable capital, the OCC and the VCC are unaffected by relaxing the assumption that the value of labour power is equal to its price, since they are all defined in terms of wages. This means we can start with the following expression derived in the previous chapter, after substituting $(s - u)$ for s:

$$\frac{s_{t,t+1} - u_{t,t+1}}{C_{t,t+1}} = \frac{\frac{(s_{t,t+1} - u_{t,t+1})}{w_{t,t+1}} \times nv_{t,t+1} \times \frac{y_{t,t+1}}{ys_{t,t+1}}}{VCC_t + 1} = \frac{\frac{s_{t,t+1}}{w_{t,t+1}} \times nv_{t,t+1} \times \frac{y_{t,t+1}}{ys_{t,t+1}} \times \frac{(s_{t,t+1} - u_{t,t+1})}{s_{t,t+1}}}{\frac{VCC_t + 1}{OCC_t + 1} \times (OCC_t + 1)}.$$

Similarly, we can take the results that

$$\frac{VCC_t + 1}{OCC_t + 1} = \frac{C_t}{C_i \times \frac{QC_t}{QC_i}} \times \frac{L_{t,t+1}/nv_{t,t+1}}{L_{i,i+1}/nv_{i,i+1}} \times \frac{v_i}{v_t}$$

and

$$\frac{L_{t,t+1}}{L_{i,i+1}} \times \frac{vr_{i,i+1}}{vr_{t,t+1}} = \frac{w_{i,i+1}/L_{i,i+1}}{\frac{y_{i,i+1}}{ys_{i,i+1}}} \Big/ \frac{w_{t,t+1}/L_{t,t+1}}{\frac{y_{t,t+1}}{ys_{t,t+1}}}.$$

We can re-arrange this last expression as follows:

$$\frac{L_{t,t+1}}{L_{i,i+1}} \times \frac{vr_{i,i+1}}{vr_{t,t+1}} = \left(\frac{w_{i,i+1}}{r_{i,i+1}} \Big/ \frac{w_{t,t+1}}{r_{t,t+1}}\right) \times \left(\frac{r_{i,i+1}/L_{i,i+1}}{\frac{y_{i,i+1}}{ys_{i,i+1}}} \Big/ \frac{r_{t,t+1}/L_{t,t+1}}{\frac{y_{t,t+1}}{ys_{t,t+1}}}\right).$$

Next, since

$$ROSV_{t,t+1} = \frac{s_{t,t+1}}{r_{t,t+1}} = \frac{L_{t,t+1} - r_{t,t+1}}{r_{t,t+1}} = \frac{L_{t,t+1}}{r_{t,t+1}} - 1,$$

$$\frac{r_{t,t+1}}{L_{t,t+1}} = \frac{1}{ROSV_{t,t+1} + 1}.$$

Therefore

$$\frac{L_{t,t+1}}{L_{i,i+1}} \times \frac{vr_{i,i+1}}{vr_{t,t+1}} = \left(\frac{w_{i,i+1}}{r_{i,i+1}} \Big/ \frac{w_{t,t+1}}{r_{t,t+1}}\right) \times \frac{\frac{y_{t,t+1}}{ys_{t,t+1}} \times (ROSV_{t,t+1}+1)}{\frac{y_{i,i+1}}{ys_{i,i+1}} \times (ROSV_{i,i+1}+1)}$$

and

$$\frac{VCC_t+1}{OCC_t+1} = \frac{\frac{w_{i,i+1}}{r_{i,i+1}}}{\frac{w_{t,t+1}}{r_{t,t+1}}} \times \frac{C_t}{C_i \times \frac{QC_t}{QC_i}} \times \frac{\frac{y_{t,t+1}}{ys_{t,t+1}}}{\frac{y_{i,i+1}}{ys_{i,i+1}}} \times \frac{ROSV_{t,t+1}+1}{ROSV_{i,i+1}+1}$$

(since $vr_{t,t+1} = v_t \times nv_{t,t+1}$).

Applying this to the rate of profit,

$$\frac{s_{t,t+1}-u_{t,t+1}}{C_{t,t+1}} = \frac{\frac{w_{i,i+1}}{r_{i,i+1}}}{\frac{w_{t,t+1}}{r_{t,t+1}}} \times \frac{\frac{s_{t,t+1}}{w_{t,t+1}}}{ROSV_{t,t+1}+1} \times nv_{t,t+1} \times \frac{C_i \times \frac{QC_t}{QC_i}}{C_t} \times \frac{y_{i,i+1}}{ys_{i,i+1}} \times$$

$$(ROSV_{i,i+1}+1) \times \frac{1}{OCC_t+1} \times \frac{(s_{t,t+1}-u_{t,t+1})}{s_{t,t+1}} = \frac{w_{i,i+1}}{r_{i,i+1}} \times \frac{\frac{s_{t,t+1}}{r_{t,t+1}}}{ROSV_{t,t+1}+1} \times$$

$$nv_{t,t+1} \times \frac{C_i \times \frac{QC_t}{QC_i}}{C_t} \times \frac{y_{i,i+1}}{ys_{i,i+1}} \times (ROSV_{i,i+1}+1) \times \frac{1}{OCC_t+1} \times \frac{(s_{t,t+1}-u_{t,t+1})}{s_{t,t+1}}$$

$$= \frac{w_{i,i+1}}{r_{i,i+1}} \times \frac{ROSV_{t,t+1}}{ROSV_{t,t+1}+1} \times nv_{t,t+1} \times \frac{C_i \times \frac{QC_t}{QC_i}}{C_t} \times \frac{y_{i,i+1}}{ys_{i,i+1}} \times (ROSV_{i,i+1}+1) \times$$

$$\frac{1}{OCC_t+1} \times \frac{(s_{t,t+1}-u_{t,t+1})}{s_{t,t+1}}.$$

The exponential growth rate of the rate of profit can therefore be expressed as:

$$\log\left(\frac{s_{f,f+1}-u_{f,f+1}}{C_{f,f+1}}\right) - \log\left(\frac{s_{t,t+1}-u_{t,t+1}}{C_{t,t+1}}\right) = \log\left(\frac{ROSV_{f,f+1}}{ROSV_{f,f+1}+1}\Big/\right.$$

$$\frac{ROSV_{t,t+1}}{ROSV_{t,t+1}+1}\right) + \log\left(\frac{nv_{f,f+1}}{nv_{f,f+1}}\right) + \log\left(\frac{C_i \times \frac{QC_u}{QC_i}}{C_f}\Big/\frac{C_i \times \frac{QC_t}{QC_i}}{C_t}\right) + \log\left(\frac{w_{i,i+1}}{r_{i,i+1}} \times\right.$$

$$\frac{r_{i,i+1}}{w_{i,i+1}} \times \frac{y_{i,i+1}}{ys_{i,i+1}} \times \frac{ys_{i,i+1}}{y_{i,i+1}} \times \frac{ROSV_{i,i+1}+1}{ROSV_{i,i+1}+1}\right) + \log\left(\frac{OCC_f+1}{OCC_t+1}\right) +$$

$$\log\left(\frac{ROSV_{f,f+1}}{ROSV_{f,f+1}+1}\Big/\frac{ROSV_{t,t+1}}{ROSV_{t,t+1}+1}\right)$$

$$= \log\left(\frac{s_{f,f+1}-u_{f,f+1}}{s_{f,f+1}}\Big/\frac{s_{t,t+1}-u_{t,t+1}}{s_{t,t+1}}\right) + \log\left(\frac{nv_{f,f+1}}{nv_{t,t+1}}\right) - \log\left(\frac{\frac{C_f}{QC_f}}{\frac{C_t}{QC_t}}\right) +$$

$$\log\left(\frac{OCC_t+1}{OCC_f+1}\right) + \log\left(\frac{ROSV_{f,f+1}}{ROSV_{f,f+1}+1}\Big/\frac{ROSV_{t,t+1}}{ROSV_{t,t+1}+1}\right).$$

In other words, the decomposition is the same as before (and, following the steps in the previous chapter, can be extended to distinguish devaluation of existing capital from the cheapening of new capital), except that by removing the stipulation that the price of labour power is equal to its value we have made it more general.

We can use the same kind of approach to decompose changes in rates of profit on production. Below we will do this for the pre-tax, corporate measure of the rate of profit on production.

First we need an estimate of the surplus value produced in the corporate sector alone. This is just for the purposes of the decomposition, so we do not need to be too precise. The results make estimates of employment and compensation in the productive corporate sector, multiply employment by the MELT to estimate value produced, and subtract productive corporate employees' consumption to estimate surplus value. They then estimate surplus value appropriated (before tax) by first estimating total value appropriated as compensation of employees of non-financial corporations plus pre-tax corporate profits from production plus TSSI depreciation for non-financial corporations, then subtract depreciation back out along with consumption of productive corporate employees. This allows us to incorporate the ratios of corporate surplus value appropriated to corporate surplus value and corporate pre-tax profits from production to corporate surplus value appropriated pre-tax into the decomposition. We also need to calculate the OCC, devaluation, etc. as it applies to the non-financial corporate sector only. The decomposition itself uses essentially the same approach as for the s – u rate of profit above.

CHAPTER 5

Marx on Finance

We now have a method for measuring the rates of profit that are most important for determining productive investment and the rate of accumulation, and we can measure the most important influences on them that Marx identifies. Next, we want to explain how movements in these rates of profit are connected to rates of return on financial investments. This chapter will set out the foundations for doing this through a discussion of Marx's writing on finance in *Capital.*

1   Money Dealing and Interest-Bearing Capital

Most of Marx's work on finance is in Part 5 of Volume 3 as edited by Engels. Although it is not a complete *theory* of finance as such, it contains the foundations we need to specify the relationship between the average rate of profit and rates of return on financial assets. The preceding sections of Volume 3 explain how competition creates a tendency for rates of profit on productive capital to equalise (Part 2); why this rate of profit has a tendency to fall and its consequences (Part 3); and how commercial capital appropriates surplus value and tends to earn the average rate of profit, even though the workers it employs do not produce new value (Part 4). At the end of Part 4 Marx moves on to consider money-dealing capital. He explains that:

> A certain section of capital must always exist as a hoard, as potential money capital: a reserve of means of purchase and payment, of unoccupied capital in the money form, waiting to be utilized ... On top of the taking-in and paying-out of money, and book-keeping, the hoard itself has to be looked after, which is again a special operation.[1]

Money-dealing capital performs these operations. Marx argues that it develops originally to service merchants' need to convert their local currencies into gold, silver and other currencies.[2] Unlike commercial capital, money-dealing cap-

---

1   Marx 1981, p. 432.
2   Marx 1981, p. 435.

ital does not buy and sell non-monetary commodities. Thus its self-expansion takes the form of $M–M'$: money-dealing capital advances its initial capital M, and receives $M' = M + \Delta M$, without the mediation of C.

Initially the money-dealing capitalist simply functions as a cashier, charging a fee to safeguard hoards of money, balance accounts, and convert currency (or profits from a spread between buying and selling prices).[3] Later this is integrated with the functions of lending and borrowing for profit; i.e. interest-bearing capital. Marx characterises the transaction between the moneylender and the actually functioning capitalist this way:

> What the buyer of an ordinary commodity buys is its use-value, what he pays is its value. What the borrower of the money buys is likewise its use-value as capital; but what does he pay for this? Certainly not its price or value, as with other commodities. The value does not change its form between lender and borrower, as it does between buyer and seller, so that this value exists at one point in the form of money, and at another in the form of a commodity. The identity between the value given out and that received back is displayed here in a completely different way. The sum of value, the money, is given out without an equivalent and returned after a certain period of time.[4]

If the sum of money being lent is a direct representation of a quantity of the money commodity, e.g. gold, this characterisation makes sense. The lender gives out the ownership title to a quantity of gold, which has a value. Immediately she receives back a promise to pay, which has no value in itself; during the course of the loan she receives interest, which has (or directly represents ownership over) value; and at the end of the loan she receives back the principal, again in the form of either the gold itself or a direct title of ownership over it.

But lending can also be an exchange of equivalent for equivalent. Suppose, rather than lending ownership over gold, the lender lends inconvertible fiat currency (i.e. currency whose issuer will not redeem it for precious metal). In this case, the object being lent has zero value (since the labour time required to print the currency is negligible and unproductive), and whatever intrinsic use value the currency might have for the borrower (e.g. as wallpaper or heating fuel) does not interest her. What interests the borrower is its exchange value – i.e. the quantity of any other commodity for which it can be exchanged – and it is this which gives it its use value as capital. In exchange for this currency, the borrower gives the lender another object with zero value and similarly irrelevant intrinsic use values: her promise to repay the principal with interest. This promise to pay has a use value as interest-bearing capital. If this promise to pay can be sold on (e.g. if it is a tradeable bond), then it also has an exchange value equivalent to its price (which may differ from its face value). Therefore this transaction is in fact an exchange of equivalent for equivalent. The borrower writes a promise to pay (or the banker records it), which has a use value as interest-bearing capital, and possibly an exchange value on the bond market, but no value. She exchanges this with the lender for inconvertible currency, which has an exchange value, a use-value as potential capital (amongst others), but again, no value.

It is important to note that such promises to pay are assets for their owners, and liabilities for their issuers. Often the two will balance, but not always. For example, if a company issues a bond and its perceived credit worthiness worsens, this does not reduce the liability that the bond represents for the company, but it is likely to reduce the price that bond holders can obtain for selling the bond before maturity.

2   Currency

Marx attaches particular importance to the connection between currency and precious metals. He even argues that the existence of inconvertible fiat money (i.e. money not convertible by its issuer to precious metals) is impossible:

> Paper money is a symbol of gold, a symbol of money. Its relation to the value of commodities consists only in this: they find imaginary expression in certain quantities of gold, and the same quantities are symbolically and physically represented by the paper. Only in so far as paper money represents gold, which like all other commodities has value, is it a symbol of value.[5]

In a footnote to this passage he ridicules Fullarton's view that 'all the monetary functions which are usually performed by gold and silver coins, may be performed as effectually by a circulation of inconvertible notes' that may 'supersede even the necessity for a standard'.[6]

---

5   Marx 1976, p. 225.
6   Ibid.

But on this issue history has proved Fullarton right. It is not necessary for notes and coins to be redeemable for precious metals for them to function as money. They only need to be widely exchangeable for commodities. Currencies which were previously promises to pay their bearer their equivalent in gold have now ceased to be promises to pay anything at all.

A similar process may currently be underway with bank deposits. A bank deposit is a promise to pay the depositor currency on request. It can be redeemed by visiting a bank or an automatic teller machine. But increasingly there is no need to do this to perform a transaction. For example, when a customer pays for their shopping using an electronic funds transfer, or even a cheque, they agree to give the shop ownership over a portion of their bank account, mediated by a transaction between their bank and the shop's bank. There is no need for physical currency to be involved. Similarly, and in part for this reason, 'base money' increasingly consists of electronic deposits held by banks in a central bank, rather than physical notes and coins. It is conceivable that electronic deposits could eventually eliminate the need for physical currency altogether, without necessarily causing any major change to the financial system or to social relations generally.

The parallel between this hypothetical scenario and the various suspensions and abandonments of the gold standard is not exact, since these *were* bound up with significant changes in the financial system. But the similarity is that financial instruments which were originally issued as promises to pay the holder some more 'basic' form of money can themselves take on that more basic function.

3   Social Relations and Interest

Marx sees interest-bearing capital as one of the most irrational, mystifying and fetish-inducing expressions of capitalist social relations. Observation of only the legal relations and forms of appearance of interest-bearing capital not only obliterates from view the source of profit in the exploitation of the working class, it obliterates from view the process of production altogether:

> In the real movement of capital, the return is a moment in the circulation process. Money is first transformed into means of production; the production process transforms it into a commodity; by the sale of the commodity it is transformed back into money, and in this form it returns to the hands of the capitalist who first advanced the capital in its money form. But in the case of interest-bearing capital the return, like the giving out, is

simply the result of a legal transaction between the owner of the capital and a second person. All that we see is the giving-out and the repayment. Everything that happens in between is obliterated.[7]

For the owner of a bank account, it is not even necessary to bear in mind that they receive interest as part of a social relation they enter into with the bank, let alone to discover that this interest is ultimately the product of surplus value produced by workers. All they need to know is that by leaving their money in an interest-bearing bank account it expands over time; they do not need to enquire into the social relations that make this expansion possible, and in turn make it possible for them to use this money to purchase commodities. They can tacitly treat money as though this thing itself possesses powers of self-expansion: i.e. they can treat money as though it possesses powers that it does not really have, fetishising it.

In reality, of course, money does not itself produce profit. If I leave two \$50 notes in my wallet they will not breed and create another (and even if they *did*, this would not produce surplus value). Instead 'interest ... is nothing but a particular name, a special title, for a part of the profit which the actually functioning capitalist has to pay to the capital's proprietor, instead of pocketing it himself.'[8] Marx calls the profit left after interest has been paid 'profit of enterprise'.

4   Dynamics of the Interest Rate (I)

For Marx, there is no predictable tendency for the proportion in which interest and profit of enterprise are divided to move towards a particular level, even assuming a given borrowed capital and a given rate of profit. For ordinary commodities:

> If supply and demand coincide, the market price of the commodity corresponds to its price of production, i.e. its price is then governed by the inner laws of capitalist production, independent of competition, since fluctuations in supply and demand explain nothing but divergences between market prices and prices of production.[9]

---

7   Marx 1981, pp. 470–1.
8   Marx 1981, p. 460.
9   Marx 1981, p. 477.

But for the rate of interest 'competition does not determine divergences from the law, for there is no law of distribution other than that dictated by competition ..., there is no "natural" rate of interest'.[10] Indeed, '[t]he minimum limit of interest is completely indeterminate. It could fall to any level, however low. But countervailing circumstances constantly enter to raise it above this relative minimum.'[11] However, the maximum limit of interest that can be paid is profit after subtracting managers' wages (though Marx says that in special cases even this limit might be exceeded). If we assume a more or less constant ratio between profit of enterprise and interest,

> the functioning capitalist will be able and willing to pay a higher or lower interest in direct proportion to the level of his profit rate. Since we have seen that the level of the profit rate stands in inverse proportion to the development of capitalist production, it follows that the higher or lower rate of interest in a country stands in the same inverse proportion to the level of industrial development, particularly in so far as the variation in the rate of interest expresses an actual variation in the profit rate. We shall see later on this need by no means always be the case. In this sense one can say that interest is governed by profit, and more precisely by the general rate of profit. And this kind of regulation applies even to its average.
>
> At all events, the average rate of profit should be considered as ultimately determining the maximum limit of the interest.[12]

This passage suggests that Marx saw this as a long-term tendency, driven by the tendency of the rate of profit to fall. He also thinks there is an independent tendency for the interest rate to fall, as (1) the relative number of *rentiers* increases, and (2) the development of the credit system reduces the length of time that savings lie idle.[13]

---

10   Marx 1981, p. 478.

11   Marx 1981, p. 480.

12   Marx 1981, pp. 481–2.

13   Marx 1981, p. 483. I have doubts about the connection between (1) and movements in interest rates, since the issue is more complex than Marx presents it. Assuming no change in the mass of interest, as Marx is by assuming a constant rate of profit and constant ratio of profit of enterprise to interest, an increase in the number of *rentiers* will only result in a fall in the interest rate if it results in a higher propensity to save income in interest-bearing securities. But assuming the propensity to save increases as income increases, if a given interest income is spread between more people, then they will tend to save less of it, and hence purchase a smaller value of interest-bearing securities.

Over the course of the business cycle, Marx argues there is instead likely to be an inverse relationship between the rate of profit and the rate of interest:

> If we consider the turnover cycles in which modern industry moves – inactivity, growing animation, prosperity, overproduction, crash, stagnation, inactivity, etc., cycles which it falls outside the scope of our argument to analyse further – we find that a low level of interest generally corresponds to periods of prosperity or especially high profit, a rise in interest comes between prosperity and its collapse, while maximum interest up to extreme usury corresponds to a period of crisis ... Yet low interest can also be accompanied by stagnation, and a moderate rise in interest by growing animation.[14]

These hypothesised long- and short-term relationships are also discussed below.

When Marx discusses rates of interest, he may also be referring to dividend yields on shareholdings. He writes that the formation of 'joint-stock companies' involves:

1. Tremendous expansion in the scale of production, and enterprises which would be impossible for individual capitals. At the same time, enterprises that were previously government ones become social.

2. Capital, which is inherently based on a social mode of production and presupposes a social concentration of means of production and labour-power, now receives the form of social capital (capital of directly associated individuals) in contrast to private capital, and its enterprises appear as social enterprises as opposed to private ones. This is the abolition of capital as private property within the confines of the capitalist mode of production itself.

3. Transformation of the actual functioning capitalist into a mere manager, in charge of other people's capital, and of the capital owner into a mere owner, a mere money capitalist. Even if the dividends that they draw include both interest and profit of enterprise, i.e. the total profit ... this total profit is still drawn only in the form of interest, i.e. as a mere reward for capital ownership, which is now as completely separated from its function in the actual production process.[15]

---

14   Marx 1981, pp. 482–3.
15   Marx 1981, pp. 567–8.

As an aside, it is worth highlighting that this passage shows Marx does not see capitalism as synonymous with private ownership of the means of production. Indeed, now that share-issuing corporations dominate the economy, 'the abolition of capital as private property within the confines of the capitalist mode of production itself' has largely been achieved. Marx sees this as

> a necessary point of transition towards the transformation of capital back into the property of the producers, though no longer as the private property of individual producers, but rather as their property as associated producers, as directly social property. It is furthermore a point of transition towards the transformation of all functions formerly bound up with capital ownership in the reproduction process into simple functions of the associated producers, into social functions.[16]

However,

> the transformation into the form of shares still remains trapped within the capitalist barriers; instead of overcoming the opposition between the character of wealth as something social, and private wealth, this transformation only develops this opposition in a new form.[17]

The more important point for our present purposes is that profit is now overwhelmingly drawn in this 'form of interest'. This may have important implications for the tendency of rates of profit to equalise and fall, as Marx argues:

> Since profit here simply assumes the form of interest, enterprises that merely yield an interest are possible, and this is one of the reasons that hold up the fall in the general rate of profit, since these enterprises, where the constant capital stands in such a tremendous ratio to the variable, do not necessarily go into the equalization of the general rate of profit.[18]

When Marxists measure the average rate of profit, we rightly include share-issuing corporations. Marx does not elaborate on the observation above, but he seems to be suggesting that corporations with a high organic composition of capital might be able to attract investment, even in their equity, at something like the general rate of interest, or in any event at a rate of return lower than

---

16   Marx 1981, p. 568.
17   Marx 1981, p. 571.
18   Marx 1981, p. 568.

the general rate of profit. Perhaps he draws this conclusion by making the unjustified assumption that it is possible, in general, to attract equity capital by offering rates of return similar to debt capital (which would seem to fit with his idea that dividends are a form of interest).

However, it is possible that he had something more interesting and useful in mind, or perhaps was working from a valid observation about rates of profit in practice. In many cases, high organic composition of capital businesses will have fewer competitors. Businesses with high 'sunk costs' tend to be monopolies or oligopolies, because these sunk costs function as barriers to entry (e.g. infrastructure businesses). This does not automatically makes these businesses more profitable, since the profit maximising price, even under monopoly conditions, is a function of only marginal costs, and not sunk costs. But it may make them more likely to deliver dependable profits over a long period, if the high sunk costs function as a barrier to competitors establishing new and potentially more efficient operations that might push down prices, and if the assets with the high sunk costs are also comparatively long lived (again, think of infrastructure). If this is true, it may create the (accurate) perception that investment in these businesses is less risky, and hence make investors prepared to accept a lower rate of return on their capital (both debt and equity). Thus these businesses could obtain the money capital to make investments with lower rates of profit than average.

Duménil and Lévy find that businesses which have a high ratio of fixed capital to wages (and are therefore likely to have high organic compositions of capital) do in fact tend to make lower rates of profit than those with lower organic compositions of capital.[19] This evidence and the reasoning above suggest there is more likely to be a tendency for 'risk adjusted' rates of profit to equalise, rather than rates of profit themselves, but this is an issue we cannot explore further here.

5   Money Capital and Fictitious Capital

So far, we (and Marx) have used the term 'money capital' somewhat loosely. But what is 'real' money capital, from the point of view of capital as a whole? This is an important issue because, in the next chapter, we will need to calculate the average rate of return on all financial capital, which means we need to distinguish this from 'genuine' capital.

---

19   Duménil and Lévy 2002, pp. 417–36.

While discussing 'interest-bearing securities, government bonds, stocks, etc.', Marx explains that:

> These securities ..., if they are in government bonds, are capital only for the person who has bought them, to whom they represent his purchase price, the capital he has invested in them. They are not capital in themselves, but simple creditor's claims; if they are in mortgages, they are simple claims on future payments of ground-rent; and if they are stocks of some other kind, they are simple property titles which gives the holder a claim to future surplus-value. None of these things are genuine capital, they do not constitute any component of capital and are also in themselves not values. By similar transactions, money that belongs to the bank can be transformed into deposits, so that the bank becomes a claimant for this money instead of its owner, and holds it under a different title. Important as this is for the bank itself, it in no way affects the amount of capital stored in the country, or even the money capital.[20]

Marx goes on to call these instruments 'fictitious capital':

> With the development of interest-bearing capital and the credit system, all capital seems to be duplicated, and some points triplicated, by the various ways in which the same capital, or even the same claim, appears in various hands and in different guises. The greater part of this 'money capital' is purely fictitious. With the exception of the reserve fund, deposits are never more than credits with the banker, and never exist as real deposits.[21]

But even concerning the reserve fund:

> Just as everything in the credit system appears in duplicate and triplicate, and is transformed into a mere phantom of the mind, so this also happens to the 'reserve fund', where one might finally expect to lay hold of something solid ...
>
> Ultimately ..., what these reserve funds actually boil down to is the reserve fund of the Bank of England. But this reserve fund, too, has a double existence. The reserve fund of the Banking Department is equal

---

20   Marx 1981, p. 590.
21   Marx 1981, p. 601.

to the excess of notes that the Bank is authorized to issue over the notes
that are actually in circulation. The legal maximum note issue is £14 million (the amount for which no metal reserve is required, this being the
approximate sum of the government's debt to the Bank), plus the Bank's
total reserve of precious metal. So if this reserve is also £14 million, the
Bank can issue £28 million in notes, and if £20 million of these are already
in circulation, the reserve fund of the Banking Department is £8 million.
This £8 million in notes is then the legal banking capital that the Bank
has at its disposal and at the same time the reserve fund for its deposits.[22]

So, for Marx, the reserve fund for deposits ultimately amounts to the central
bank's stock of precious metals plus its holdings of government bonds (i.e. the
government's debt to the central bank), which was the legal limit of notes it
could issue, less currency in circulation.

But in a passage quoted above, Marx also identified government debt as fictitious capital. So a significant component of what is, for the bank, its reserve
fund, is in fact also fictitious capital. It follows that the non-fictitious component of the central bank's reserve fund reduces to its holdings of precious metals;
i.e. to its holdings of commodity money, as opposed to its holdings of credit
money.

While Marx does not say this explicitly, it does seem to follow from this that
for capital in general, 'genuine' money capital can only consist of commodity money; i.e. *produced* capital, such as precious metals. It also seems logical
to count the value of commodity money as a component of genuine capital
for capital in general, since, unlike paper money and bank deposits, precious
metals require a non-negligible amount of productive labour time to produce.

Fictitious capital, on the other hand, is not produced by productive labour,
so should not be counted as genuine capital. This is no mere scholastic distinction. A capitalist making an investment decision does not have to consider how
much fictitious capital they must advance to invest in a project *in addition to* the
constant and variable capital they must advance. Rather, one way of obtaining
the credit money capital with which to pay for the constant and variable capital
is to borrow it or issue shares. That is, one way of obtaining productive capital is
to obtain it from an outside investor, in exchange for a corresponding fictitious
capital.

---

22   Marx 1981, pp. 603–4.

6   Fictitious Capital and the Dynamics of the Interest Rate (II)

It is worth discussing what fictitious capital represents in more detail. As Marx explains:

> The formation of fictitious capital is known as capitalization. Any regular periodic income can be capitalized by reckoning it up, on the basis of the average rate of interest, as a sum that a capital lent out at this interest rate would yield.[23]

This is now known as determining the net present value (NPV) of an expected future payment stream.

As this expected future payment stream and the interest rate vary, the prices of financial instruments can move up or down independently from the value of genuine capital advanced:

> The independent movement of these ownership titles' values, not only those of government bonds, but also of shares, strengthens the illusion that they constitute real capital besides the capital or claim to which they may give title. They become commodities, their prices having a specific movement and being specifically set. Their market values receive a determination differing from their nominal values, without any change in the value of the actual capital (even if its valorization does change) ...
>
> In so far as the rise of fall in value of these securities is independent of the movement in the value of the real capital that they represent, the wealth of a nation is just as great afterwards as before.[24]

This last sentence is particularly important. Movements in the prices of securities do not, in themselves, represent any increase in real wealth. Yet for their owners these capital gains *are* profits. Here Marx is describing how the expansion of fictitious capital can lead to *fictitious profit*.

These movements are linked to movements in the interest rate. For this reason, Marx argues that, perversely, a falling rate of profit can lead fictitious capital to *expand*:

> Their values, i.e. their listings on the stock exchange, have a necessary tendency to rise with the fall in the rate of interest, in so far as this is a

---

23   Marx 1981, p. 597.
24   Marx 1981, pp. 597–8.

simple result of the tendential fall in the rate of profit, independent of the specific movements of money capital, so that this imaginary wealth, which according to its value expression gives each person his aliquot share of a definite original nominal value, already expands for this reason as capitalist production develops.

Profits and losses that result from fluctuations in the price of these ownership titles, and also their centralization in the hands of railway magnates etc., are by the nature of the case more and more the result of gambling.[25]

Thus Marx's account of the connection between financial markets and underlying profitability goes deeper than simply asserting that capitalists tend to speculate more when the rate of profit on production is low (although this may also be true). Above, Marx does not invoke any such tendency, but instead argues that a falling interest rate tends to create an expansion of fictitious capital. This is a situation out of which those adept at gambling on financial markets are best positioned to profit.

Expressed in modern terminology, Marx's idea here seems to be that since the net present value of an income stream is an inverse function of the current interest rate, a lower interest rate will, *ceterus paribus*, mean a higher net present value. So, if shares are trading at their net present values, then a lower interest rate will mean higher share prices.

The problem with this logic is that the falling profit rate (that Marx assumes) will also tend to lead to declining profits over time on any given investment. Indeed, it follows from the equation for NPV that if the rate of interest declines by the same proportion as the mass of surplus value on a given investment declines (i.e. as the rate of profit declines) then the NPV will be unchanged.

Marx's proposed short-term relationship between the rate of interest and the business cycle might appear to suggest a more promising explanation of stock market bubbles. If, as Marx argues, the rate of interest is at its lowest point near the peak of the cycle, this would indeed coincide with a higher than usual ratio of stock market prices to productive capital advanced, if stock prices were determined by their NPV. Then, as business activity declined and interest rates rose, stock prices would fall.

However, from the point of view of supply and demand for investment, it is not clear if the interest rate *should* be at its short-term minimum at the peak of the business cycle as Marx predicts. During an economic upturn demand for credit is likely to be relatively high, as businesses borrow money to fund new

---

25   Marx 1981, pp. 608–9.

investments – hence the supply of bonds is likely to be high. This should tend to push *up* interest rates, contrary to Marx's observations.

Instead, however, if we regard bonds as just one financial instrument amongst others, then we can make sense of both the general pattern of movements in share prices and the short-term dynamics of the interest rate that Marx observes. At the beginning of an upswing in economic activity, share prices of existing companies tend to increase as their genuine capital is revalued upwards, or at least devalued downwards more slowly, and perhaps also because companies with existing assets are generally better placed to take advantage of an upswing than those which have not yet started producing. This means that expected dividend yields tend to be high at the beginning of the upswing, and to decline as share prices rise.

The dynamic for the interest rate is likely to be similar. Sellers of bonds compete with sellers of shares for investors' money. This means that declining dividend yields will tend to put downward pressure on bond yields: i.e. they will tend to put downward pressure on interest rates.

Then, as the downswing commences, the process is likely to tend to be reversed. Genuine capital will be devalued more rapidly, and potentially fictitious capital along with it. Investors may start to sell down their share holdings and hold more of their wealth in 'cash' and term deposits, tending to push down share prices. If this happens to a large enough extent, dividend yields will tend to increase, pushing up the interest rate. Then, with the onset of crisis, the interest rate in most cases will spike dramatically, with the increased risk of bankruptcy.

However, these are just somewhat speculative hypotheses. To better understand the relationship between rates of profit and rates of return on financial instruments, we need a method for quantifying them.

7   Conclusions

Interest is one of the most mystifying and fetishised forms of appearance of surplus value, and cannot be understood without penetrating beneath the legal relations established between lender and borrower.

Lending is the exchange of a new promise to pay for either an existing one, or a commodity (though this is not how Marx characterises it).

Currency is either a promise to pay gold, or it only represents a claim over a portion of commodities offered for sale in that currency. Again, this differs slightly from Marx's approach because Marx did not think inconvertible fiat money was possible.

Shares, bonds, bank deposits and other financial assets are 'fictitious' capital. This does not mean that they are unimportant, or that their existence is
illusory. Rather, it means that an expansion of this capital does not, in itself,
expand either a nation's real wealth or its genuine capital. This does not apply
to commodity money – i.e. precious metals used as money – which require a
non-negligible amount of labour time to produce.

Any promise to make future payment (or payments) can be capitalised into
a fictitious capital if that promise can be sold. The method Marx discusses for
doing this is a version of what is now called 'net present value', and is a function
of expected future payments, the current interest rate and future interest rates.

There is no 'natural' rate of interest, it is determined purely by the supply
of and demand for loanable funds. However, Marx argues the rate of interest
tends to move within limits set by the rate of profit, since interest is a component of profit. This means there is a (weaker) tendency for the rate of interest to
fall, along with the rate of profit. However, over the short- to medium-term business cycle, Marx suggests an inverse relationship between the rate of profit and
the level of business activity. The relationship between the dynamics of the rate
of interest and the stock of fictitious capital may help to explain movements in
share markets.

CHAPTER 6

The Rate of Profit and Financial Rates of Return

As we have seen, fictitious capital can grow in a way that is not directly determined by profitability from producing and selling commodities. This chapter shows that when fictitious capital grows in this way it can create 'fictitious profits': an imbalance between the total profit that investors appropriate for themselves as individuals, and the surplus value available to 'pay for' these profits. This has implications for the relationship between the average rate of profit and the average rate of return on financial assets, which can help to explain 'bubbles' and 'crashes' on financial and property markets.

The chapter begins with some simplified representations of financial markets to show how fictitious profits emerge. It then discusses the general relationship between fictitious profits, non-fictitious profits and surplus value after unproductive expenditures, and which measure of the stock of capital is relevant for calculating the average rate of return on individuals' investments in financial assets, non-corporate businesses and rental property. It also introduces the 'non-fictitious' rate of return on individuals' capital, which measures what their average rate of return would be if total fictitious profit were zero. It shows how changes in this rate of return can be decomposed into the effect of changes in the rate of profit and changes in the ratio of what counts as capital for *individuals* to the stock of produced capital over which individuals' capital is ultimately a claim. Then it shows how a similar approach can be used to calculate the average rate of return and the non-fictitious rate of return on individuals' financial capital only (i.e. excluding investments in businesses or rental property they own which are not mediated through financial instruments). Finally it discusses the implications this has for movements in rates of return and interest rates over the long- and short-term, and how this accords with Marx's observations.

1   The Separation between Financial Profits and Profits from Production

So far we have dealt with one form of appearance of surplus value, profits from production, and seen how this differs from surplus value and surplus value after unproductive expenditures. Profits from production (and profits from secondary exploitation) are profits which *businesses* record on their balance sheets.

But businesses and their assets are ultimately owned by *people* (and mostly by members of the capitalist class) whether through direct ownership, through share certificates, or more indirectly through money lent by individuals to banks.

To explore some of the complexities involved in determining the relationship between rates of return on these forms of capital, and rates of return for businesses themselves, we will start with a simplified representation of a financial market. Suppose the global economy consists of two firms, A and B; suppose in each case their profit from production are equal to the surplus value their workers produce, after deducting unproductive expenditures, and suppose they distribute all these profits to their shareholders as dividends. Further suppose that, initially, the total market capitalisation of each company is equal to the value of their stock of genuine capital (fixed assets plus inventories). Market capitalisation is the total number of shares held by all investors in a company, multiplied by the current share price. Assume this is $100 trillion for A, and $200 trillion for B.

Now suppose that A's profit from production is $10tn, and B's is $20tn. It follows that the rate of profit for each company is 10% ($10tn / $100tn = $20tn / $200tn). Also assume each has issued 1tn shares; since we have given the market caps, this means A's share price is $100tn / 1tn = $100, and B's share price is $200tn / 1tn = $200. Since we assume all profits are distributed as dividends, the dividend per share will be $10tn / 1tn = $10 for A, and $20tn / 1tn = $20 for B. It follows that the dividend yield for A is $10 / $100 = 10% and for B is $20 / $200 = 10%.

In this example the connection between the rate of profit and the rate of return on financial instruments is very simple. Because there are no capital gains, because all surplus value is realised as profit which is paid out as dividends, and because market capitalisations are equal to capital advanced, we have the result that the rate of profit, the rate of return on financial instruments and the dividend yield are all equal.

In reality, market capitalisations are generally higher than the current market value of a company's net assets. This is because, in most cases, investors are prepared to pay a premium for ownership of an established company, because established companies tend to be less risky investments, because buying a financial instrument means it is not necessary to amass the whole capital required to start a new business, and because buying a financial asset is much simpler than the messy business of exploiting workers oneself. On the other hand, companies with market caps below the current value of their net tangible assets are at risk of being bought out and having their assets sold off, because, theoretically, this would make these investors a quick profit (though the risks involved mean that this does not always happen in practice).

Returning to the example, let us suppose there is a 5% increase in the share prices of A and B, creating a small divergence between the each company's market capitalisation and its genuine capital. This means A's market cap becomes $105tn, and B's becomes $210tn. A's dividend yield will be $10tn / $105tn = 9.5%, and B's dividend yield will be the same. Note that, in this way, dividend yields have fallen independently of movements in the rate of profit, purely driven by increased demand for these stocks.

The increase in the share prices also creates capital gains, which we need to incorporate into our measure of the rate of return on the shares. The capital gain on each A share is $105 – $100 = $5, and on each B share it is $210 – $200 = $10. So the total return (capital gain + dividends) on each A share is $10 + $10 = $20, and on each B share it is $20 + $20 = $40. The rate of return relative to the initial share price for A shares is $20 / $100 = 20%, and for B shares is $40 / $200 = 20%, giving us a rate of return figure for individuals who own shares in both companies that is considerably higher than the rates of profit for these companies themselves.

Note that, in this case, this extra financial profit is not a deduction from the wealth of the investors who bought in at this higher price. Their personal wealth is unchanged: they have just exchanged a sum of money for shares with an equivalent exchange value. It is not even necessary that large numbers of investors 'buy in' at this new price: the 'market value' of the shares is just determined by the price at which they last traded. The result is that all investors who owned shares before the change in the share price make a capital gain. This capital gain is part of their rate of return, because it constitutes an increase in their wealth. The increase in wealth is 'fictitious' in the sense that it does not constitute an increase in *genuine* wealth, across society as a whole; but for the beneficiaries of these capital gains this increase in wealth is quite real, and could be realised by selling their shares.

This is similar to the result from Chapter 2, where we saw that incorporating capital gains on productive assets makes it possible for companies' total profit to exceed or fall below their total surplus value after unproductive expenditures and their total profits from production. Here we have just applied the same reasoning to financial assets.

Capital gains can also have consequences for the mass of the dividends paid by companies. For example, company A might own shares in company B. If it realises the profits from its capital gains and distributes them to its shareholders as dividends, then even the total dividends paid out to shareholders would exceed $s - u$ and profits from production.

In both these examples, the difference between shareholders' profit and surplus value after unproductive expenditures is 'fictitious' profit. We will define this concept more precisely below. Note here that the fictitious *profits* discussed in these examples are all the result of the creation of more fictitious *capital*.

There is no absolute theoretical limit to the generation of fictitious profits. For example, there is no theoretical limit to how high share prices can be bid. If investors are prepared to pay ever higher prices for a stock then its share price will rise ever higher, creating continual fictitious profits for existing owners of the stock. In practice such bubbles do not last forever, because eventually investors are not prepared to make ever larger bets that others will buy the stock for a higher price than they have. Under the right conditions, however, investors have repeatedly demonstrated that they are willing to make financially irrational decisions.

The creation of fictitious profits does not *automatically* create a bubble. As we will see, it may simply depress the future rate of return on financial assets relative to the rate of profit. Indeed, as mentioned above, in the normal course of events, we would expect market capitalisations to be higher than the stock of capital owned by companies, and, after excluding fictitious profits, for the average rate of return on financial assets to be lower than the average rate of profit. If we can understand and quantify these relationships we are likely to be in a better position to explain the relationship between rate of profit and financial crises.

To do this, we first want appropriate measures of the average rate of return on individuals' capital and their average yield: that is, the ratio of individuals' profits to their capital both including and excluding capital gains. To do this, we need an appropriate measure of the total stock of individuals' capital.

A problem we immediately encounter is that, as Marx puts it, 'everything in the credit system appears in duplicate and triplicate'.[1] For example, banks lend on sums of money that they receive from depositors to borrowers. This multiplies the claims on what we could call 'gross financial income' and gross financial income itself. For example, suppose person X lends $100 to bank Y, and Y lends $100 to company Z. In this situation, total gross debt is $200, and $200 of fictitious capital has been created. Assuming there is no revaluation, X has a claim worth $100 on interest from Y, and Y has a $100 claim on interest from Z. But if Y has lent this $100 on at an interest rate greater than or equal to the interest rate it pays X, then Y can pay its interest bill out of the money it receives from Z. In effect, bank Y has made it possible for person X to lend to company Z without X having to seek out Z, assess its credit worthiness, and directly bear the risk that Z will default. In playing this role, Y has doubled

---

1   Marx 1981, p. 603.

gross debt, and doubled gross fictitious capital. So if we simply measured the stock of fictitious capital as the gross stock of financial assets across all entities, transactions like this would make our measure of fictitious capital larger, and potentially much larger than a situation in which X lent directly to Z.

However, the fact that bank Y acts as an intermediary does not mean that company Z needs to appropriate twice as much profit to keep the rate of return on X's fictitious capital constant. The bank only keeps the difference between the interest it charges Z and the interest it pays X (the 'spread' between the two interest rates, multiplied by the value of the loan); and, after the bank has paid its expenses, this income can be returned to its creditors and shareholders.[2]

For our purposes here, the only financial assets that are relevant are those held by individuals. Financial arrangements between companies ultimately only function to re-distribute ownership of assets and claims on future value between companies, but do not, in themselves, change the total claims held by individuals over the business sector as a whole (though they may do so indirectly, by affecting prices of shares held by individuals). For example, if a person owns shares in a company which in turn owns shares in another company, in effect that person's investment is divided between the two companies. To avoid double counting, we need to count just the financial assets owned by individuals, and not also the financial assets owned by companies in each other.

2   Fictitious and Non-fictitious Profits

Next we want to define non-fictitious profit more precisely. What does it mean for a profit to be either 'fictitious' or 'non-fictitious'? Marx himself does not explicitly make this distinction, but we need it if we are trying to explain financial profits using value theory. One candidate for 'non-fictitious' profit is total profit from production after-tax. But as the last chapter explored, this would create the implication that 'non-fictitious' profit can be created through government borrowing. It would also mean that 'non-fictitious' profit cannot be extracted through secondary exploitation.

Another possibility is that fictitious profit is equal to individuals' capital gains. As mentioned in the last chapter, Marx observes that capital gains in stock markets do not, in themselves, make any difference to the real wealth of a nation. This is because they cannot produce value: a capital gain in a share

---

2   It follows that measuring the average rate of return as the ratio of profits to a gross measure of financial assets, as Freeman does, creates an artificially low estimate of the rate of return. Freeman 2012.

certificate cannot make any difference to the use values of the commodities produced over a year, and neither, therefore, can it add to their value. But in some cases, capital gains in financial assets can (indirectly) embody genuine increases in wealth. For example, if a company invests in produced capital out of profits it retains, this will tend to increase the market value of the shares it has issued, and appear as capital gains for the individuals who own them. So just as it is possible for dividends to represent fictitious profit (as we saw above), it is also possible for capital gains to be the result of genuine increases in wealth.

A better starting point is to ask: what is the value of the commodities these profits 'could be' used to buy, without increasing debt? This includes commodities bought directly by individuals themselves (e.g. for their own consumption) and commodities bought for investment by the businesses they own. More precisely, what is the actual total value of domestic net investment and consumption out of non-wage income, less net borrowing from the rest of the world? This is what we will call 'non-fictitious' profit. This is what total domestic profit for individuals ultimately 'counts for'; i.e. the value of the commodities it can be used to obtain.

Our framework is well-suited to measuring this. Chapter 4 gave a method for calculating $s - u$, which is equivalent to the sum of consumption out of non-wage income, net domestic investment and net exports of produced commodities. We just defined non-fictitious profit as consumption out of non-wage income, plus net domestic investment, less net borrowing from the rest of the world (otherwise known as the capital account surplus). So, if we use the letter Ψ for non-fictitious profit, this definition is equivalent to:

$$\Psi \equiv s - u - net\ exports\ of\ produced\ commodities - capital\ account\ surplus$$

Throughout this chapter we will use Greek letters to denote magnitudes related to individuals' profit, as opposed to profits direct appropriated by businesses.[3]

As it is defined here it is possible to measure Ψ using the national accounts, but it is useful to unpack this expression further. By definition, the capital account surplus is equal to the current account deficit: that is, the difference between national income and national expenditure must, by definition, be covered by net national borrowing. The current account deficit is equal to net

---

3   In Chapter 4, however, we did make an exception to this rule in order to use the letter 'π' to stand for profits from production. This is because using 'π' for 'profit' will be familiar to most readers.

imports (as defined by the national accounts, including net imports of both commodities and financial services, insurance, patents and licenses) less 'net foreign sourced income' (*NFSI*): i.e. net payments of interest, dividends and other income by the rest of the world to domestic recipients (including businesses, governments and individuals). Non-fictitious profit can therefore be expressed as:

Ψ = *s* − *u* − *net exports of produced commodities* − (*net imports of produced commodities* + *net 'imports' of financial services, insurance, patents and licenses* − *NFSI* = *s* − *u* + *NFSI* + *net 'exports' of financial services, insurance, patents and licenses* = *s* − *u* + *NTPF*

where *NTPF* ≡ net transfer payments from foreign entities.

That is, non-fictitious profit is the surplus value remaining after unproductive expenditures plus net profits appropriated from transfers from the rest of the world (which, in the national accounts, takes the form of *NFSI* plus net 'exports' of financial services, insurance, patents and licenses); or, more strictly, surplus value remaining after unproductive expenditures plus the difference between the total price and total value of output (which, recall from Chapter 4, is incorporated in our measure of *s* − *u*) plus net profits from transfers from the rest of the world.

Tacitly, this assumes all new domestic investment is made by businesses wholly owned by US residents, and that US residents do own businesses which make investments in the rest of the world. We will relax this assumption a little further on. First, however, let us consider how we can use this definition of non-fictitious profit. There are two goals we want to achieve: to compare non-fictitious profit with the relevant measure of total profit for individuals, in order to identify 'fictitious' profit; and to calculate the 'non-fictitious rate of return' on all capital owned by individuals – that is, what the rate of return for individuals would be if there were no fictitious profit.

We will define total nominal before-tax profit for individuals as the net increase in US residents' wealth brought about by dividends, interest, or any income from businesses they own (excluding the 'wages' we impute to proprietors), and capital gains on all capital owned by US residents, including their financial assets, their equity in non-corporate businesses and the market value of their rental property, net of all personal liabilities (including personal debt and mortgages). The best source of data for this purpose, which can be easily integrated with the framework we have developed so far, is the US Integrated Macroeconomic Accounts (IMAs). These integrate data from the US Flow of Funds Accounts and the US National Income and Product Accounts, to produce, among other things, 'balance sheets' for the US household, business and government sectors. This allows us to calculate net individual profit as net interest, dividends and 'withdrawals from non-corporate business' for households (less proprietors' imputed 'wages'), plus revaluation (i.e. capital gains) for financial assets and equity in non-corporate businesses net of any revaluation of liabilities. In the IMAs, 'non-corporate businesses' includes rental property owned by households (and equity in non-corporate businesses incorporates the land value of rental properties). The full definition for individuals' nominal profit after-tax, Λ, is given in the Appendix. We will work with after-tax figures because this is what matters to individuals, and because it is consistent with our measure of $s - u$ and hence non-fictitious profit.

The total capital owned by individuals is their financial assets plus non-corporate equity net of liabilities, which we will call Φ. 'Financial assets' here incorporate everything from share certificates to pension funds to ordinary bank deposits (which, since they pay interest, are a form of capital), and is defined precisely in the Appendix. As mentioned, equity in non-corporate businesses includes not only households' equity in assets owned by actual unincorporated businesses, but also in rental property. The ratio of individuals' profit to their capital is their average rate of return, Λ / Φ.

Over any given period, there is likely to be a wide distribution of rates of return on different types of asset. Investigating this distribution is not the purpose of this book, but here we will simply note that less 'risky' assets will often provide profit predominantly or exclusively in the form of an income stream (e.g. bank deposits, 'safer' stocks and property investments) while more 'risky' assets will often be more reliant on giving their owners capital gains. Although they are rarely owned directly by households, Treasury bonds are among the least risky assets, so we would expect them (and hence the interest rate on government debt) to give a below average rate of return that is also less variable than other instruments.

Another major type of asset owned by individuals is owner-occupied dwellings and land. Although these can be a source of capital gains, because they are owned for their direct usefulness and do not generate income, they are not capital, and therefore are not included in measuring Φ.

We also want to calculate the 'non-fictitious' rate of return on individuals' capital: that is, what the average rate of return on individuals' capital would be if individuals' profit were equal to non-fictitious profit. Before we can do this, we have to address the problem mentioned earlier, that our current measure of non-fictitious profit does not take into account investments in produced capital in other countries by companies owned (wholly or in part) by US residents; or investments in produced capital in the US by companies owned wholly or in part by non-US residents. We could only solve this problem properly with data identifying which companies US residents own (including indirectly) and their net investments in produced capital. Even then, identifying the proportion of capital gains on these financial assets which was ultimately a claim over an investment in produced capital would potentially be impossibly labourious.

Instead, we will correct the estimate of non-fictitious profit using the following approximation. First, we can calculate the net financial assets and non-corporate equity issued by US governments and the operations of businesses in the US. This is liabilities for these sectors less their financial assets, which is the net stock of financial assets that are claims on produced capital located in the US. For each year, we can then calculate the ratio between the increase in this stock of capital and net investment in US produced assets. This is a measure of the extent to which the increase in this financial capital and non-corporate equity is 'backed by' an increase in produced capital.

Next, we calculate the difference between Φ and the financial capital and non-corporate equity issued by US governments and businesses. We will call this 'US residents' net foreign capital', for which we can also calculate capital gains (by taking overall capital gains for US residents and subtracting the increase due to revaluation in financial assets and non-corporate equity issued by US governments and businesses). We will assume the ratio of these capital gains to the growth in the produced capital located outside the US over which they are a claim is the same as the ratio of capital gains to net investment in produced capital for produced assets in the US. We can then add the result this gives for the increase in net produced capital located outside the US but owned by US residents to US individuals' non-fictitious profits, which we will classify as a part of *NTPF*.

This approach is not ideal for several reasons, but in practice it only makes between zero and two percentage points difference to our estimate of non-fictitious profits (and a much smaller percentage point difference to the non-fictitious rates of return). The full method for making the estimate is given in Appendix B in Chapter 4, as well as the full definitions of non-fictitious profit and *NTPF*.

Having made this correction, we can define the non-fictitious rate of return on US individuals' capital as Ψ / Φ.

Next, we need to define and calculate fictitious profit. It sounds as though this might just be the difference between individuals' profit and their non-fictitious profit. But this does not take into account the effect of saving. Income saved by individuals accumulates as financial capital (except for their holdings of hard currency, e.g. money kept under the mattress), which adds to their total claims over produced capital. If individuals' total profit were equal to non-fictitious profit, but saving were greater than zero across all individuals, then the stock of individuals' capital would grow by more than the stock of produced capital over which individuals' capital is a claim. Part of individuals' profit would therefore be fictitious, because it would represent an increase in claims over produced capital in excess of the increase in produced capital.

For this reason, fictitious profit is individuals' profit in excess of non-fictitious profit *after subtracting* the growth in individuals' capital that is due to new injections of capital (i.e. not due to capital gains). We will call this Γ:

$\Gamma \equiv \Lambda - (\Psi -$ new capital injections by individuals) $= \Lambda - \Psi +$ growth in $\Phi -$ capital gains in $\Phi =$ Individuals' net dividends, interest and withdrawals from non-corporate businesses after 'wages' + growth in $\Phi - \Psi$.

Or, equivalently:

$\Gamma + \Psi =$ Individuals' net dividends, interest and withdrawals from non-corporate businesses after imputed wages + growth in Φ.

That is, the sum of fictitious and non-fictitious profits is equal to the growth in individuals' capital plus their net profit-type income payments. Therefore, assuming no change in profit-type income payments or non-fictitious profits, an increase in capital gains will correspond to an increase in fictitious profit.

This highlights an important dynamic. Capital gains in share and property markets tend to be strongly related to business confidence. When business confidence is rising, investors are prepared to pay higher prices for property and financial assets, creating capital gains for those who already own these stocks or property. This is why conditions of *rising* business confidence tend to be the most profitable for investors (i.e. *before* the peak in the business cycle); and often this is especially true when sentiment changes rapidly in the early phase of a recovery. In effect, these capital gains mean investors register profits 'before' the value of the commodities which are to 'stand behind' them has been produced. These fictitious profits leave a legacy. The additional capital they create increases the denominator of the average rate of return, tending to make it smaller.

When confidence worsens, these fictitious profits start to be reversed by 'fictitious losses'. A sudden loss of confidence can rapidly wipe trillions off share and property markets through capital losses. This also lays the basis for the rate of return to recover, by reducing its denominator.

Here we are discussing the dynamic for the average rate of return on individuals' capital. Unlike rates of profit, there is no direct tendency for rates of return on different financial investments to equalise. This is because their strength and order of priority as a claim on future value varies. Currency notes and coins generally have a very strong immediate claim on the value of useful commodities (they are highly 'liquid') because the conditions under which people would stop accepting notes and coins as payment within a given currency zone are usually the least likely to occur in practice. In foregoing interest, holders of these assets pay a price for this liquidity, and run the risk of inflation destroying the value of their holdings. Indeed, they are not even *capital*, because they promise no rate of return. Bank deposits introduce new risks (there might be a run on the bank) but mitigate the inflation risk and promise higher returns by paying interest. Bonds have a different risk/return profile again, and this profile depends on the credit-worthiness of the bond issuer. Equities are usually riskier still, since if a business is wound up, equity only constitutes a claim on the assets of the business after its debts have been paid. For this reason equities usually offer higher rates of return. Finally, there is a range of more 'exotic' financial instruments (a very small proportion of which are held by individuals) which offer different risk/return profiles again. It is reasonable to suppose that there is a tendency for rates of return to equalise across financial assets with risks that are perceived as similar, but not that there is a tendency for rates of return to equalise across financial assets with different risk profiles. Moreover, riskiness is not static: investors are constantly re-evaluating the types of risk entailed by different assets in light of current economic conditions and adjusting their holdings accordingly. So, for example, if sentiment about the economy worsens moderately, 'defensive' stocks might appreciate in value, while the value of 'riskier' stocks might decline; but then if sentiment worsens more severely, nearly all stocks tend to lose value.

Thus it can look as though rates of return on financial assets are purely a product of the sentiments of investors, and whether they decide to pay prices for financial assets that produce fictitious profits; and, theoretically, a financial and property market boom followed by a bust could happen independently of movements in the rate of profit. But there is also a quite direct connection between the rate of profit, with $s - u$ on the numerator, and the non-fictitious rate of return on individuals' capital. We can measure the relationship through the following decomposition:

$$\frac{\Psi}{\Phi} = \frac{s - u + NTPF}{\Phi} = \left(\frac{s - u + NTPF}{s - u} \times \frac{\Phi D}{\Phi} \right) \times \frac{C}{\Phi D} \times \frac{s - u}{C}.$$

where ΦD is net liabilities of domestic businesses and governments, and C here refers to *all* produced capital owned by businesses (not just produced capital for non-financial businesses). The two ratios within the brackets are the combined effect of non-fictitious profit from the rest of the world and capital owned by US individuals less net domestically issued financial capital. The third ratio is the ratio of US produced capital to domestically issued financial capital. This is the effect of accumulated past fictitious profits on the domestically issued part of the average non-fictitious rate of return, which, as mentioned above, is likely to be strongly related to business confidence. This ratio is similar to 'Tobin's q'.[4] The final ratio is a measure of the rate of profit. If there is a long-term tendency for the rate of profit to fall, then this is likely to be the most important determinant of the non-fictitious rate of return over the long term. By replacing this term with the decomposition of the rate of profit expressed in terms of $(s - u)$ we could also calculate the direct effect on the non-fictitious rate of return of changes in the OCC, the ROSV, turnover time, etc. As before, we can calculate the effect of each of these ratios by taking the logarithm of the initial and final levels of the non-fictitious rate of return. The actual average rate of return on individuals' capital could be decomposed similarly, by including the ratio of individuals' actual profit to their non-fictitious profits in the decomposition above.

We can also measure and decompose changes in the non-fictitious rate of return for individuals' capital excluding equity in non-corporate businesses. This is useful because non-corporate businesses are more likely to continue to exist on a relatively low rate of profit, since in many cases their owners also depend on the existence of their business for their 'wage'. Unless they can get enough proceeds from selling their business to buy another one with a higher rate of profit (a potentially very risky decision) their only alternative is to find employment for a wage elsewhere. Note, however, that the 'non-corporate business' sector as defined in the national accounts also includes rental property owned by individuals, which can be bought or sold as an investment with fewer personal consequences.

Investors in an unprofitable corporation, on the other hand, can sell their shares and buy others instead without this affecting their employment. As mentioned, this creates a tendency for rates of return to equalise across financial assets with risk profiles which are perceived as similar. This means the average rate of return across these financial assets only is a more meaningful measure. For this reason, the non-fictitious rate of return on individuals' financial assets is more likely to have a similar trend to the interest rate than the non-fictitious rate of return on individuals' total capital.

---

4   Tobin and Brainard 1976.

To refer to magnitudes excluding the non-corporate business sector, we will use the same Greek letters as above but in lower case. We will refer to individuals' capital excluding non-corporate businesses (and rental property) as 'financial assets', and profits on these assets as 'financial profits'. Note that this is shorthand for individuals' gross financial assets less liabilities, and individuals' gross financial profits less interest paid out by individuals on their personal debt and mortgages on dwellings they keep for their own use.

First, individuals' non-fictitious *financial* profit, ψ, is individuals' total non-fictitious profit less expenditures by proprietors on investment and personal consumption financed by non-corporate business profits (including rents from housing), which we called ep in Chapter 4:

$$\psi \equiv s - u + NTPF - ep.$$

Next, total financial profit is individuals' total profit less withdrawals from non-corporate businesses, plus wages imputed to proprietors (since these 'wages' are not part of individuals' total profit, but *are* part of withdrawals from non-corporate businesses):

$$\lambda \equiv \Lambda - \text{withdrawals from non-corporate businesses after 'wages'}.$$

The stock of net financial assets owned by individuals is:

$$\varphi \equiv \Phi - \text{individuals' equity in non-corporate businesses}.$$

Similarly, fictitious financial profit is:

$$\gamma \equiv \text{individuals' net dividends and interest} + \text{growth in } \varphi - \psi.$$

This makes it possible to calculate the non-fictitious rate of return on financial assets, ψ / φ, and the average total rate of return on financial assets, λ / φ. Both of these can be decomposed using the same method as above, but replacing $s - u$ with $s - u - ep$, and excluding fixed assets and inventories for the non-corporate business sector.

3   The Non-fictitious Financial Rate of Return and the Interest Rate

Finally, here are some hypotheses concerning the relationship between the growth in financial assets and movements in interest rates. As mentioned above, capital gains on financial markets tend to be largest when economic confidence is rising. If investors' expectations concerning future profitability improve, and people are sufficiently confident about their financial situation to move their savings into riskier classes of financial asset, then fictitious capital is likely to expand at a faster rate than produced capital, tending to bring down the non-fictitious rate of return and yields on financial assets. Conversely, when economic confidence worsens, investors revise down their estimates of the NPV of financial assets, especially riskier ones, bidding down their prices and hence shrinking the total stock of financial assets, tending to increase the non-fictitious rate of return and yields. So at the peak of the cycle, with confidence at its highest point, we would expect the non-fictitious rate of return and yields to be at their lowest (which also makes it cheapest and easiest to obtain money for more speculative investments); and we would expect the reverse to be true at the bottom of a trough, once financial assets and property have suffered their maximum devaluation.

This is the same dynamic Marx observes for interest rates. Recall from last chapter that Marx observed interest rates to be at their highest during a crash, then to fall as activity starts to pick up, continue to fall until the peak of the cycle, then to rise between the peak of the cycle and the next crash. In general, we would expect interest rates to move in a similar direction to yields on other financial assets, since they are just the yields on the least risky financial assets. We would therefore expect interest rates to move in a similar direction to the non-fictitious rate of return on financial assets. So Marx's observations concerning movements in interest rates seem to fit well with the framework outlined here.

Finally, over the long term, if there is a declining non-fictitious rate of profit, then this is likely to be the most important influence on the non-fictitious rate of return on individuals' financial assets, yields, and interest rates. This is consistent with Marx's view that the interest rate tends to fall along with the rate of profit over the long term, despite his observation that interest rates tend to move in the opposite direction to the business cycle in the short-term.

All these movements could have significant influences on the real economy. Our hypothesis from Chapter 2 is that the main influence on the rate of accumulation, and hence on the rate of growth, is movements in the rate of profit over the long term. But over the short-term, movements in financial markets have their own effect on the rate of accumulation, and do not merely reflect movements in the underlying rate of profit. This happens most dramatically during a financial market crash, when the supply of credit is drastically curtailed. Not only does this mean investment declines drastically but many firms stop production, lay off their workers or go bankrupt because they cannot sell their output and cannot borrow.

On the other hand, fictitious profits can also hide the consequences of a falling rate of profit for a time. We have seen how government borrowing can 'artificially' inflate the after-tax rate of profit on production (and the same effect applies to after-tax rates of profit from secondary exploitation); and fictitious profits can 'artificially' inflate investors' wealth and rates of return.

The interest rate cycle is likely to have a particularly significant effect on the rate of accumulation. Lower interest rates encourage people and businesses to borrow to finance consumption and investment, tending to increase the rate of accumulation, the current account deficit and potentially also the value of output (insofar as this investment is spent on employing more living labour). If Marx's hypothesis is true, and interest rates tend to be at their short-term minimum at the peak of the cycle, then movements in the interest rate would aggravate the short-term business cycle itself (or perhaps even explain it).

4   Conclusion

Marxists have tended to pay more attention to Marx's theory of money than his unfinished work on finance. They have paid even less attention to the relationship between finance, the rate of profit and his theory of value. We have shown that by doing so, we can develop a theory that reproduces some of Marx's conclusions and can be applied to existing data. Unlike the previous chapters, this is more an *extension* of Marx's theory than an interpretation as such.

This completes the formalism set out in this work. The next chapter presents the results obtained by applying it.

5   Appendix: Accounting Definitions for Financial Rates of Return

5.1   *Individuals' Capital*
Including non-corporate equity: $\Phi \equiv$ Households' financial assets (IMAs S3 line 103) – Households' liabilities (IMAs S3 line 131).

Excluding non-corporate equity: $\varphi \equiv \Phi$ – Households' equity in non-corporate business (IMAs S3 line 122).

5.2   *Individuals' Total Profit*
Including non-corporate profits: $\Lambda \equiv$ Households' received property income (IMAs S3 line 14) – Households' interest paid (IMAs S3 line 19) + Revaluation of

households' financial assets (IMAs S3 line 89) – Imputed wages paid to proprietors (see Chapter 4, Appendix A).

Excluding non-corporate profits: $\lambda \equiv$ Households' received property income (IMAs S3 line 14) – Households' interest paid (IMAs S3 line 19) + Revaluation of households' financial assets (IMAs S3 line 89) – Households' withdrawals from non-corporate business (IMAs S3 line 18) – Revaluation of households' equity in non-corporate business (IMAs S3 line 92).

5.3   *Individuals' Non-fictitious Profit*

Individuals' total non-fictitious profit (including profits from non-corporate business) $\equiv \Psi \equiv s - u + NTPF$.

Individuals' financial non-fictitious profit $\equiv \psi \equiv s - u + NTPF - ep$ (see Chapter 4, Appendix A).

Here *NTPF* (net transfer payments from foreign entities) $\equiv$ Net exports of financial services, insurance, patents and licenses (see Chapter 4, Appendix A) + Net foreign-sourced income (NIPA 1.7.5 line 2 – line 1) + Net investment in foreign produced capital owned directly and indirectly by US residents;

> where: Net investment in foreign produced capital owned directly and indirectly by US residents $\equiv$ (Estimated net claims by US households on foreign produced assets / US produced capital) × [Gross investment in non-residential business fixed assets (FA 4.7 lines 2 + 3 – 66 – 67 – 70 – 71 – 74 – 75) – TSSI depreciation of business fixed assets + Net investment in inventories (NIPA 1.4.5 line 5) + Gross investment in tenant-occupied residential fixed assets (FA 5.7 line 12) – TSSI depreciation of tenant-occupied residential fixed assets] and:
>
> Estimated net claims by US households on foreign produced assets $\equiv$ [Φ – Net liabilities for US business and government (IMA S4 line 104 + IMA S5 line 129 – IMA S5 line 103 + IMA S6 line 131 – IMA S6 line 106 + IMA S7 line 129 – IMA S7 line 101 + IMA S8 line 101 – IMA S8 line 79)] × US produced capital / Φ;
>
> US produced capital $\equiv$ Non-residential business fixed assets (FA 4.1 lines 2 + 3 – 66 – 67 – 70 – 71 – 74 – 75) + Residential fixed assets occupied by tenants (FA 5.1 line 12) + Business inventories at end of year (see Chapter 4, Appendix A);
>
> TSSI depreciation of non-residential business fixed assets $\equiv$ Current cost depreciation of business fixed assets (FA 4.4 lines 2 + 3 – 66 – 67 – 70 – 71 – 74 – 75) × [Price index for non-residential private investment$_{t-2,t-1}$ (NIPA 1.1.4 line 9, previous year) / Price index for non-residential private investment$_{t-1,t}$ (NIPA 1.1.4 line 9)] × $n_{t-2,t-1}$ / $n_{t-1,t}$.

TSSI depreciation of tenant-occupied residential fixed assets ≡ Current cost depreciation of tenant-occupied residential fixed assets (FA 5.4 line 12) × [Price index for residential private investment$_{t-2,t-1}$ (NIPA 1.1.4 line 13, previous year) / Price index for residential private investment$_{t-1,t}$ (NIPA 1.1.4 line 13)] × $n_{t-2,t-1}$ / $n_{t-1,t}$.

CHAPTER 7

Results

The results below are presented and discussed in roughly the order in which the formalism was developed in previous chapters. The discussion focuses on whether the results support Marx's hypotheses and what they imply regarding the causes of the Great Recession.

1   Output and Surplus Value

1.1   *Output of Commodities*
The measure of output we are using is the total price of commodities produced each year for final consumption or investment. Figure 3 compares the real rate of growth of this measure with the rate of growth of real GDP; and Figure 4 graphs the ratio of the level of GDP to our measure of output.[1] They show that while the changes affect the *level* of output significantly, they make very little difference to the measure of the real rate of growth of output. They therefore give almost identical measures of economic 'performance' year-by-year; measuring the total price of the output of commodities is mainly important to allow for a more accurate measure of surplus value.[2]

---

1   Real output is calculated in a similar way to real GDP. Real GDP is nominal GDP (GDP at current prices) divided by the GDP deflator for the current year, multiplied by the GDP deflator for the 'base' year. We could obtain a good estimate of our measure of real output by applying exactly this same approach. The GDP deflator, however, is an index of the price level for all GDP, and our estimate of output excludes some parts of GDP. We have obtained a more accurate estimate of real output by breaking nominal output down into parts (e.g. personal consumption expenditure, investment) and deflating each part by the relevant price index. Chapter 4 already defined our estimate of output on this basis: we identified which components of PCE, exports, imports, gross private investment and government spending are commodities. The NIPA publish price indexes for each of these categories, so we use them to calculate real output. A minor problem is that we only estimate net 'exports' of financial services and insurance, not gross 'exports' and gross 'imports' of these non-commodities, and the price indexes apply only to exports and imports in gross terms. For the purposes of working backwards from 'exports' and 'imports' as defined in the NIPA to exports and imports of commodities, we have just assumed that gross 'exports' of financial services is equal to net 'exports' of financial services, and therefore also that gross 'imports' of financial services is zero. This should only make a very small difference to the estimates of real output, and would make no difference at all if we were using price indexes at a finer level of detail.

2   However, it is also interesting to note that as this small difference in growth rates accumu-

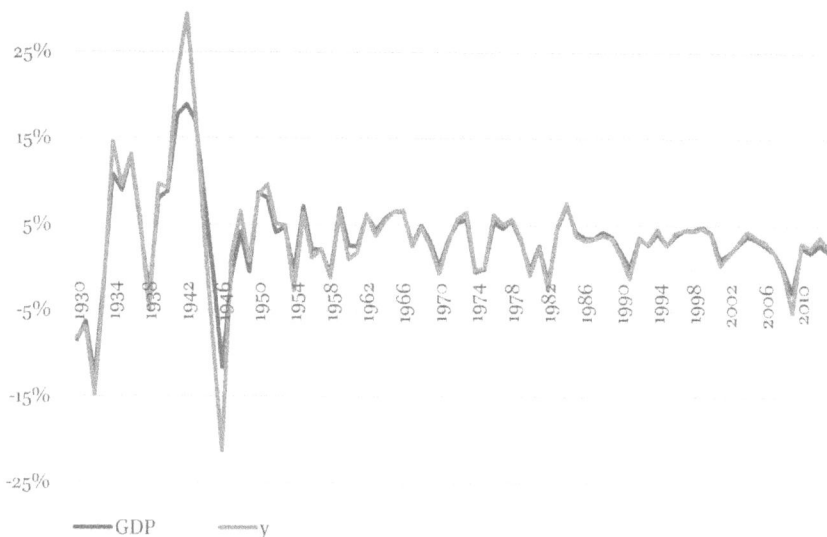

FIGURE 3   Real growth rates of two measures of output

1.2   *Consumption, Saving and Secondary Exploitation*

Our measure of surplus value also depends on estimating the proportion of wages that workers spend buying commodities for consumption. We are assuming that the average propensity to consume employees' compensation (p) is equal to the average propensity to spend any personal income on commodities for consumption including housing depreciation. Personal income can also be saved in various forms (e.g. in financial assets or investment in housing net of depreciation) or it can be extracted from productive workers through secondary exploitation.[3] Figure 5 graphs the proportions of personal income spent, saved or appropriated in these ways. It separates secondary exploitation into four categories: housing rent and mortgage interest above the value of housing depreciation; costs of financial services, insurance premiums net of claims and net losses from gambling; personal taxes and social insurance; and interest on personal loans plus other transfer payments to business and government.

---

lates over time it leads to an increasing ratio of GDP to the total output of commodities. (I am grateful to an anonymous referee for this point.) This means that if it is interpreted as a proxy for a Marxist measure of output, because it includes unproductive sectors GDP progressively overstates the total value of US output.

3   It can also be extracted from people other than productive workers through the same forms as secondary exploitation (taxes, interest and rent), but strictly speaking this is not a form of *exploitation* since only productive workers produce value.

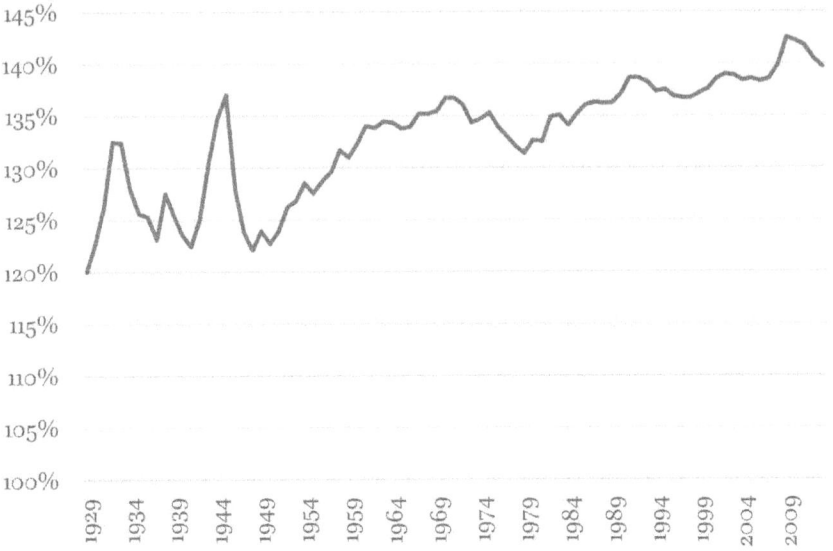

FIGURE 4   *GDP/y*

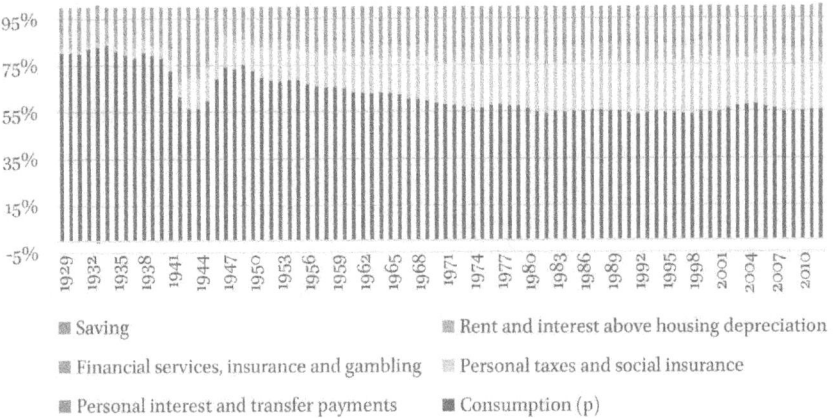

■ Saving   ■ Rent and interest above housing depreciation

■ Financial services, insurance and gambling   ▨ Personal taxes and social insurance

■ Personal interest and transfer payments   ■ Consumption (p)

FIGURE 5   Uses of personal income

From the end of WWII until around 1982, the tendency is for the propensity to consume to decline over time. This is due to increases in all forms of secondary exploitation as a proportion of income, and, to a much lesser extent, an increase in the savings rate. Then until 1998 *p* stays roughly constant, while, proportionately, value extracted through secondary exploitation continues to grow. The savings rate therefore declines significantly, and continues to decline until the Great Recession. This means that the fall in the savings rate begins well before the Federal Reserve's policy of keeping interest rates low to boost con-

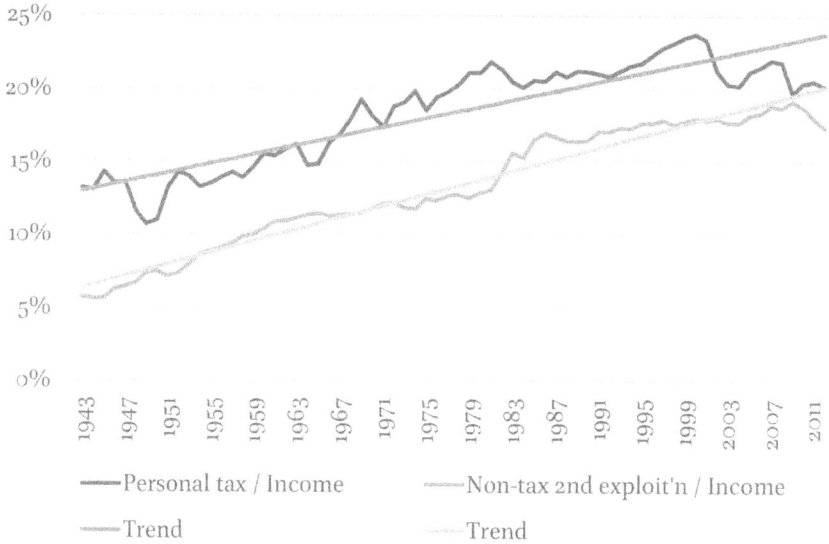

FIGURE 6   Forms of secondary exploitation

sumption during the 2000s; indeed, it starts when interest rates were at record *highs* in the early 1980s. The decline in the savings rate seems more likely to be related to the nature of the recovery from the crises of the 1970s; specifically, as we will see below, the fact that the recovery was not underpinned by a substantial increase in the underlying profit rate or the rate of accumulation of produced capital.

From 1999 until 2005 p increases significantly. We can see why more clearly in Figure 6 below. It shows that during the postwar period there was a clear trend for personal taxes to increase as a proportion of personal income *until* 2001; after which the downward trend is clear. This looks to be the result of the Bush tax cuts, which essentially financed reductions in marginal tax rates (especially at higher incomes) by increasing government borrowing. These tax cuts appear to have had the largest effect on the propensity to consume, and a much more significant effect than the decline in the savings rate. This also suggests that the true increase in the average propensity to consume for *workers* is not as large as the measure we are using, since the Bush tax cuts favoured higher income earners, and we are assuming the general average propensity to consume is equal to workers' average propensity to consume.

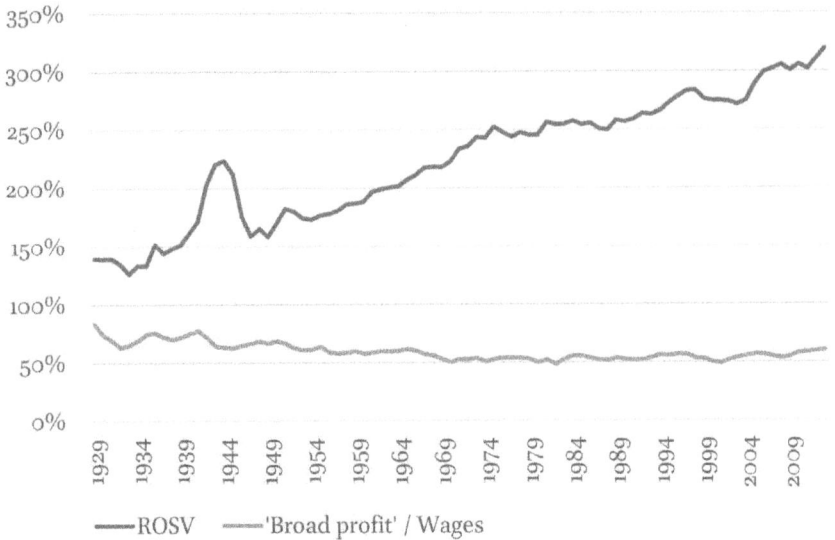

FIGURE 7   Estimates of the rate of surplus value

1.3   Rate of Surplus Value

We are measuring 'surplus value' as the total price of output net of productive depreciation less the value of the labour power expended by productive workers and productive members of the petty bourgeoisie, and the rate of surplus value (ROSV) as the ratio of surplus value to the value of productively expended labour power. This means the ROSV is quite different from the ratio of 'capital income' or 'broad profits' to total wages, which is often used as a proxy for the ROSV. Nor is the ROSV a proxy for income inequality, or the relative 'strengths' of capital and labour, because surplus value includes the consumption of workers who are unproductive, unemployed or retired. The ROSV as defined here is only intended to measure what Marx intended it to measure: the ratio of surplus labour to necessary labour for productive workers. Figure 7 below compares it to the 'rate of surplus value' as it is more usually estimated, the ratio of 'broad profits' to wages.[4] We can see these two measures have very different levels and trends.

In *Capital* Marx mostly assumes there is a process of the production of relative surplus value; i.e. a tendency for the rate of surplus value to rise as productivity improvements bring down the cost of reproducing labour power. We

---

4   Where 'broad profits' / wages is defined as (GDP – consumption of fixed capital – employees' compensation) / employees' compensation.

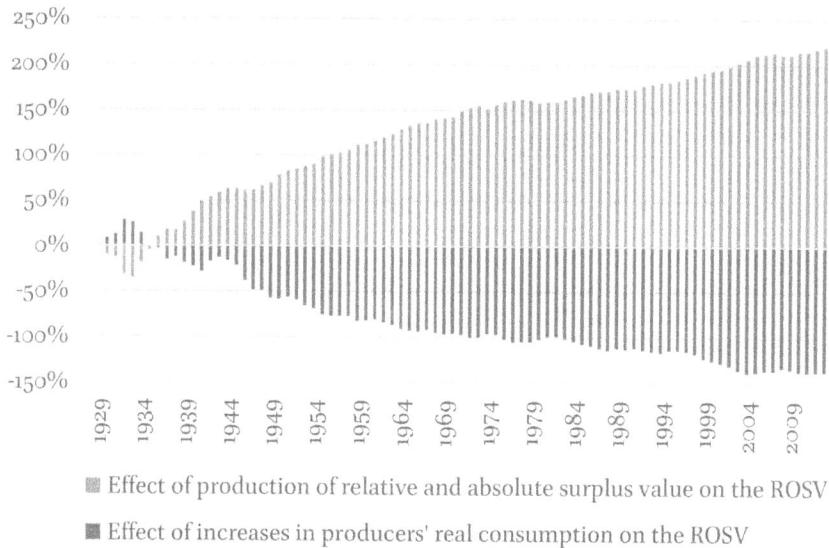

Effect of production of relative and absolute surplus value on the ROSV

Effect of increases in producers' real consumption on the ROSV

FIGURE 8   Influences on the rate of surplus value

can see from the graph above that unlike the ratio of 'broad profits' to wages, the measure of the ROSV used here is consistent with that assumption. On the other hand, if the ratio of 'broad profits' to wages were a good proxy for the ROSV, then the tendency until the end of the postwar boom would have been for the ratio of surplus to necessary labour to *fall* over time; the opposite of Marx's assumption.

Chapter 4 also gave a method for decomposing changes in the ROSV into the effect of increases in productive workers' real consumption and the effect of the production of relative and absolute surplus value.[5] Figure 8 graphs the cumulative effect of these two influences. They have the effects we would expect: over time, productivity improvements reduce the SNLT required to produce a given bundle of commodities, producing relative surplus value, but this is offset to some extent by increases in workers' real consumption.

Figure 9 graphs real yearly compensation for employees in productive sectors, adjusted for inflation in the Personal Consumption Expenditures (PCE)

---

5   Separating out the effects of the production of relative from absolute surplus value could be done using estimates of hours worked per full-time equivalent employee, making this the basis for defining the MELT, and then distinguishing the effect on the ROSV of changes in total hours worked per full-time equivalent employee and the cheapening of commodities consumed by workers.

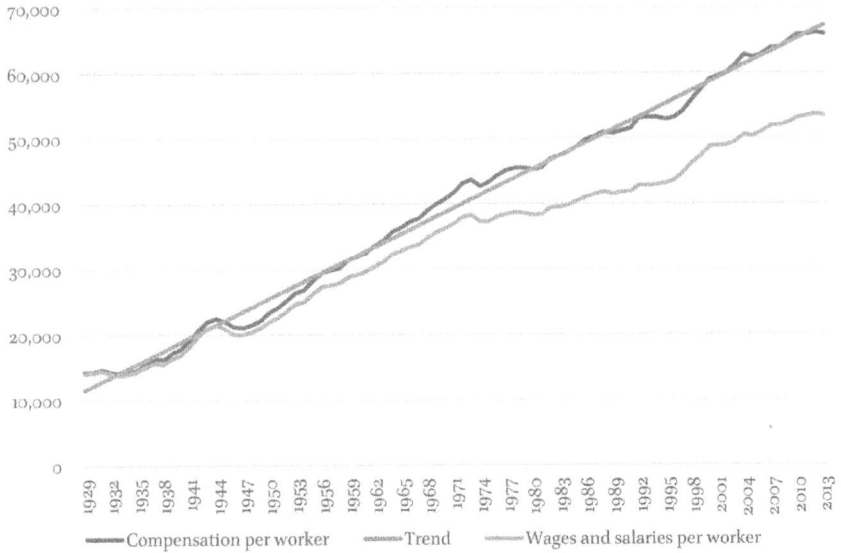

FIGURE 9   Average yearly real employee compensation and wages and salaries per full-time
equivalent productive worker

index. As for all our measure of 'wages', this is *total* employee compensation,
which is not just wages and salaries but also employer contributions to pension
funds and social security. This is the total wage that *employers* pay. The income
available for *employees* to spend or save is their compensation after secondary
exploitation.

Figure 9 also graphs real 'wages and salaries' per full-time equivalent employee
in productive sectors. This is not a measure of employees' pre-tax income, pre-
tax income after contributions to social insurance, after-tax income, income
available to spend or save, or the price paid for labour power by employers. It is
included in Figure 9 to illustrate the source of the easy to develop impression
that wages have fallen behind so far behind profits that the rate of profit cannot
have declined.

We can see that if we instead use a correct measure of the money paid to
employees by employers adjusted for 'ordinary' inflation, real total compensation per full-time equivalent employee, there is extraordinarily little variation
around its linear trend; the R squared between the two is 0.992. Bear in mind:
this says nothing about how the growth in wages was distributed between different groups within the category of 'employees'; this is not a measure of compensation per hour worked; and 'employees' is a much broader category than

that of the working class proper. This growth in employee compensation has almost certainly disproportionately benefitted supervisors and managers, and a growing proportion of compensation has been spent on healthcare and education (which must especially be borne in mind when making comparisons with countries where these services are lower cost or free). Investigating this question fully would require more detailed analysis than is possible within the scope of this work. The important point for understanding trends in rates of profit is that regardless of who benefitted from this growth in employee compensation, it was a cost that businesses paid instead of appropriating it as profit available for dividends or investment.

Looking at all the data for surplus value and wages period-by-period, we can see that there is a large increase in the actual ROSV during the postwar boom, even though, for employees as a whole, their share of national income increased. This suggests that the relative surplus value produced by the productivity increases of the postwar boom was largely spent employing unproductive workers (e.g. in the military during the Cold War). There was also a sharp spike in the ROSV during WWII as productive workers' exploitation was increased to boost military spending. Again, this is not captured by the ratio of 'broad profits' to wages because a large portion of this surplus value was spent unproductively, especially by the military.

After the postwar boom the ROSV grew more slowly until the early 1990s, because productivity increased more slowly, producing relative surplus value at a slower rate. Then the recession of 1991 and the 'jobless recovery' which followed coincided with a sharp increase in ROSV, while the real wage rate stagnated; indicating that a high rate of unemployment allowed bosses to keep wages down. From 1998–2003 the effect of this stagnation was reversed, as employees won higher than average real wage increases. Real employee compensation returned to its long-term trend and the ROSV fell back to around its trend level since the end of the postwar boom. From 2004 until the Great Recession the ROSV again increased significantly.

The immediate effect of the Great Recession was to halt the production of relative surplus value and the increases in the ROSV. Its tendency to increase then resumed while the economy recovered during 2012 and 2013.

The most important limitation of these results is the definition of employees in productive sectors. It probably includes significantly more workers in industries that are not productive than it excludes employees in industries that are productive. This means it overestimates the number of productive workers and their wages, and this overestimate probably gets proportionately worse over time as the true ratio of unproductive to productive workers grows. This means our measure of the ROSV becomes a progressively larger underestimate. On our figures, the ROSV more than doubles between 1929 and 2015, so the true ROSV almost certainly increased by even more. The estimates also depend on adopting and extending Mohun's estimates of the ratio of supervisory to non-supervisory employees and their compensation (see Chapter 4). Relying, as they must, on the categories used to define occupations by the Bureau of Labor Statistics, these estimates are inherently somewhat imprecise. Fortunately these issues make no difference to our estimates of rates of profit (except insofar as they affect some measures of inflation), since compensation of all employees is a deduction from revenue, whether or not they are productive.

The results therefore strongly support Marx's hypothesis that the development of the forces of production tends to produce relative surplus value and raise the ROSV. This is important because a great deal of Marx's analysis throughout *Capital*, but especially in Volume 1, works with this assumption.

It also matters because of what it says about the possibilities for improved standards of living and human development under socialism. A higher rate of surplus value means a relatively smaller number of productive workers support a relatively larger value of unproductive expenditures. Some of this labour is unproductive for capital, but socially useful (e.g. healthcare and education not provided for profit) and therefore does not necessarily represent labour time that could be spent differently to improve living standards. But almost certainly a much larger proportion of this surplus labour does not contribute to fulfilling human need, at least not for workers. Some is embodied in consumption goods for capitalists, some in actively harmful use values such as weapons, but by far the largest amount is spent on reproducing the labour power of unproductive wage earners. Much of this is only 'necessary' because capitalism makes this the case: e.g. much of the retail sector, finance and administration. A great deal is also devoted to a directly repressive and harmful social function: e.g. the military, prison guards, police, supervisors and managers. We can only imagine the possibilities for human development we would liberate if this labour power were instead expended directly satisfying human need, or freed up by shortening the working day; even setting aside the enormous creative and productive potential which ending alienation would unleash.

If it is instead measured as the ratio of 'broad profits' to wages, this aspect of the meaning of the ROSV no longer applies, and we are left with a ratio which at best describes a distributive relationship.

Chapter 4 also defined two measures of the rate of exploitation: the rate of primary exploitation and the total rate of exploitation. The first is the ratio of net output less the total price of productive labour power to the total price of productive labour power. The second replaces productive *wages* in the numerator and the denominator with the *value* of productive labour power plus the

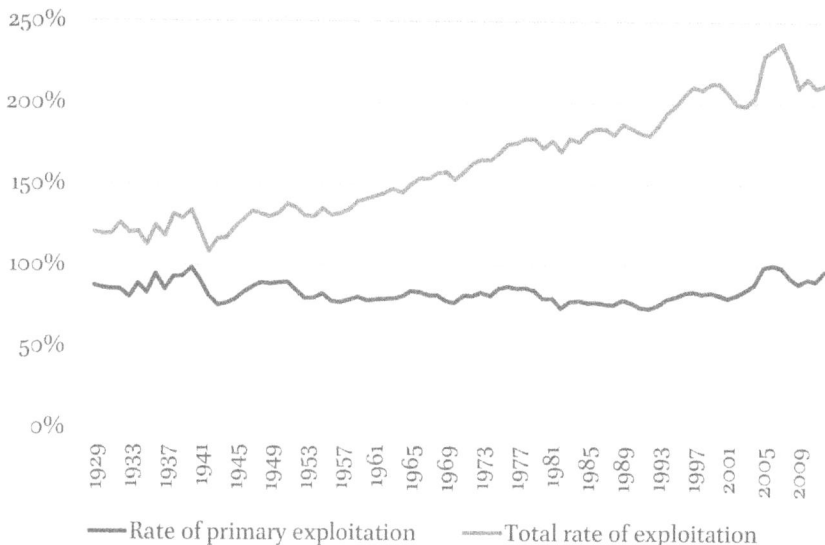

FIGURE 10   Rates of exploitation

portion of these wages retained as savings. This is productive workers' and proprietors' wages after subtracting the value extracted from them through rent, income taxes and interest.

Figure 10 below graphs both these measures. As we might expect, the rate of total exploitation has a similar trend to the rate of surplus value. Perhaps more surprisingly, the rate of primary exploitation is essentially trendless until 1992. This is because secondary exploitation becomes an increasingly important source of profit and tax revenue. This highlights another major problem with using the ratio of 'broad profits' to pre-tax 'wages' as a proxy for the ROSV: by ignoring secondary exploitation, especially through taxes, it grossly underestimates the level of and growth in the ROSV. Therefore it is not even a reliable measure of the distribution of income between capitalists and workers.

1.4   Unproductive Expenditures of Surplus Value
Now we will look at unproductive expenditures of surplus value more directly. Chapter 4 suggested that it is likely that, over time, there is an increase in the proportion of surplus value used to buy inputs and labour power for unproductive sectors. Figure 11 below suggests this is roughly true, but not the entire story. It graphs $(s - u) / s$ and $(s - u - ep) / s$, which is the proportion of surplus value 'left over' for net investment and for business owners' personal consumption for all businesses and for corporations respectively. The difference between

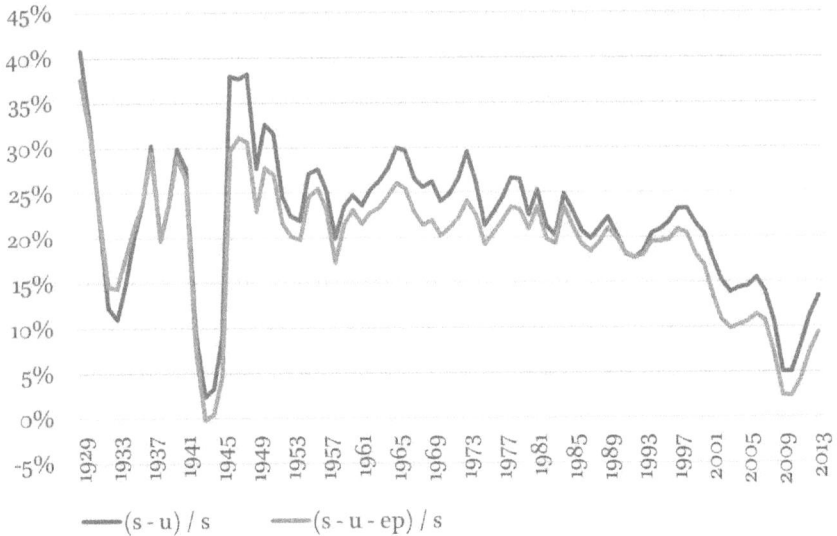

FIGURE 11   Surplus value 'left over' after unproductive expenditures

the two is that the latter excludes consumption and investment funded out of non-corporate profits (*ep*), and the former depends on our less than ideal method for imputing a value to the labour power of petty-bourgeois producers.

The most important aspect of the graph is the sharp drop in the ratios from 1998 until the Great Recession. By 2009 only 4% of surplus value remains 'left over' for businesses as a whole, and only 2% for corporations. What explains this quite dramatic change? Figure 12 and Figure 13 break down unproductive expenditures of surplus value as a proportion of surplus value by institution and by function from 1959 onwards.[6] Figure 12 shows there is a tendency for unproductive expenditures by both government and business to increase over time as a proportion of surplus value. But between 1992 and 1997 government unproductive expenditures fall considerably in proportional terms. The large fall in $(s - u) / s$ from 1998 is explained in part by the increase in government

---

6   NIPA table 3.15.5 gives estimates of government spending by function, and the text below describes how these categories have been grouped according to a Marxist interpretation. We cannot simply use the estimates of government consumption expenditures and gross investment by function supplied by the NIPA, however, because we have defined these include the pre-tax wages paid to government employees, and not just government employees' consumption. We instead assume that this data gives us the correct proportional breakdown of government spending by function. It is then straightforward to estimate unproductive government expenditures by function.

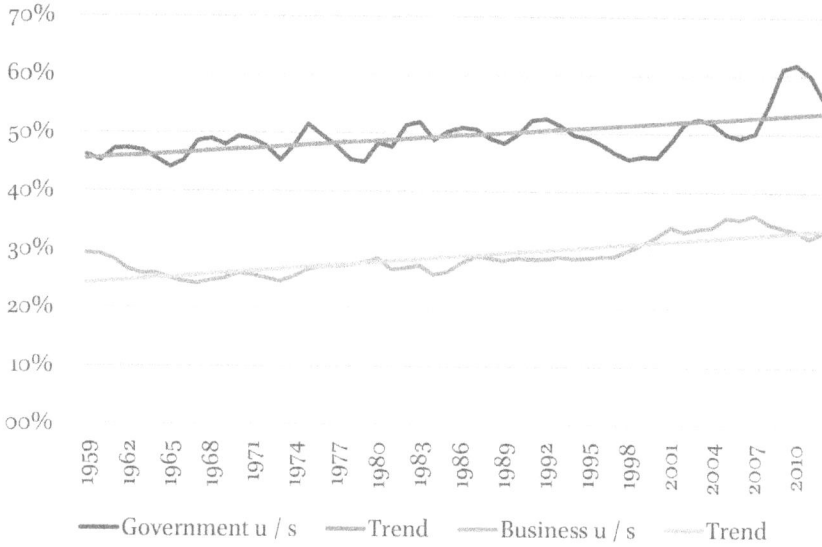

FIGURE 12   Unproductive expenditures by government and business

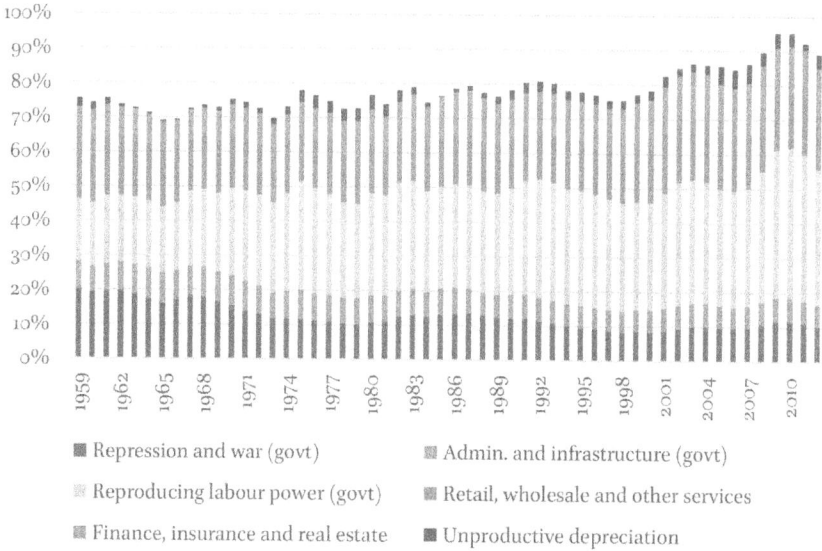

FIGURE 13   Unproductive expenditures by function as percentages of surplus value

spending as a proportion of surplus value between 2000 and 2002 back to trend levels; but by 2005 it had fallen back to trend. The more important change before the recession is an increase in unproductive expenditures by businesses as a proportion of surplus value.

Figure 13 breaks this down further. It uses the NIPA's newly available data for government expenditure by function and combines them according to a Marxist interpretation. 'Repression and war' is defined as unproductive expenditures on 'national defense' and 'public order and safety'; 'administration and infrastructure' is spending on 'general public service' plus 'economic affairs'; and 'reproducing labour power' is consumption spending on 'housing and community services', 'health', 'recreation and culture', 'education', 'income security' (which is the cost of administering income security payments only) plus gross government social benefits paid to persons (which includes income security payments themselves). In all cases this covers spending only on the *value* of labour power (rather than all wages, since we are dealing with expenditures of surplus value) and the cost of buying commodities either consumed as intermediate inputs or bought as fixed assets.

Spending on repression and war as a proportion of surplus value nearly halves over the period, with the end of the Cold War and the Vietnam War. This is balanced out by an increase in government spending on reproducing labour power. A great deal of this is probably due to the large increase in the unemployment rate after the postwar boom, and the increased unemployment benefits the state has to pay as a result. *During* the Great Recession this leads to a sharp increase in government expenditure, pushing unproductive government spending up to around 55% of surplus value. But, as mentioned, immediately *before* the Great Recession government unproductive expenditures as a proportion of surplus value are still below trend.

For unproductive expenditures of surplus value by business, the increases in unproductive expenditures are shared roughly evenly between retail, wholesale and other services and finance, insurance and real estate.

The increase in unproductive expenditures as a proportion of surplus value may be an important part of the explanation for the Great Recession. To see if it is, and to judge its relative importance, we first need to examine measures of the rate of profit and the various influences on them.

2 Measures of the Rate of Profit

2.1 'Standard' Measures

To give a point of comparison, we will start by looking at the results produced by some more 'standard' measures of the rate of profit, and some conclusions others have drawn from them. As discussed in Chapters 1 and 2, Marxists do not agree over whether to measure fixed assets at current or historical cost. As mentioned in Chapter 4, they also use many different numerators. A broad definition of 'profit' is gross domestic product less depreciation of fixed assets and compensation of employees. Then there are other business payments which may or may not be treated as deductions from this 'broad profit': taxes on production less subsidies, net proprietors' income (i.e. income for owners of non-corporate businesses), net interest payments, net rental income of persons (which is rent paid for housing, including an imputation for the rent that the national accounts treat owner occupiers as 'paying to themselves'), current surplus of government enterprises, and taxes on corporate profits.[7] If we deduct all of these, we get what the national accounts call 'corporate profits after tax'.

Basu and Vasudevan measure the US rate of profit using nearly all possible combinations of the methods listed above (and some others). They conclude:

> [A]ll the measures display similar trends: there is a break in the declining trend in profitability in the early 1980s; the subsequent period is marked by either a trendless or a slowly rising trend in profitability. The only exception is a measure of the rate of profit that uses historical cost valuation for the capital stock and before-tax (both direct and indirect taxes), before-interest profit flow; this measure displays a secularly declining trend for the whole postwar period.
>
> The weight of evidence thus suggests clearly that the current crisis was not preceded by a prolonged period of declining profitability. In fact, the current crisis was preceded by a period of rising profitability, buoyed by favourable trends in both the profit share and technology. Capital productivity increased through the 1990s along with rising labour productivity and declining capital intensity. The tentative hypothesis provided here is that these favourable trends can be explained as the outcome of the specificities of information technology, globalisation and the global relocation of production, and the intensification of managerial control to enforce a steep increase in labour productivity.[8]

---

7   This list is not exhaustive.
8   Basu and Vasudevan 2012, p. 83.

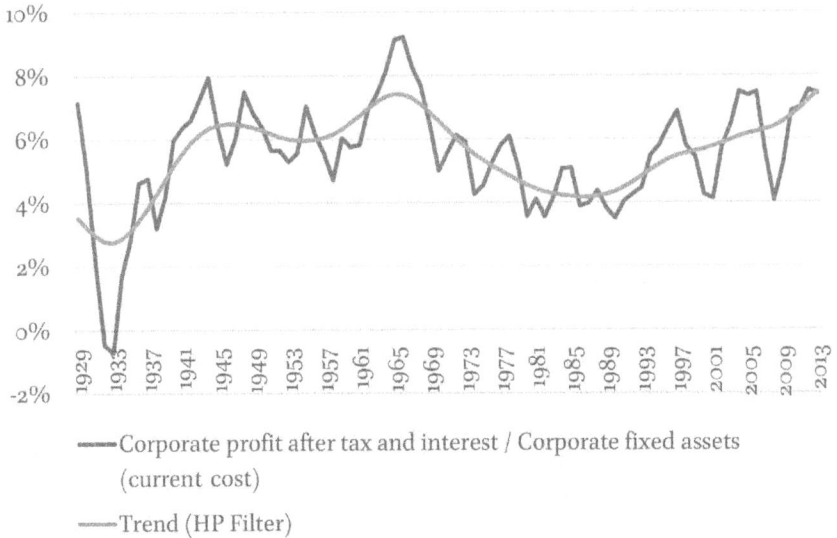

——Corporate profit after tax and interest / Corporate fixed assets
   (current cost)
——Trend (HP Filter)

FIGURE 14   'Narrow' current cost 'rate of profit'

Determining trends in this way, by calculating linear trends between 'breaks' identified by the researcher, can be problematic.[9] Nevertheless, some of the measures of the rate of profit listed above *do* have an upward trend in the lead up to the Great Recession, even if we use a better method to calculate the trend. Figure 14 below gives the rate of profit calculated as the ratio of corporate profits after tax (and after interest) to corporate fixed assets at current cost. It also includes a trend line calculated using a Hodrick-Prescott (HP) filter, which 'smooths' the data series to fit a polynomial function, making it easier to identify trends and inflection points.[10]

After 1990 this 'rate of profit' becomes very volatile, though there does appear to be a rising trend. At the other extreme, if we use a broad measure of 'profit' and corporate fixed assets at historical cost, then there is a clear downward trend during the 1980s and 1990s, and the rate of profit remains low in the lead up to the Great Recession. This is graphed in Figure 15 below. Yet even on this measure, there is no actual *decline* in the rate of profit in the lead up to the Great Recession; and, if anything, there is small upward trend during the 2000s.

9   Kliman 2011, pp. 104–5.
10   Hodrick and Prescott 1997.

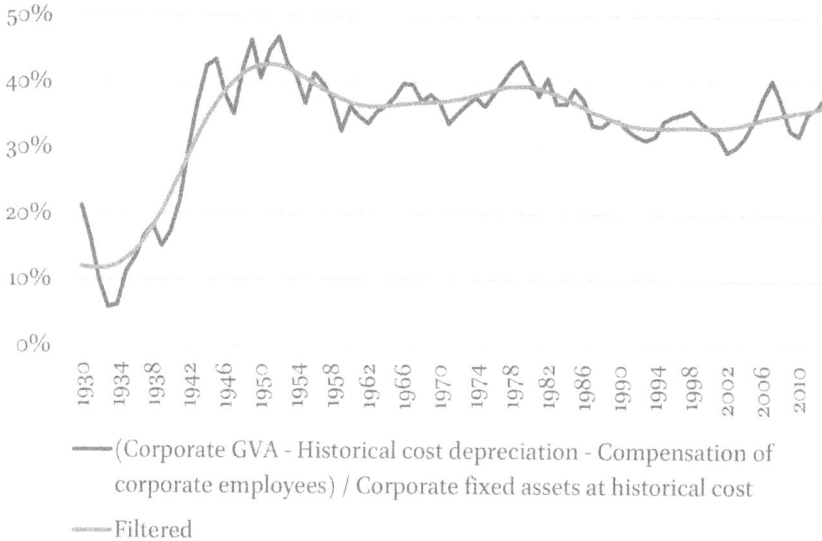

——(Corporate GVA - Historical cost depreciation - Compensation of
corporate employees) / Corporate fixed assets at historical cost

———Filtered

FIGURE 15   Broad, historical cost 'rate of profit'

Different measures of the rate of profit such as these have been used to justify very different explanations of the crisis. One debate mentioned in Chapters 1 and 2 is whether to use a historical cost or a current cost measure of fixed assets.

Duménil and Lévy, who use current cost measures of the rate of profit, argue there has been a significant divergence between the rate of profit and the rate of growth of real corporate output.[11] We can see this by comparing the trends in Figure 16 below and Figure 14 above.

If this reflected a genuine divergence between the rate of profit and the rate of growth, it would be a surprising and interesting result. Duménil and Lévy argue this characterises a distinctively 'neoliberal' 'régime of accumulation', established in the US and elsewhere during the 1980s. They argue that, after WWII, a 'social democratic compromise' was established between the 'popular' and 'managerial' classes, which left the 'capitalist' class (which, for them, is basically equivalent to large shareholders) marginalised compared with other periods. This compromise was centred on:

(1) a financial sector targeted to the growth of the real economy, and not to 'administration' of capitalist collective interests as in neoliberalism;

---

11   Duménil and Lévy 2011, p. 152.

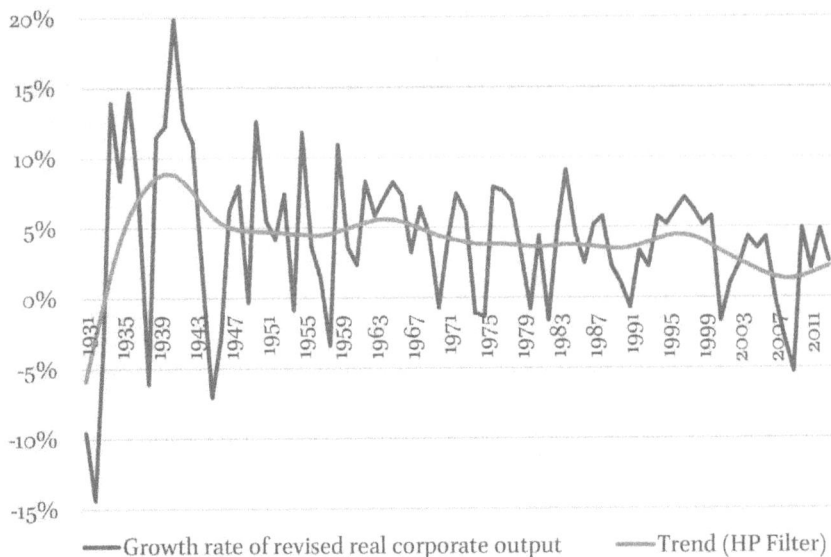

──Growth rate of revised real corporate output   ──Trend (HP Filter)

FIGURE 16   Growth rate of revised real corporate output

(2) a lesser concern vis-à-vis shareholders (that is, a management aiming at accumulation instead of capital income), low real interest rates, and a 'not-too-performing' stock market; and (3) possibly diminished profits that would result from higher labour costs.[12]

For Duménil and Lévy, this class compromise broke down with the profitability crisis of the 1970s, and a new 'neoliberal compromise' was formed between the 'managerial' and 'capitalist' classes. Under this arrangement, corporate managers' remuneration became increasingly tied to their companies' share prices, which they boosted with higher dividend payouts at the expense of retaining profits to expand production. They argue this is why the rate of profit stayed relatively high (as they measure it), but the rate of accumulation and rate of growth of output were relatively low.[13] This is the main reason they characterise the Great Recession as a crisis of *neoliberalism* and financialisation rather than a crisis of capitalist production.[14]

Kliman, on other hand, uses historical cost measures of the rate of profit to argue that there was no divergence large enough to warrant this explanation:

12   Duménil and Lévy 2011, pp. 16–17.
13   Duménil and Lévy 2011, p. 152.
14   Duménil and Lévy 2011, pp. 22–6.

that, instead, the underlying cause of the Great Recession was the persistently low level of the rate of profit since 1970s. Thus, for Kliman, and for others who advance a falling rate of profit explanation, the financial crash of 2007–08 and the Great Recession which followed were expressions of a contradiction within capitalist production *itself*, not the fault of a particular *type* of capitalism.[15]

2.2   New Measures of the Rate of Profit

None of these measures of the rate of profit are good approximations of the rate of profit Marx's law is designed to explain. This book has set out two alternative types of measure of the rate of profit: ones based on surplus value after deducting unproductive expenditures, and ones based on profits from production. We will calculate the first type for the corporate sector and for the business sector as a whole, and the second type for the corporate sector only, on a before- and after-tax basis. This gives four definitions of the rate of profit to measure, graphed in the figures below. We can only calculate these accurately from 1947 onwards, since 1947 is the first year for which inventories data is published; but below we will also include some less reliable estimates for some measures from 1930 onwards.

Here we will focus on Marx's hypothesis that the rate of profit tends to decline in the lead up to economic crises, and recovers if and when sufficient capital is devalued or destroyed. Further below we will test Marx's hypothesis that the rate of profit tends to fall over the long term, using (less reliable) estimates of the US rate of profit stretching back to 1869.

Figure 17 below graphs the two measures of the rate of profit most appropriate for explaining rates of accumulation: one for the whole business sector (with $s - u$ on the numerator, and produced capital for productive and commercial businesses on the denominator) and one for the corporate sector only (with $s - u - ep$ on the numerator, and produced capital for productive and commercial corporations on the denominator). Both measures have downward trends over the period as a whole, and the trend is a little more pronounced for the corporate sector. The R squared with the linear trend for the corporate sector measure is 0.52, and for the business sector as a whole it is 0.40. This is significant variation around the trend, consistent with a cyclical movement.

We can visually identify 5 main inflection points: a declining trend from 1947–58, a rising trend from 1958–66, a declining trend from 1966–83, a rising trend from 1983–98, a declining trend from 1998–2010, and a rising trend from

---

15   Kliman 2010; Kliman 2011; Harman 2009; Carchedi 2011; Roberts 2009; Freeman 2012.

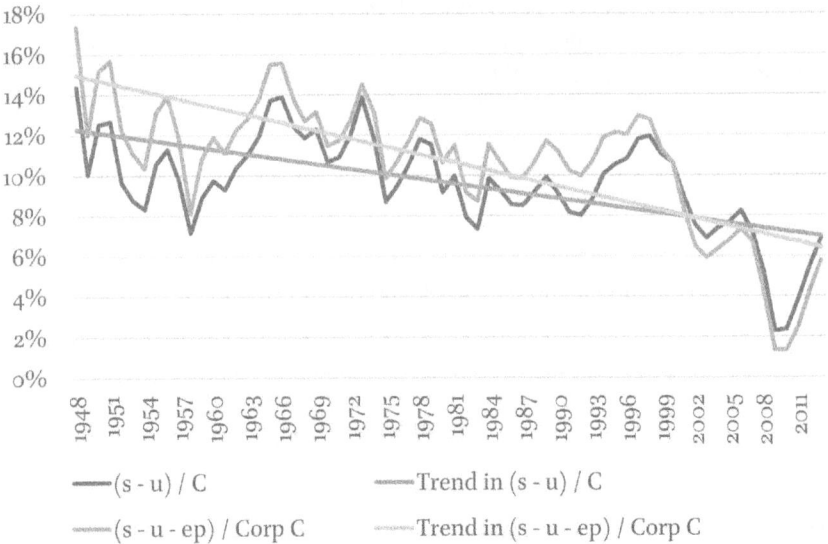

FIGURE 17   Rates of profit based on $s - u$ with linear trends

2010–13. This is consistent with the results from applying an HP filter, graphed in Figure 18 (apart from the last possible trend). Most importantly, there can be little doubt that these measures of the rate of profit decline in the lead up to the two major periods of crisis: the crises of the 1970s and the Great Recession.

Both of these measures of the rate of profit also recover to a limited extent after the steep increase in interest rates in 1983 at the end of the crisis which started in the 1970s, and more substantially with the 'jobless' economic recovery starting in 1992. Both measures also recover when the Great Recession ends in 2010; and though by 2013 the recovery in these rates of profit is around as large as the recovery during the 1990s, this still leaves both measures of the rate of profit below their levels at the beginning of the recession in 2007.

The next pair of measures of the rate of profit are graphed in Figure 19 below. These are the rates of profit on production for the corporate sector before- and after-taxes and subsidies on production and taxes on corporate income. Again in both cases there is a definite downward trend across the period as a whole, but there are turning points around this trend. The R squared measure of correlation with the trend on the before-tax measure is 0.57, and on the after-tax measure it is 0.28. Until 2002 the main points of inflection appear to be mostly the same, sometimes one year earlier: 1958, 1966, 1982 and 1997. However, the steep decline in all four measures of the rate of profit after 1997 comes to a halt in 2002. Then until 2005 there is sharp increase in both measures of the corporate rate of profit on production, followed by a levelling off until the steep

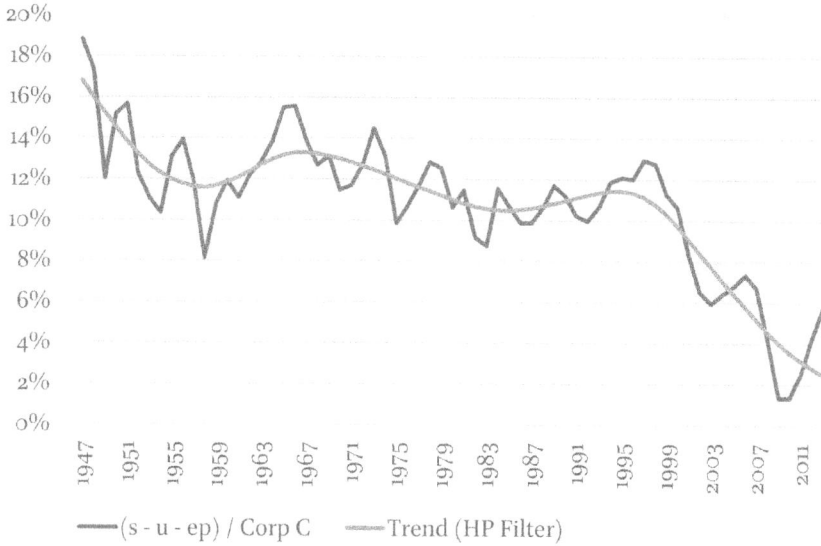

FIGURE 18 $(s - u - ep) / Corp\ C$ with filter

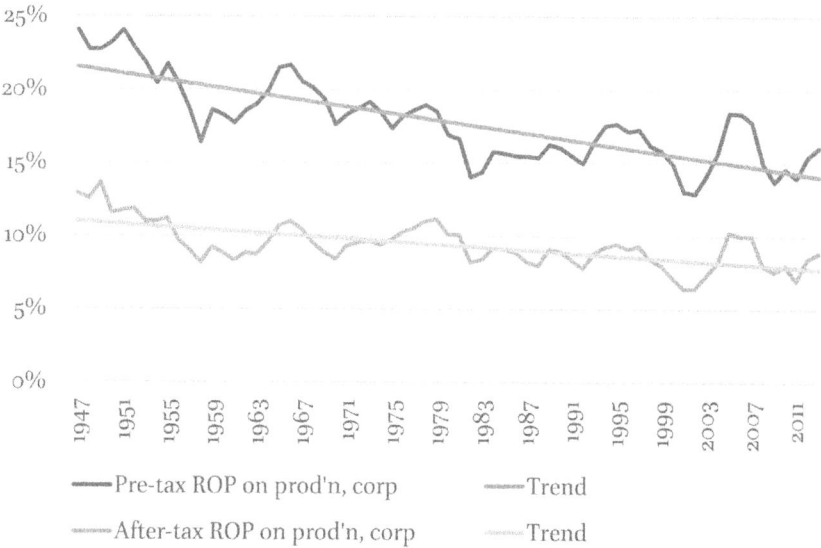

FIGURE 19   Corporate rates of profit on production

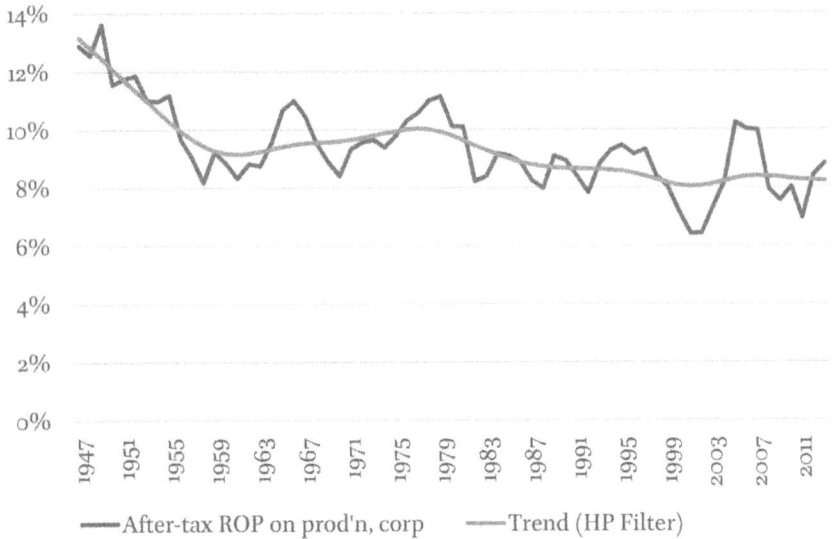

FIGURE 20   After-tax corporate rate of profit on production with filter

decline once the recession starts. There is only a much smaller increase in the rates of profit defined in terms of $s - u$. This is discussed further below.

Finally, if we assume no change in the ratio of inventories to fixed assets from 1930–46, we can extend our estimates of the rate of profit back to 1930. This is graphed in Figure 21 for the corporate sector defined in terms of $s - u$ and in terms of corporate profits from production after-tax. As we would expect, there is a steep decline in both measures during the Great Depression, followed by a large recovery from 1933 until the end of WWII. The $s - u$ measure also falls dramatically but temporarily during the war, because much more surplus value is spent unproductively by the state, funded partly by borrowing. From 1943–44 it falls below zero, suggesting so much surplus value is spent unproductively that more than the entire value of output is spent on consumption for proprietors and wage earners and consumption and investment by the state. This does not imply there was zero (or less than zero) consumption and investment by capitalists, since this can also be funded by transfers of profit and borrowing from overseas.

Most importantly, these measures show rates of profit that reach comparable lows during the Great Recession and the Great Depression, helping to explain why these were economic crises of comparable severity.

These results strongly support the hypothesis that the rate of profit tends to fall in the lead up to major economic crises. This is arguably the most important aspect of Marx's LTFRP, since the main purpose of Marx's law is to explain

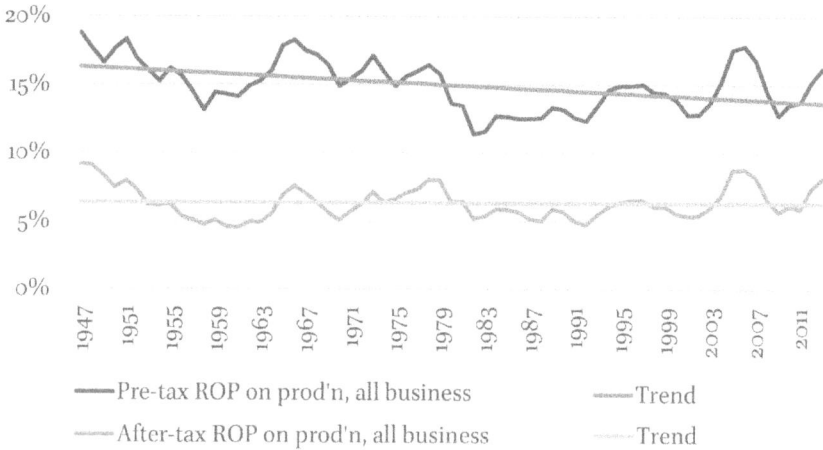

FIGURE 21   Rates of profit since 1930, based on estimated inventories from 1930–46

crises. Measures of the rate of profit used by other Marxists do not generally give the result that the rate of profit actually *fell* in the lead up the Great Recession, or that it fell to levels as low as those reached in the Great Depression.

2.3   The Rate of Profit, the Rate of Accumulation and the Rate of Growth

Another reason to measure the rate of profit is to see if it can explain movements in other economic aggregates that interest us, such as the rate of growth of output. Chapter 2 hypothesised that the rate of profit would influence the rate of growth through its influence on the rate of accumulation. The idea was that a falling rate of profit would provide less surplus value to invest (relative to the existing stock of capital), and hence slow the rate of accumulation. The slowing rate of accumulation would reduce the rate of growth of the capacity to produce real output, which in turn would reduce the actual rate of growth of output. Chapter 4 argued this was most likely to apply when the numerator of the rate of profit is defined as $s - u$.

This applies to trends over the medium- to long-term. In the shorter-term, the rate of growth of output can vary considerably as the rate of capacity utilisation changes. When economic conditions worsen, companies lay off workers, and so produce less real output using the existing stock of fixed assets and other capital. This causes a fall in the rate of growth independent of any decline in the rate of accumulation (though a decline in the rate of accumulation is also likely). Then, when conditions recover, growth can bounce back rapidly, even without any investment in new fixed assets, as companies re-hire workers and bring capacity utilisation back up to a higher level. If there is a sustained depression, then there might be a sustained period over which movements in

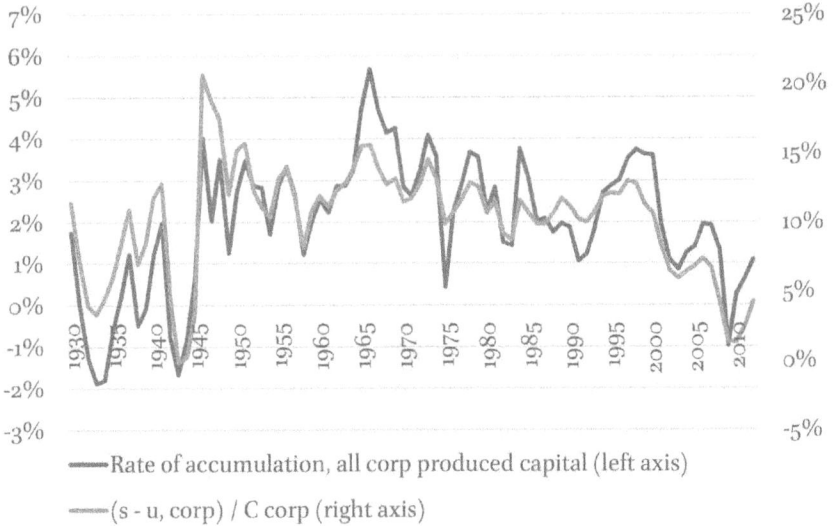

FIGURE 22   Rate of accumulation vs. rate of profit, corporations

the rate of accumulation are not similar to movements in the rate of growth. First we will look at the relationship between the rate of accumulation and the rate of profit. Figure 22 does this for the corporate sector, and Figure 23 for all businesses.

Both relationships are quite close. The R squared coefficient of correlation between the rate of profit and the rate of accumulation for the corporate sector is 0.71, and for the business sector as a whole it is 0.84. Unlike standard measures of the rate of profit, these measures strongly indicate that the decline in the rate of accumulation after 2000 was due to the decline in the rate of profit from 1998 onwards. There is no evidence of a change in the 'willingness' of capitalists to invest the surplus value that was available for investment or for their personal consumption.

As mentioned, the relationship between the rate of accumulation and rate of growth of output is likely to be less close over the short-term. Figure 24 and Figure 25 below graph the rates of accumulation for the corporate and business sectors against growth in real revised output for the corporate sector and in general.

In both cases the R squared coefficients are near zero, because the rates of accumulation are much less volatile than the rates of growth. However, the rates of accumulation do give reasonable indications of trends in the rates of growth, as we can see more clearly by comparing them with the rates of growth after applying an HP filter (with a smoothing value of 100, as used throughout).

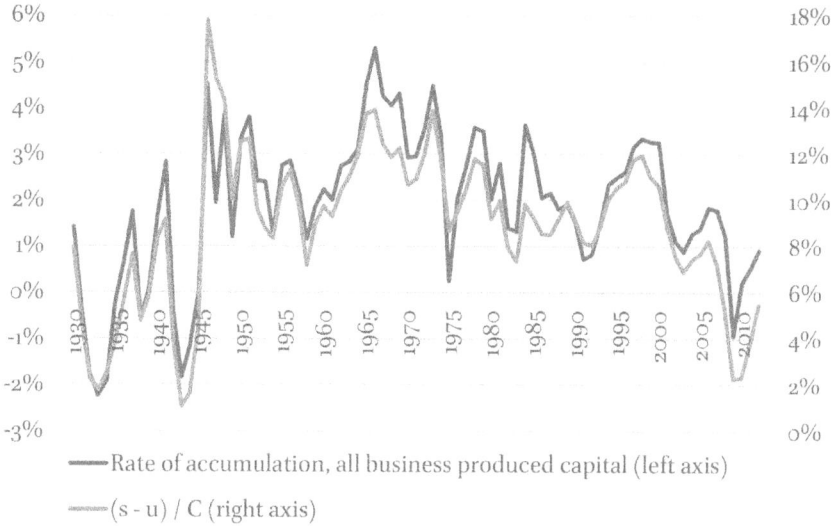

FIGURE 23   Rate of accumulation vs. rate of profit, all businesses

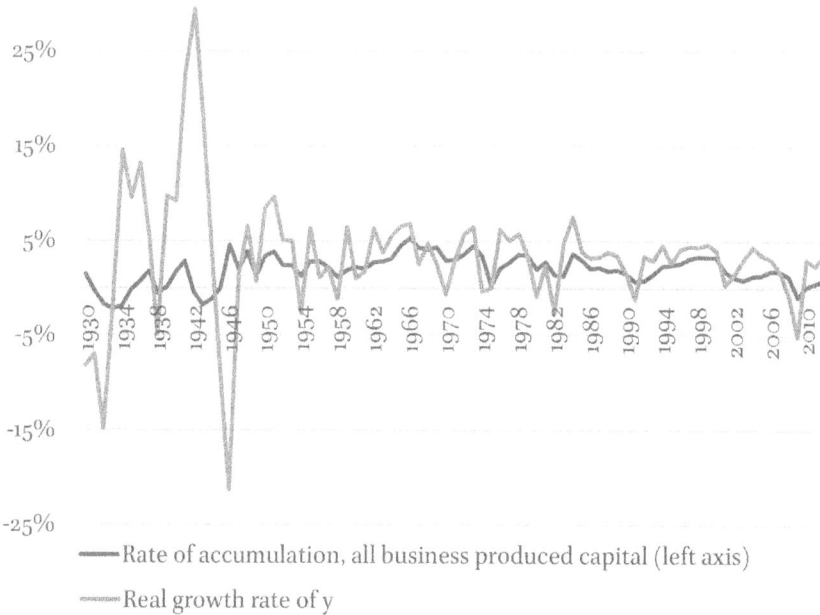

FIGURE 24   Rate of accumulation vs. growth rate, all business

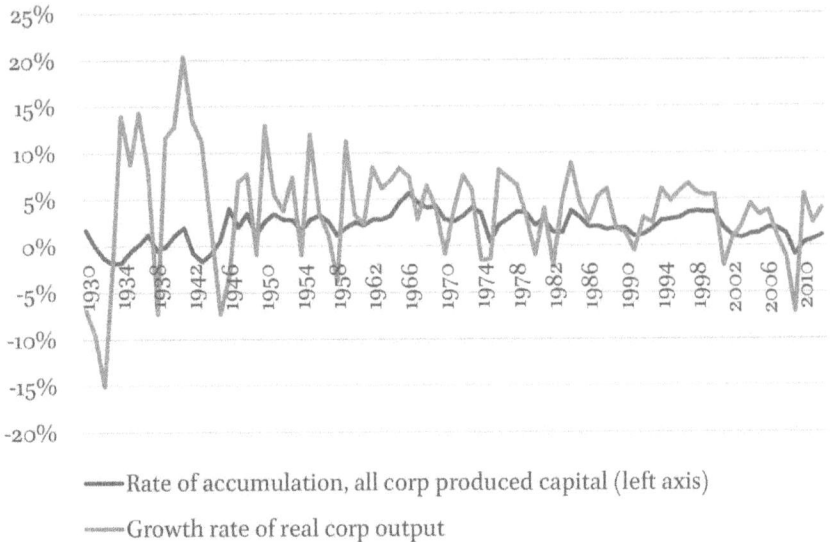

——Rate of accumulation, all corp produced capital (left axis)

——Growth rate of real corp output

FIGURE 25   Rate of accumulation vs. growth rate, corporations

From the mid-1960s onwards the relationship between the two series is reasonably close, but before then, and especially before the end of WWII, the trends are quite different. It is likely that the Great Depression caused a very large fall in capacity utilisation, and so, during the recovery of the mid- to late-1930s, capacity utilisation increased by a correspondingly large amount back towards more 'normal' levels. This would account for the combination of a high rate of growth and a low rate of accumulation: the rate of growth was high, because there was so much idle capacity to be taken up, which also meant that firms could expand output without investing a great deal in new fixed assets.

So the hypothesis that the rate of accumulation and rate of growth have the same trend holds up reasonably well, except when there is significant unused capacity. One problem with the hypothesis is determining the direction of causation: is it that changes in the rate of accumulation lead to changes in the rate of growth, or *vice versa*? It is likely that to some extent there is a reciprocal relationship between the two; and, in the short-term, the results above suggest that changes in the rate of growth might 'lead' changes in the rate of accumulation.

Overall, we can say that the rate of profit defined in terms of $s - u$ eliminates the 'mystery' surrounding the relationship between the rate of profit, the rate of accumulation and the rate of growth of output. All three have similar downward trajectories over the postwar period, and leading up to the two major

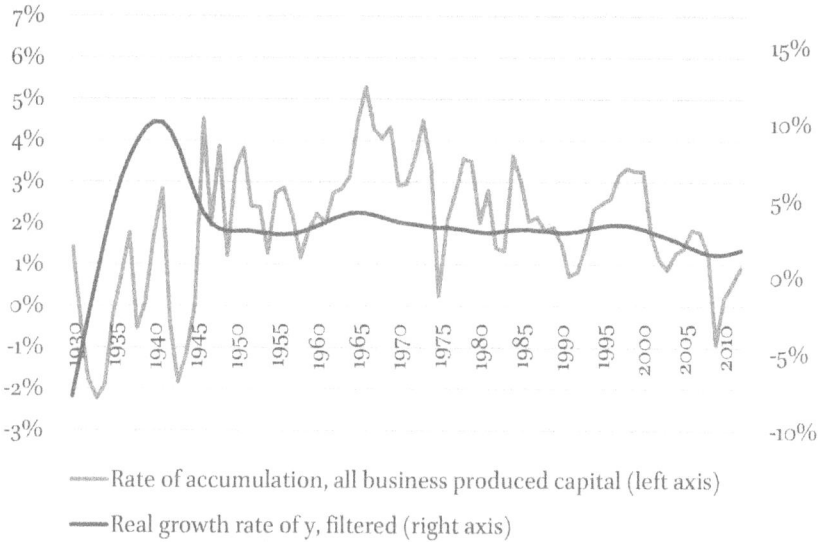

Rate of accumulation, all business produced capital (left axis)

Real growth rate of y, filtered (right axis)

FIGURE 26   Rate of accumulation vs. filtered growth rate, all business

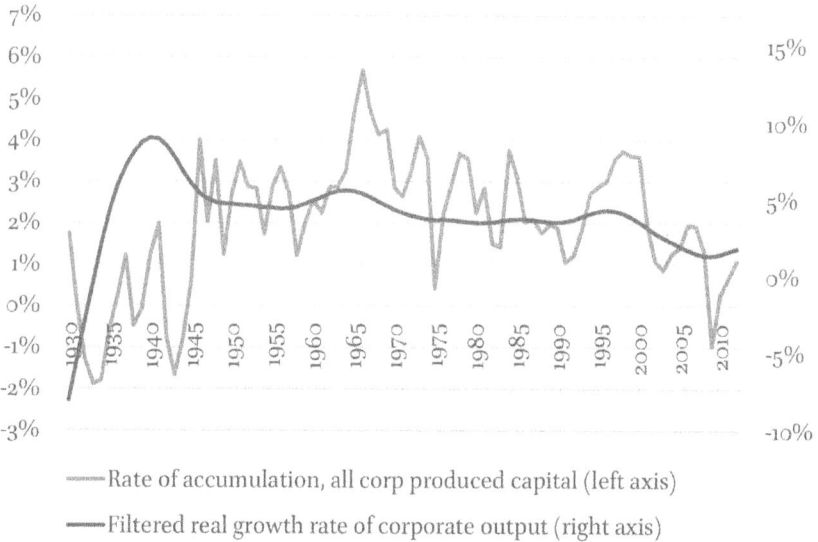

Rate of accumulation, all corp produced capital (left axis)

Filtered real growth rate of corporate output (right axis)

FIGURE 27   Rate of accumulation vs. rate of growth, corporations

crises (the crises of the 1970s and the 2000s). The rate of profit on production also declines over the postwar period, though does increase sharply between 2002 and 2005.

The evidence therefore confirms a falling rate of profit explanation for the Great Recession. But does it fit with *Marx's* explanation for the falling rate of profit: i.e. *his* LTFRP? To answer this question, we need to look at *why* the rate of profit fell.

3   Why the Rate of Profit Fell

We have seen that the fall in the rate of profit was certainly *not* due to a fall in the rate of surplus value, which rises throughout the postwar period, and more than doubles from 1929 to 2015. On the other hand, this increased exploitation did not necessarily translate into profits, because spending on unproductive inputs also tended to increase. Marx's law does not focus on these issues. For him, the decisive influence on the rate of profit is the rising organic composition of capital. Was this the case in reality?

3.1   *Turnover Time, the OCC and the VCC*

As argued in Chapter 3, we cannot measure the OCC or its influence on the rate of profit without first trying to estimate the turnover time of variable capital. That chapter gave a method for estimating this, and argued the method should give similar results to dividing inventories by final sales (after allowing for the different definitions they use for productive labour). Figure 28 below gives estimates for the average turnover time of variable capital each year using both methods.

Four phases are evident: a phase in which turnover time shortened from 1948 to 1969; a period of volatility from 1969 to 1984; another shortening phase from 1981 to around 2002; and then a period in which turnover time increased a little until 2012 before shortening again. As we might expect, improvements in turnover time are associated with periods of expansion, when there is more investment in improving production and distribution techniques. During crises, turnover time also tends to increase due to the build-up of inventories. Importantly, across the postwar period as a whole, average turnover time declines by more than half, which fits with Marx and Engels' hypothesis that it tends to fall with the development of the forces of production.

Calculating turnover time also involves calculating the stock of variable capital 'tied up' in capital advanced, v, at the beginning of each year. First we will

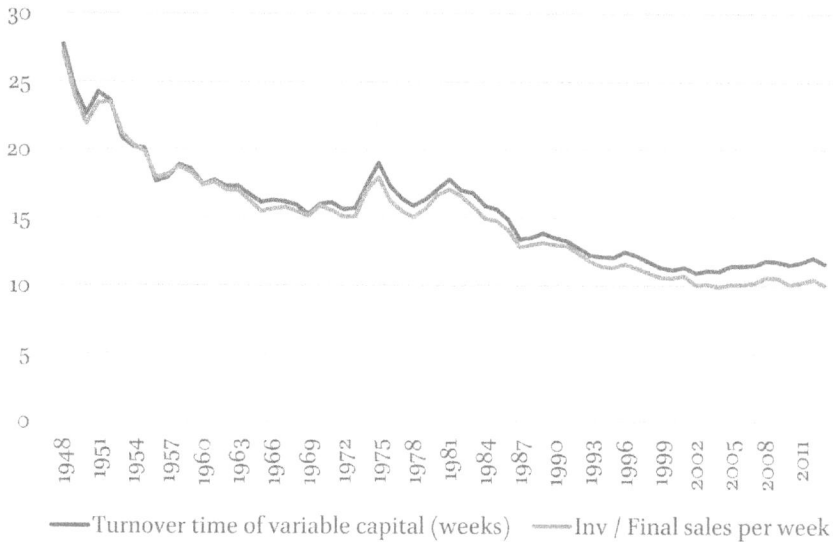

FIGURE 28   Turnover time

use this to calculate the *annual* rate of surplus value – the ratio of surplus value produced in the year, *s*, to the *stock* of variable capital, *v*, for the private sector.[16]

We can see from the graph below that the only significant periods during which the annual ROSV did not increase were associated with crises: 1973–82 and from 2007–12. It generally increased significantly faster than the actual rate of surplus value.

Now to the value composition of capital (VCC) and the organic composition of capital (OCC). The VCC is the ratio of the stocks of constant to variable capital; the OCC is the VCC assuming no changes in prices. The OCC needs to be measured relative to a base year: here this is 1947.

The results indicate strong tendencies for both the VCC and the OCC to rise. They both increase less rapidly during the postwar boom than during the 1980s and 1990s, which may help to explain the boom's longevity. However, during the two periods of crisis both were stagnant. Before the Great Recession, both start to stagnate from 2001. This is around the time the $s - u$ rate of profit and the rate of accumulation fall dramatically, which makes sense: the decline in investment meant a slower growth in the ratio of dead labour to living labour.

---

16   The estimate does not cover government enterprises because their stocks are not included in the BEA's estimates of inventories.

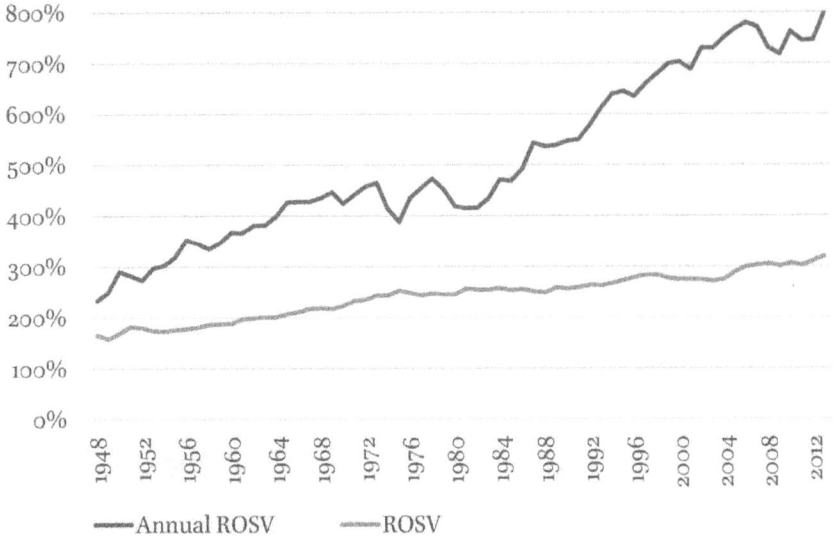

FIGURE 29   Annual rate of surplus value for the private sector

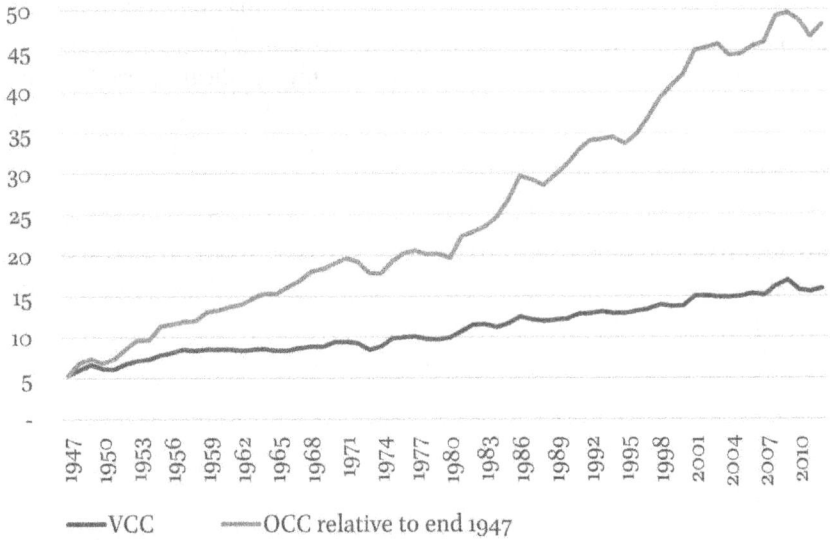

FIGURE 30   The value and the organic compositions of capital

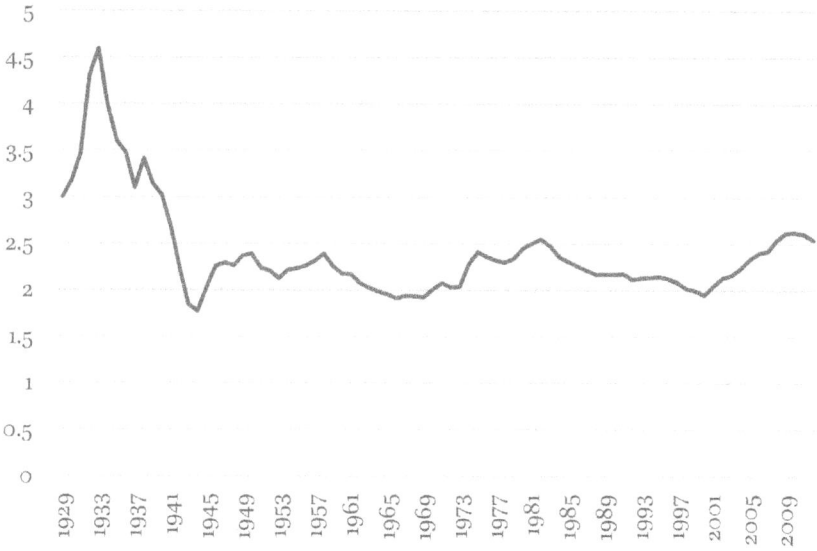

FIGURE 31   Corporate fixed assets / compensation of corporate employees

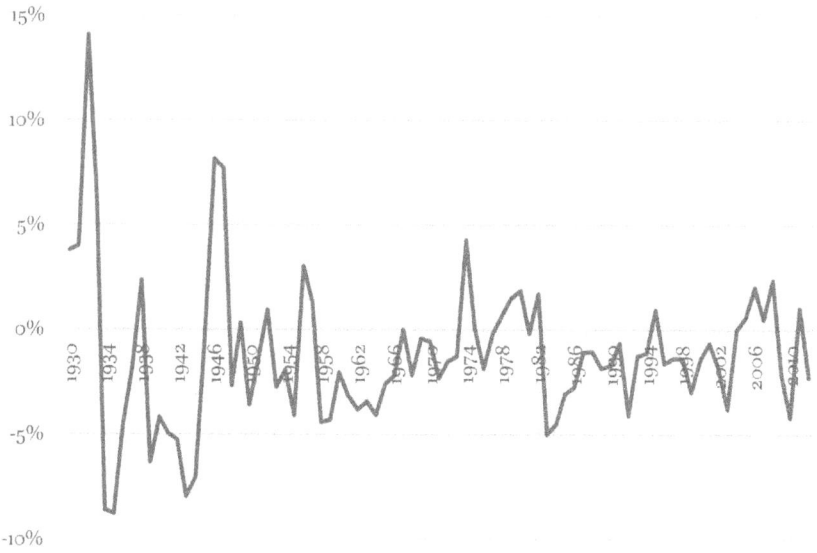

FIGURE 32   Revaluation of business fixed assets / business fixed assets before revaluation

As we would expect, the OCC rises faster than the VCC, reflecting the tendency for constant capital to be cheapened over time with improvements in productivity. Bear in mind however that, as discussed in Chapter 3, the method used here to estimate the OCC tends to over-estimate this difference, because when measuring the OCC it does not increase depreciation to account for the fact that the OCC excludes the effect of devaluation on the stock of constant capital.

Compare this with a measure of the 'VCC' or 'OCC' as the ratio of corporate fixed assets to corporate compensation of employees. Here only the faintest trace of an increasing 'OCC' is evident over the postwar period, combined with long periods in which this 'OCC' actually declines. It also appears as though the 'OCC' was dramatically higher before WWII than for the entire period afterwards. If this were a true measure of the OCC or the VCC it would refute Marx's hypothesis that the OCC and VCC tend to increase as the forces of production develop (at least for the US) and hence Marx's LTFRP.

Let us now look at devaluation and revaluation directly. The graph below takes revaluation of productive fixed assets, as defined in Chapter 2, and divides it by productive fixed assets excluding that year's revaluation. So it is the percentage of the value of productive fixed assets that is gained through revaluation (or, if negative, lost through devaluation).

First, we can see here the exceptionally high rate of devaluation from 1934–44 which, combined with disinvestment in net terms, lays the basis for the postwar boom. We can also see that there was a relatively high rate of devaluation in the early phase of the postwar boom, suggesting significant 'moral' depreciation through productivity improvements.

Also notice that when there is *re*valuation (i.e. when the graph is positive), this tends to be associated with recessions, and often precedes them. The spike in revaluation in 1930–32 occurs during the Great Depression; the spike in 1938 occurs during the recession of 1937–38; the spike from 1945–47 precedes the recession of 1949; the spike in 1956–57 precedes the recession of 1958; the spike in 1974 occurs during the recession of 1973–75; again the 1978–80 spike precedes the recession of 1980; and there is an extended period of revaluation in 2004–08 before the Great Recession. This is likely to be registering the asset price bubbles which tend to occur before recessions.

On the other hand, larger than usual devaluation tends to occur immediately after or during recessions (with the exception of the high rate of devaluation during the postwar boom). When the devaluation is large, it tends to lead to periods of recovery. So after the recession of 1973–75, there was some devaluation in 1975–76, but not a large amount, and a recovery did not follow. However, after the early 1980s recession, there was a sharp devaluation of fixed assets in 1983–86, followed by a period of expansion. There was also devaluation in 2009–10, but not enough to make a great deal of difference to the value of the stock of fixed assets. The cumulative effect of revaluation from 2004 to 2012 was −0.14 %, at an average of −0.02 % per year. This is significantly less devaluation than the average rate of revaluation over the period as a whole (−1.1 % per year), which helps to explain why the recovery from the Great Recession has been so sluggish.

3.2   *Full Decomposition*

Now we are in the situation Marx reaches at the end of his chapter called 'The Law of the Tendential Fall in the Rate of Profit'. We have shown there has been a substantial, long-term tendency for the OCC and the VCC to increase; and so, as Marx puts it:

> If we consider the enormous development in the productive power of social labour ... and particularly if we consider the enormous mass of fixed capital involved in the overall process of social production quite apart from machinery proper, then instead of the problem that occupied pre- vious economists, the problem of explaining the fall in the profit rate, we have the opposite problem of explaining why this fall is not greater or faster. Counteracting influences must be at work, checking and cancel- ling the effect of the general law and giving it simply the character of a tendency, which is why we have described the fall in the general rate of profit as a tendential fall.[17]

Chapters 3 and 4 gave a method for separating out six influences on changes in the $s - u$ measure of the rate of profit: the ratio of surplus value after unproduct- ive expenditures to surplus value; the rate of surplus value; the turnover time of variable capital; revaluation of existing capital; the cheapening of newly pro- duced capital; and the OCC. Figure 33 graphs the cumulative effect of each on $(s - u)/C$ for the business sector as a whole.

The long-term effect of each on the rate of profit is as we would expect from Marx's theory. The OCC has the largest effect on the rate of profit, pulling the rate of profit down as it rises. The ratio of $(s - u)$ to s also pulls the rate of profit down over time as it declines, as a result of increasing unproductive expendit- ures of surplus value, especially from 1998 onwards (as we found earlier). On the other hand, the rising rate of surplus value, shortening turnover time, and

---

17   Marx 1981, p. 339.

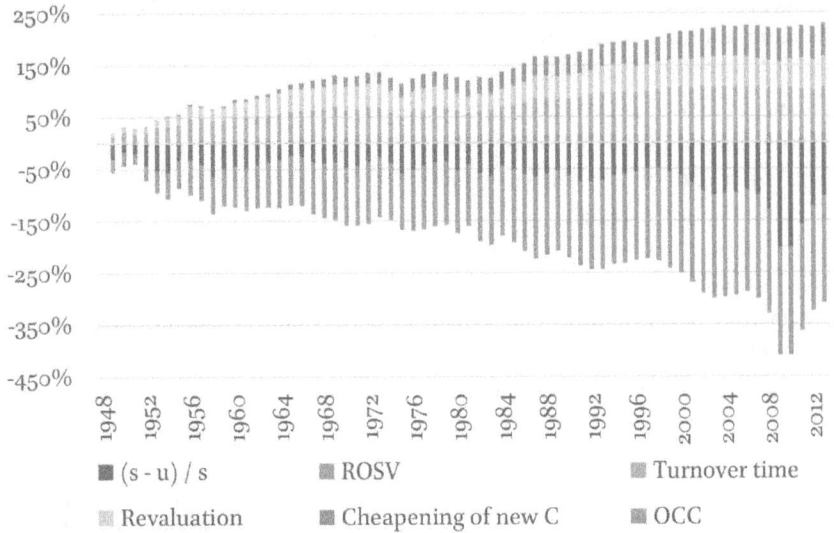

FIGURE 33   Influences on (s – u) / C

the devaluation and cheapening of constant capital all tend to be counteracting factors to the falling rate of profit.

Overall, this fits remarkably well with Marx's hypotheses in *Capital*. First, there is a clear tendency for the organic composition of capital to rise, and this is the largest influence on the rate of profit. Second, there is also a clear tendency for the rate of surplus value to rise, but its effect on the rate of profit is much smaller than the rising OCC. Third, the other potential counteracting factors considered here do in fact tend to exert upward pressure on the rate of profit. Fourth, these counteracting factors operate in the way Marx describes them, in that they do not eliminate the tendency for the rate of profit to fall, but counteract it to some extent.

The only aspect of this analysis which Marx does not identify so clearly is the tendency for $(s - u) / s$ to decline over time. These results suggest the decline of this ratio from 1998 due to higher unproductive outlays was the most important *immediate* cause of the fall in the rate of profit leading up to the Great Recession. But over the longer-term the rising OCC has been the most important reason for the fall in the $s - u$ measure of the rate of profit. Let us see if we get similar results from decomposing movements in the corporate before-tax rate of profit on production. This is graphed in Figure 34 below.

Here the effect of the rising OCC on the falling rate of profit is even clearer. We can also see that the reason for the increase in the rate of profit in the early 2000s was mainly due to a fall in the difference between wages paid to

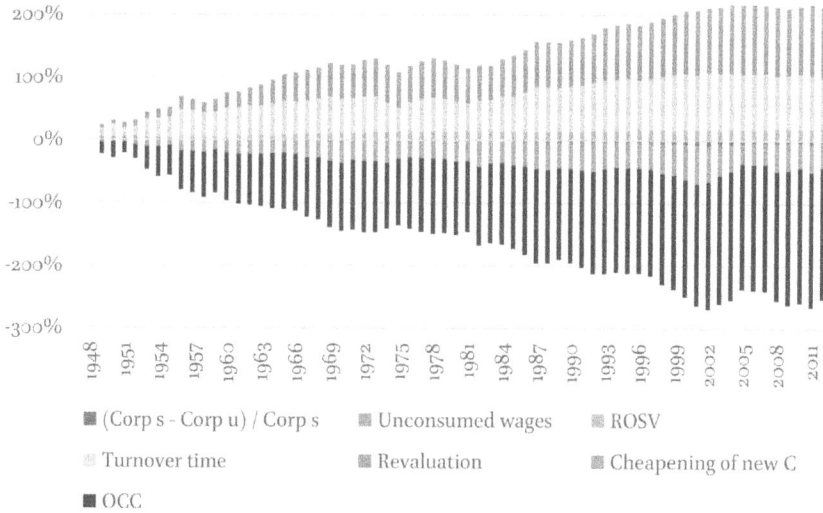

FIGURE 34   Influences on the corporate pre-tax rate of profit on production

employees in productive sectors and the value of their labour power; i.e. an increase in the proportion of wages spent on consumption. As we saw above, this was mainly due to the effect of the Bush tax cuts on disposable personal income. In so far as these tax cuts affected compensation for employees of non-financial corporations, they made it possible for these employees' after-tax pay to increase without winning raises from their bosses.[18] Its effect alone accounts for around 78% of the 5.7 percentage point increase in the pre-tax corporate rate of profit on production between 2002 and 2006 (i.e. the other effects tended to balance one another out over the period). The tax cuts therefore had roughly their intended result: even insofar as the *incidence* of the tax cuts applied to workers' incomes, their *effect* appears to have helped business and the rich generally, and possibly helped to delay the onset of recession (though perhaps increasing its severity), by allowing pre-tax wages to stagnate.[19] But

---

18   However, as mentioned above, the Bush tax cuts disproportionately benefited people on higher incomes. This makes no difference to our results for the pre-tax corporate rate of profit on production, since that is based on subtracting *pre*-tax employee compensation, not after-tax compensation. But it is likely to make a difference to the extent to which we attribute the increase in the rate of profit from 2002 to the effect of a change in the difference between the price and value of labour power and the extent to which we attribute it to an increase in the rate of surplus value (however there is also the difference between the true and the estimated rates of employees' saving to consider).

19   This does not mean workers would have been better off without the tax cuts that applied to them, since it is possible that without them their after-tax real wages would have fallen.

since the tax cuts mostly did not correspond to reductions in government unproductive expenditures, and were instead deficit-financed, they contributed to the general build-up of fictitious capital relative to genuine capital in the lead up to the recession, as we will see further below. That is, the boost they gave to profits from production through government borrowing was fictitious.

4   The Rate of Profit and Financial Rates of Return

Chapter 7 theorised the relationship between the rate of profit and financial rates of return. The main idea was that the net stock of financial assets (or 'fictitious capital') owned by individuals is generally larger than the stock of produced capital over which it is a claim. This means that the average non-fictitious rate of return on financial assets is generally lower than the $s - u$ rate of profit. The difference between the stock of fictitious and genuine capital is the result of the past accumulation of fictitious profit; and if enough fictitious profit is produced, then the actual rate of return on financial assets can be higher than the non-fictitious rate. The production of fictitious profits is essentially the result of share market traders and property investors bidding up prices of financial assets and land, but government borrowing can also push after-tax profits on production above non-fictitious profits and create additional fictitious capital.

This is an inherently unstable process. Even assuming $(s - u) / C$ remains constant, as fictitious profits accumulate the non-fictitious rate of return declines. If the accumulation of fictitious profit leads yields to fall far enough, this may trigger investors to sell financial assets at lower prices. Alternatively, a sell-off may be triggered by a falling underlying rate of profit and the effect this has on earnings. Either way, this puts the process into reverse: average rates of return on financial assets fall (though yields may rise), and potentially plummet, as investors sell their financial assets at lower prices. Real investment may also collapse, and to a lesser extent consumption spending, as investors and consumers hoard 'cash' to try to protect their savings. The fictitious losses this creates destroy fictitious capital, which may lead to a recovery in yields and in the non-fictitious rate of return once businesses are able to sell enough of their output. However, if the non-fictitious rate of profit is low, and the crisis does not lead to enough devaluation of actual capital for the rate of profit to recover, then the recovery will be long and drawn out.

How well do the data fit this theory? The data we need (the Integrated Macroeconomic Accounts) only stretch back to 1960, but fortunately this covers the two major crises of the postwar period. The first graph below gives two measures of the average non-fictitious rate of return on individuals' capital,

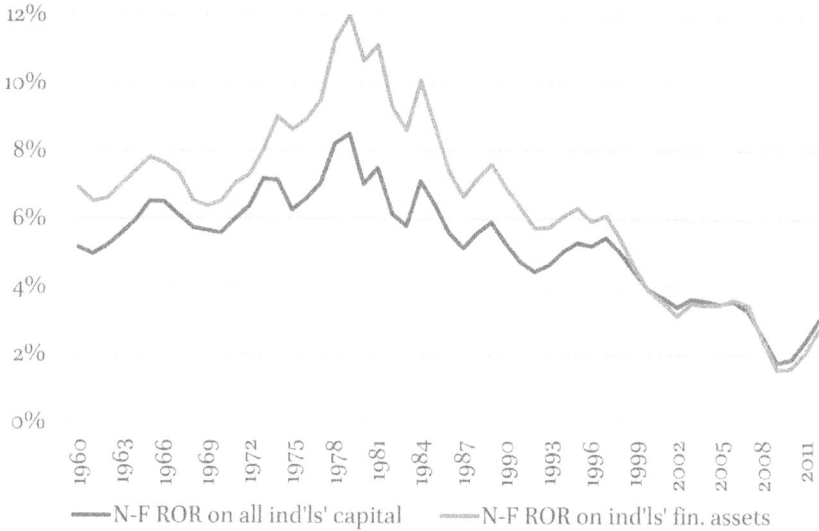

FIGURE 35   Non-fictitious rates of return on individuals' capital

one including equity in the non-corporate sector (which includes investments in rental housing) and one excluding it. These are the non-fictitious rates of return on all individuals' capital and on individuals' financial assets respectively.

We can see here one major difference between trends in these rates of return and the non-fictitious measures of the rate of profit: after the 1970s, there is a major recovery in the rate of return on individuals' fictitious capital, whereas the underlying rate of profit continues to fall. This is because, as Figure 36 shows, the crises of the 1970s destroyed a large chunk of fictitious capital, without any major devaluation or destruction of genuine capital (i.e. the ratio of individuals' capital to produced capital declined). A more significant devaluation of genuine capital did occur in the early 1980s (leading to an increase in the ratios), but it was never enough to allow the non-fictitious rate of profit to recover.

In 1974 and 1981, the ratio of individuals' capital to actual capital briefly approaches 1.25: i.e. the value of the total claims on produced capital (and land) comes close to the current market value of the produced capital over which it is a claim. The ratio of financial assets to produced capital over which they are a claim falls below one. Note that this does not mean that the value of financial assets is below the value of *all* the assets over which it is a claim, because businesses own many assets which are not produced capital, such as land. The fall in these ratios was due to the considerable destruction of fictitious cap-

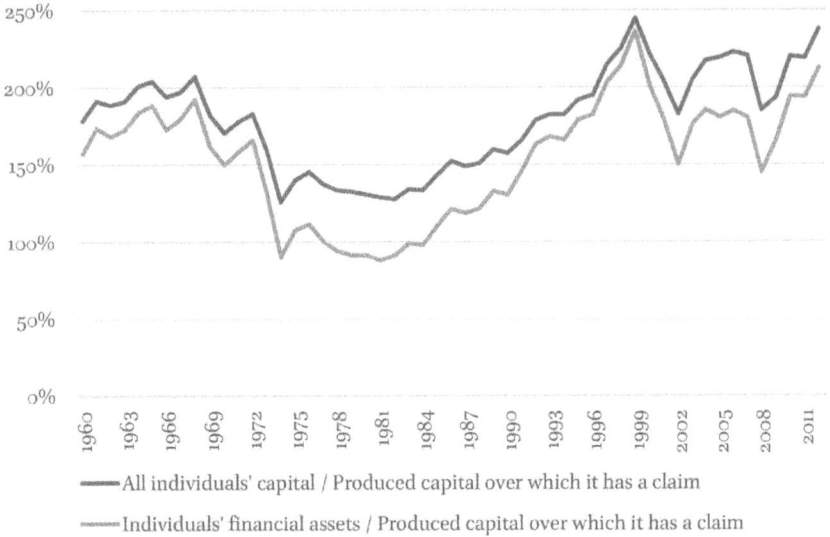

FIGURE 36   Ratios of produced capital to fictitious capital

ital which occurred over 1973 and 1974. In nominal terms, this devaluation was not large: by the end of 1974 the nominal value of individuals' capital was only 5.2% smaller than at the end of 1972. But due to inflation, in MELT-adjusted terms it fell by 18%. This inflation had the opposite effect on the value of produced capital, in MELT-adjusted terms: there was an upwards revaluation, and its value *increased* by 19%. This is probably because the high rate of inflation created an incentive to hold produced assets directly, since their prices tend to increase with the general rate of inflation. On the other hand, financial assets, especially those which are claims over debt, tend to be devalued in real terms by inflation because it reduces the value of debt in real terms. The relatively low ratio of individuals' capital to produced capital persists until the 'Volcker shock' brings down the rate of inflation through very high interest rates.

There follows a long period during which the non-fictitious rate of return declines, due to a build-up of fictitious capital relative to produced capital. This happens despite the gradual increase in the underlying rate of profit from its low in 1983. This process of the production of fictitious profit becomes significantly more rapid after 1996, and the ratio of fictitious to real capital peaks at the end of 1999. The 'dot com' crash which follows involves a sharp devaluation of fictitious capital, comparable to the devaluation of the early 1970s. But this does not go far enough to allow the non-fictitious rate of return to recover. It remains stable and low until the Great Recession. During the recession itself it falls even further, before recovering a little with the beginning of the recovery.

Interestingly, the ratio of fictitious to real capital falls less far during the Great Recession than during the early 1970s and the dot com crash. This is not explained by the fact that the property market fell by a large amount relative to the fall in the stock market, since the ratio of individuals' capital to produced capital incorporates the value of rental property. If the primary cause of the Great Recession was the financial and property market crisis, then why did financial and property markets not fall further? And when financial markets had recovered by 2011, why was the recovery in growth that accompanied it so sluggish? The financial and property market crash was clearly a *catalyst* for the Great Recession, but the fall in the underlying rate of profit is a much more plausible explanation for the recession, the crisis that triggered it, and the slow recovery afterwards. Since the end of the recession until the end of the chart the ratio of fictitious to non-fictitious capital has increased dramatically, as stock and property markets have 'recovered' while real investment has not.

In general, movements in the rate of profit defined in terms of $s - u$ give some indication of devaluations in fictitious capital relative to genuine capital. The three major devaluations since 1960 start in 1973, 1999 and 2007. In all cases these came during periods in which the underlying rate of profit had already begun to decline. However, they were not all *triggered* by declines in profitability: at least, not so far as we can tell using annual data. In particular, most measures of the rate of profit reach a small local maximum in 1973, though as part of what is clearly a broader downward trend. Nor is the devaluation of fictitious capital necessarily associated with a prior decline in the non-fictitious rate of return, which also increases between 1972 and 1973. Even the Great Recession was not *immediately* preceded by a significant fall in any measures of the rate of profit; the largest falls preceding it occurred between 1998 and 2003.

This is probably partly, perhaps mostly, explained by the Federal Reserve's conscious decision to keep interest rates 'artificially' low, and the effect of the Bush tax cuts, which together increased the incentive for investors to buy property and other riskier assets, and made more income available to the rich. These policies were responses to the underlying weakness in the rate of growth and in particular in investment, which was a result of the low rate of profit. If rates of investment and growth had returned to more 'normal' levels, no doubt the Fed would have allowed the interest rate to rise.

Finally, the decomposition below makes clear that the overwhelming reason for the decline in the non-fictitious rate of return after 1998 is the decline in the underlying rate of profit. Also note that after 2006 net foreign transfer payments (and in particular net foreign-sourced income) become an increasingly

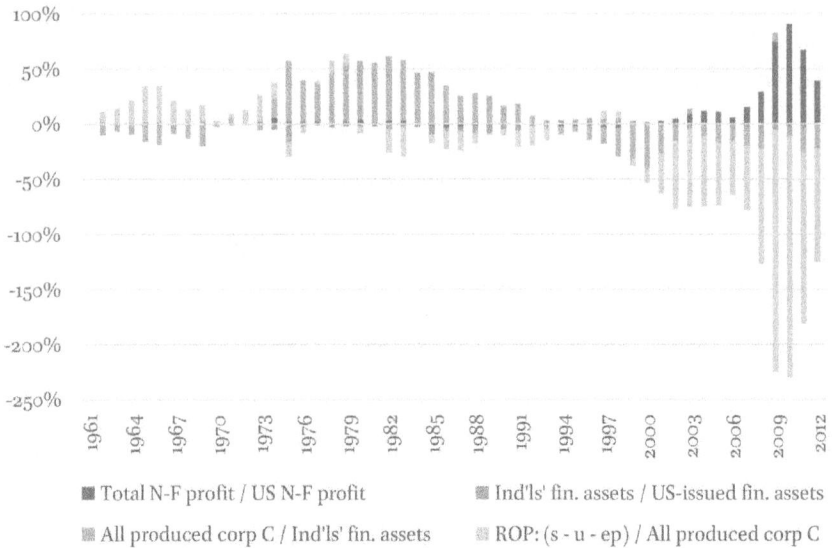

FIGURE 37   Influences on the non-fictitious rate of return on individuals' financial assets

important source of non-fictitious profit. This is probably because, with the decline in the mass of non-fictitious profit produced domestically due to the Great Recession, financial profit appropriated from other countries becomes relatively more important. Net foreign sourced income also grows considerably in absolute terms. This may be worth investigating further in other work.

4.1   *Interest Rates and Financial Rates of Return*

Chapters 5 and 6 also explored Marx's views on the dynamics of the interest rate, and hypothesised its movements would be related to movements in the non-fictitious rate of return on financial assets. As Figure 38 shows, there is quite a close relationship between trends in both measures of the non-fictitious rate of return and the Federal Funds Rate (the rate of interest paid on Treasury bonds). The R squared measure of correlation with the non-fictitious rate of return on all individuals' capital is 0.54, and with the non-fictitious rate of return on individuals' financial assets it is 0.62.

It is worth saying more about how we might explain this relationship. In general, if the non-fictitious rate of return is high, we would expect the dividend yield on stocks to also be high, because higher non-fictitious profit means more funds are available to pay dividends. A high dividend yield encourages investors into stocks and away from bonds, which pushes up the interest rate. There is also likely to be causation in the opposite direction: if, for example, the Federal Reserve 'artificially' cuts interest rates, this should temporarily increase the 'risk

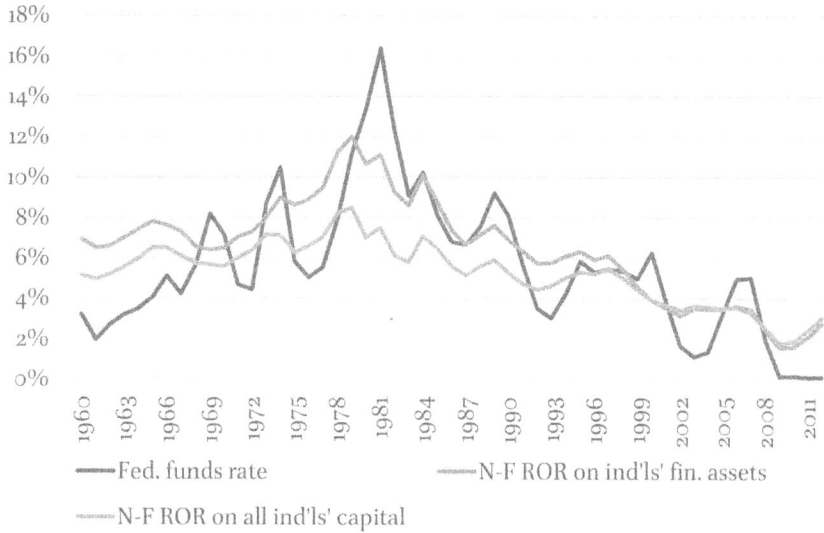

FIGURE 38   Non-fictitious rates of return and the interest rate

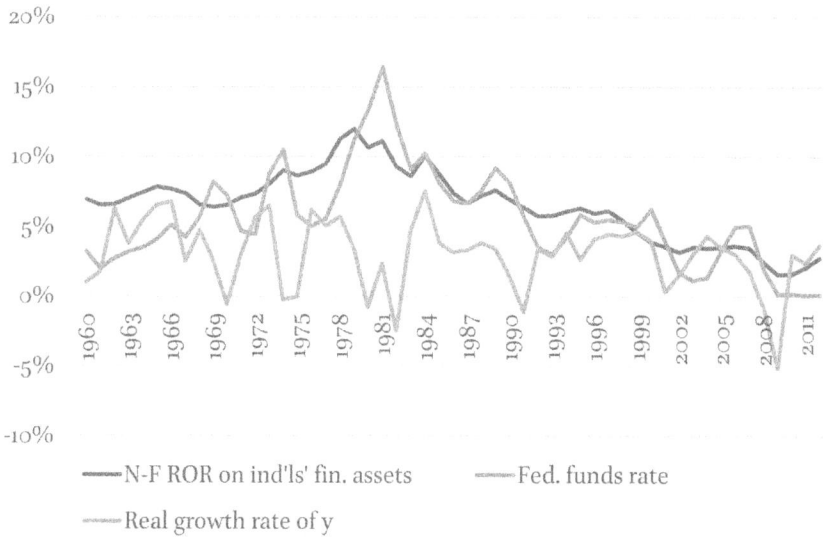

FIGURE 39   The non-fictitious rate of return, the interest rate and the rate of growth of output

premium' on offer for holding stocks and property, leading investors to bid up land and share prices, increasing the total stock of fictitious capital and pushing down the non-fictitious rate of return.

However, there is also a more cyclical movement in the interest rate which only appears to affect the non-fictitious rate of return to a smaller degree. Chapter 5 noted that Marx observed a tendency for the rate of interest to be at a local minimum at the 'height' of the business cycle, when activity is highest, then to rise between 'prosperity and its collapse', and finally to reach a maximum 'up to extreme usury' with the onset of crisis.[20] To test this, the graph below includes the Federal Funds Rate, the non-fictitious rate of return on individuals' financial assets, and the real rate of growth of output.[21]

Marx's hypothesised inverse relationship between the interest rate and the level of economic activity in the short-term does seem to be present: troughs in growth are generally near peaks in the interest rate, and *vice versa*. It is possible that troughs in growth tend to come just after peaks in the interest rate. Although there are hints of the same short-term dynamic in the non-fictitious rate of return, it is much less variable over the short-term.

The other financial results we want to investigate are the actual rates of return on fictitious capital: both rates of return incorporating capital gains, and dividend and interest yields. Figure 40 first looks at the yields compared to the non-fictitious rates of return.

As we expected, there is some similarity in the trends, though the yield on financial assets is more variable than the yield including non-corporate equity. The R squared between the non-fictitious rate of return on financial assets and the yield on financial assets is 0.44. The gap between these two series before 1982 is probably explained by corporations' higher propensity to finance investment by retaining their profits, instead of issuing new financial capital, leaving less profit to pay out as dividends.

Next, below are the total rates of return, i.e. incorporating capital gains as well as dividends, interest and withdrawals from non-corporate businesses (after subtracting proprietors' 'wages'). Figure 41 graphs this in nominal terms and then Figure 42 adjusts for inflation.

The most profitable time for individuals to own capital was after the crises of the 1970s, but before the dot com crash. Despite the low rate of profit relative to the 1960s, the total rate of return was relatively high because of the build-up of fictitious capital relative to actual capital, and the fictitious profits produced

---

20   Marx 1981, p. 482.
21   Ideally this would be based on quarterly data; this task is left for future work.

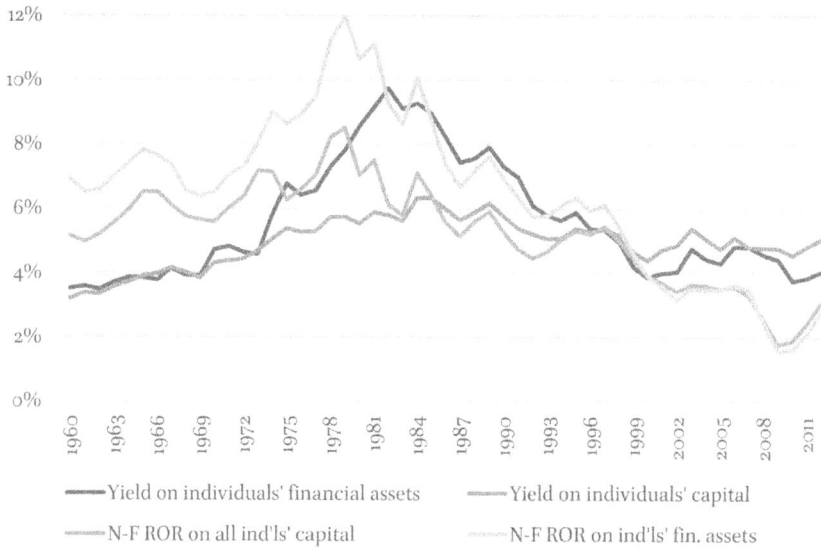

FIGURE 40   Non-fictitious rates of return and yield on individuals' capital

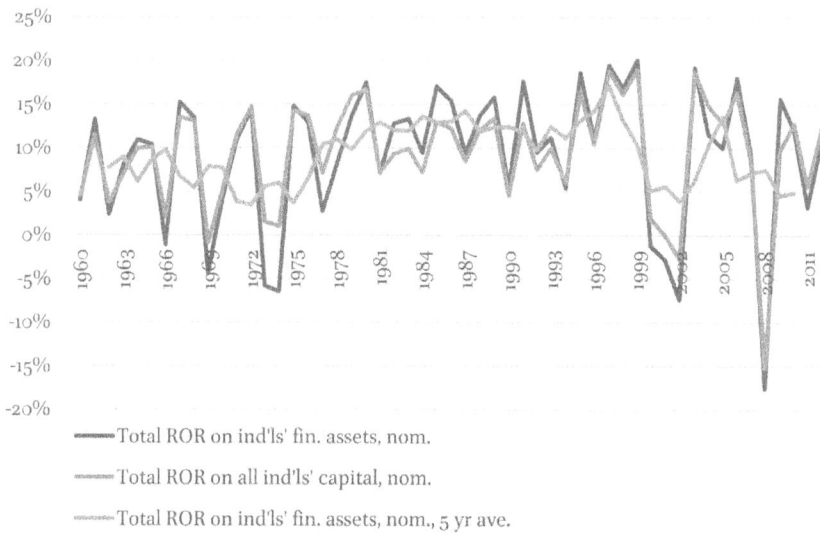

FIGURE 41   Total rates of return on individuals' capital, nominal

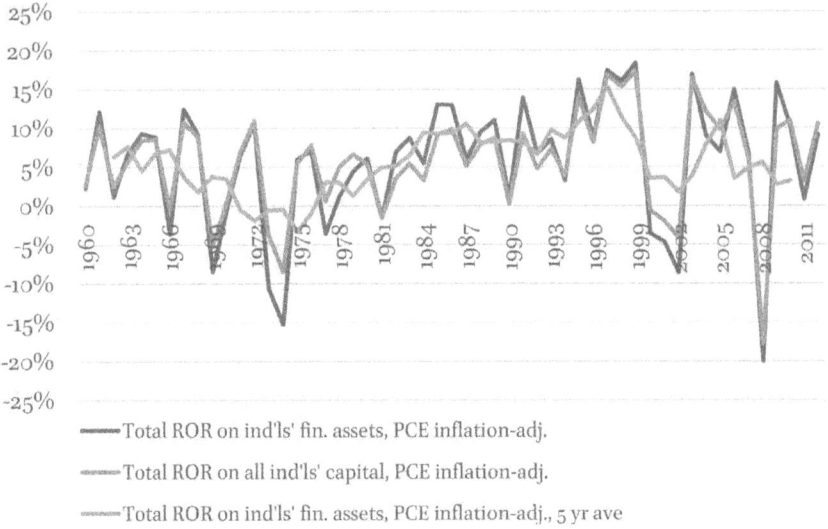

FIGURE 42   Total rates of return on individuals' capital, real

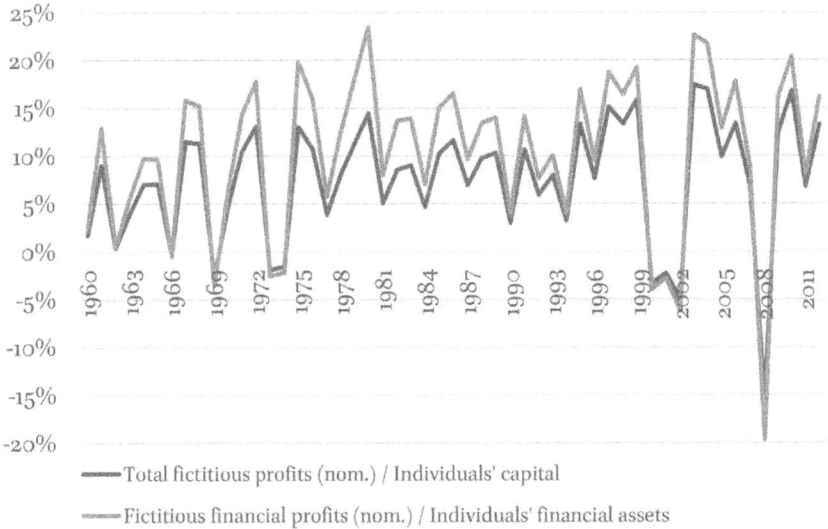

FIGURE 43   Fictitious components of nominal rates of return

as a result. Another way of seeing this same result is to calculate these fictitious profits directly, using the method outlined in Chapter 6. Below this is calculated in nominal terms and expressed as a percentage of individuals' financial assets and capital:

5   The Rate of Profit and the Interest Rate over the Long Term

Finally, we will turn to Marx's claims that there is a long-run tendency for the rate of profit to fall and that this leads to a long-run tendency for the interest rate to fall. It is difficult to get any reliable measure of the rate of profit in the US stretching back before 1929 (because this is when data collection for the most important national accounting aggregates commences), and it is probably not possible to measure the rate of profit defined in terms of $s - u$ or profits from production at all.

Duménil and Lévy have constructed estimates for the US rate of profit since 1869 using a more basic measure.[22] They define the rate of profit as net national product after wages (including an imputation for 'wages' of petty-bourgeois producers) divided by the stock of fixed assets. Figure 44 below calculates an index measure of the rate of profit by taking their estimates for the rate of profit from 1869 until 1930, and then using changes in the $s - u$ measure of the rate of profit for the corporate sector from 1930–2015.

The results fit well with Marx's hypothesis of long-term tendency for the rate of profit to fall, despite the large increase in the rate of profit associated with the devaluation and disaccumulation of capital associated with the Great Depression and WWII. The R squared with the linear trend is negligibly small, but given the effect of the increase in the rate of profit after WWII this is not surprising. It is perhaps not ideal that we start with what looks to be a peak in the rate of profit in the 1870s after the destruction of the Civil War, and end with a trough after the Great Recession, but this is the period over which we have data. It is also not clear to what extent the US rate of profit before the Civil War would have been subject to Marx's law, given the existence of slavery in the South. In any case, as we will see below, if the rate of interest is a reasonable proxy for the rate of profit over the long term, there is no evidence that starting the series earlier would give a significantly different trend.

The data available for the interest rate are more reliable, since they can be obtained by looking at quotations of interest rates actually offered by banks.

---

22   Duménil and Lévy 1994; Duménil and Lévy 2013.

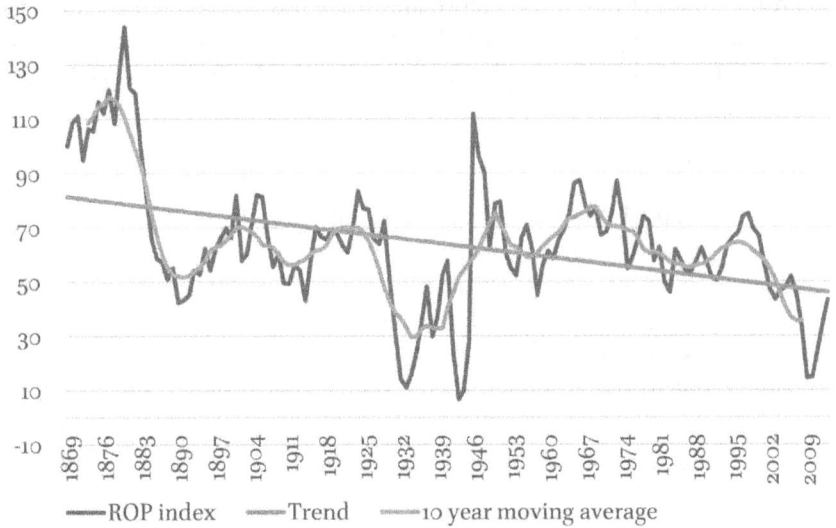

FIGURE 44   Long-term rate of profit index

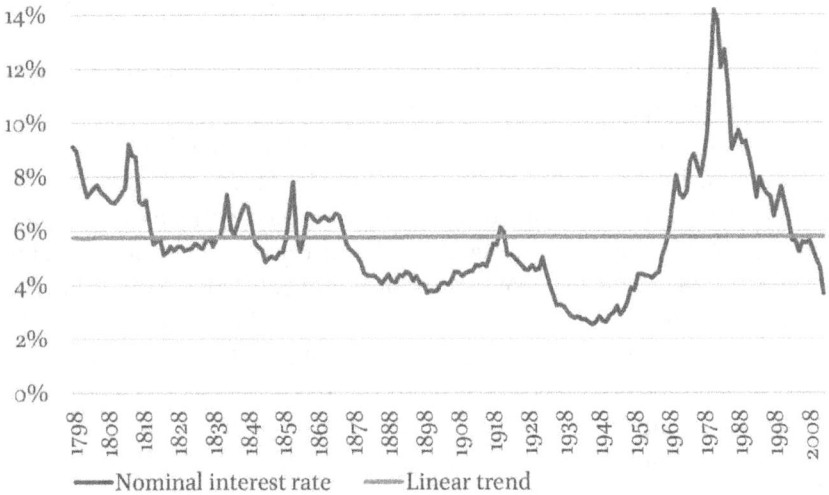

FIGURE 45   Long-term nominal rate of profit

The *MeasuringWorth* website established by Officer and Williamson publishes estimates of economic time series from the 1790s onwards, including the US interest rate.[23]

First, below is a graph of their series for the US interest rate in nominal terms starting in 1798. Across the period as a whole, the linear trend is virtually completely flat, appearing to disconfirm Marx's hypothesis.

It looks as though the main reason the series has no linear trend is because at the end of the postwar boom and especially during the crisis after it there is a large increase in the rate of inflation. Up until then the downward trend is clear. For this reason, it would be a mistake to rule out Marx's hypothesis without also looking at trends in the rate of interest after adjusting for inflation. Indeed, it is more reasonable to interpret Marx's hypothesis as a claim concerning the interest rate after inflation, since this is the cost that is relevant to a capitalist who borrows in order to invest in productive assets (because the price of these assets and the output they are used to produce also tend to increase with inflation), and since the LTFRP also applies to the rate of profit in inflation-adjusted terms.

The *MeasuringWorth* site also gives two estimates of inflation over the same period: one using a GDP deflator and the other using a consumer price index (CPI). For this purpose the GDP deflator is a better measure because it estimates the rate of inflation for all goods and services that make up GDP (including the cost of new investments) and not only the prices of goods and services purchased by consumers. Ideally, however, we would use increases in the MELT as our measure of inflation. Without national accounts data we cannot estimate the MELT directly, but we can get a very crude estimate if we use the percentage increase in nominal GDP per capita (by making the assumptions that the ratio of population to socially necessary labour time remains constant, that the value of depreciation is zero, and that GDP is equal to output of commodities).

Figure 45, Figure 46 and Figure 47 graph the estimates of the real interest rate obtained using each approach.

Using all three measures, the real interest rate has a downward trend over the long term, punctuated by sharp increases associated with crises. Note also there is evidence of a weaker downward trend in the real rate of GDP growth:

This data set also allows us to better test Marx's hypothesis that the interest rate tends to mirror the level of economic activity over the short-term (i.e. it tends to be high when activity is low and low when activity is high). Figure 49 is a graph of the real GDP growth rate and the real interest rate, adjusted for inflation in the GDP deflator. Because of the volatility in both series it is hard to say much based on comparing the two series visually.

---

23   Officer 2014; Williamson 2014; Officer and Williamson 2013.

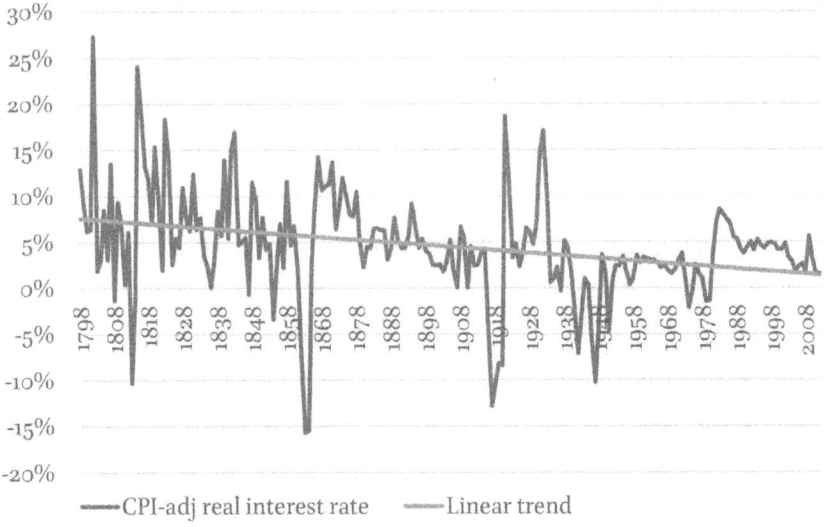

FIGURE 46   Long-term real interest rate, CPI-adjusted

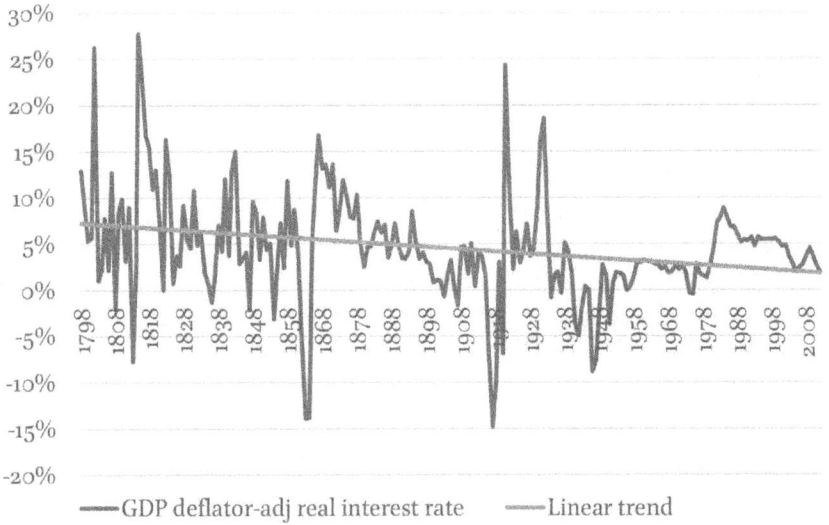

FIGURE 47   Long-term real interest rate, GDP-deflator adjusted

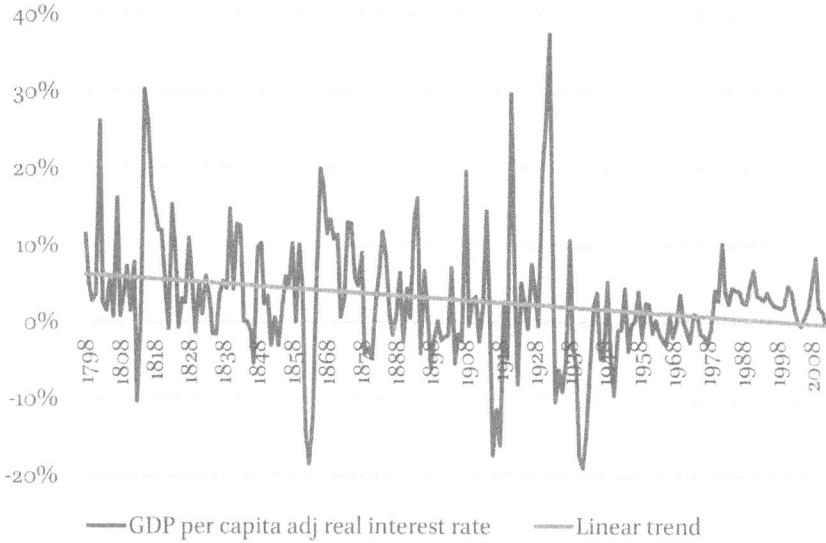

FIGURE 48   Long-term real interest rate, per capita GDP-adjusted

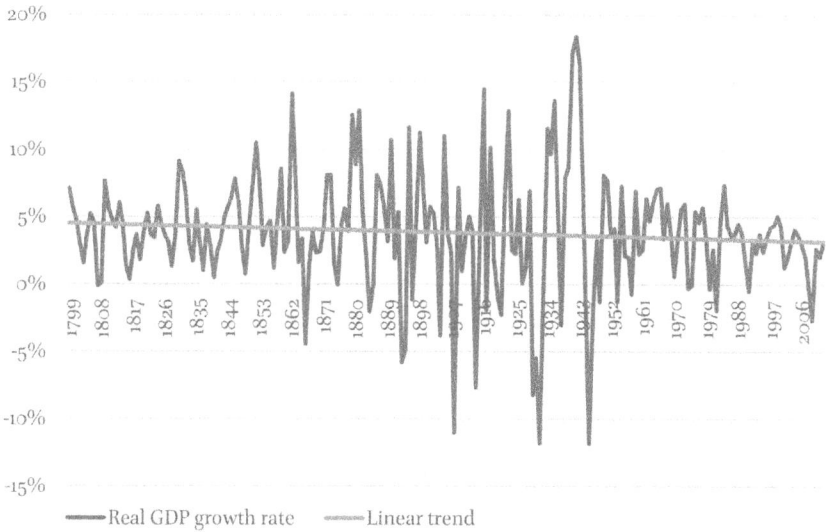

FIGURE 49   Long-term real GDP growth rate

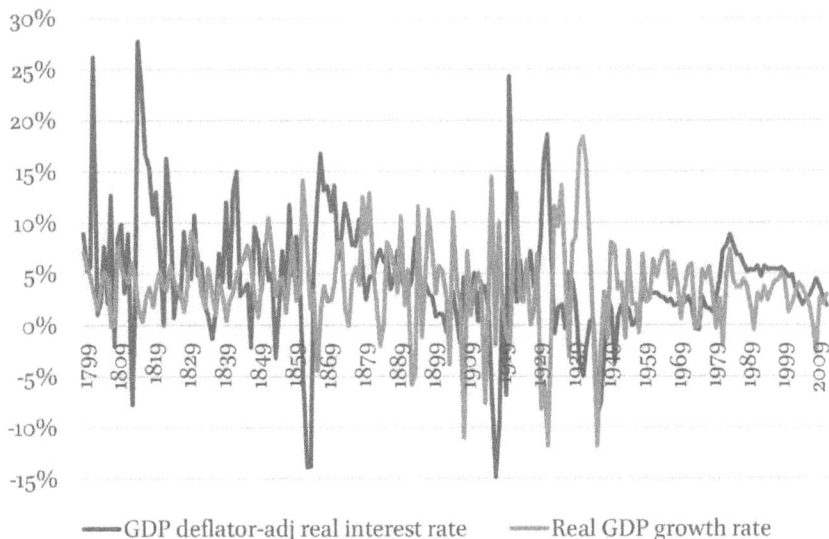

FIGURE 50   Real interest rate vs. real growth rate, long-term

After applying the HP filter to both series we get a clearer picture (in Figure 51).

First, we can see that 'maximum interest up to extreme usury corresponds to a period of crisis'.[24] The largest peaks in the real interest rate using the GDP deflator occur in 1802, 1815, 1843, 1858, 1867, 1921, 1932 and 1984. Except for 1984, these were all recession years.[25] 1984 is an anomaly, probably because the high interest rate was the result of aggressive intervention by the Federal Reserve. In any case, the peak in the interest rate in 1984 can be seen as marking the end of the crisis beginning in the mid-1970s. There was also a smaller peak in the real interest rate in 2009, associated with the fall in inflation during the Great Recession (which does not register after applying the filter).

Second, until around 1830 the real interest rate is much higher than the rate of growth. Here a comment of Marx's concerning the determination of the interest rate before capitalism has formally subsumed labour is relevant:

> When comparison is made between countries at different levels of development, and particularly between countries of developed capitalist pro-

---

24   Marx 1981, p. 482.

25   The National Bureau of Economic Research provides dates for recessions in the US from 1854 onwards (NBER 2010). Before 1854, the best resource for dating recessions are the *Business Annals* compiled by the NBER in 1926 (Thorp and Thorp 1926), which Moore and Narnowitz compile into a table with dates of economic cycles and provide useful commentary. Moore and Narnowitz 1986, pp. 743–8.

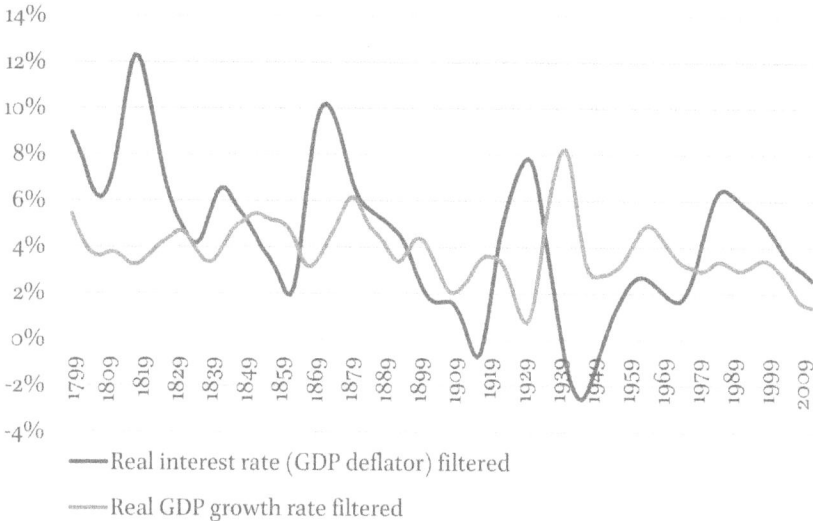

—Real interest rate (GDP deflator) filtered

------Real GDP growth rate filtered

FIGURE 51   Filtered real interest rate vs. filtered real growth rate, long-term

duction and those where labour is not yet formally subsumed by capital although in reality the worker is already exploited by the capitalist (in India, for example, where the *ryot* operates as an independent peasant farmer, and his production is not yet subsumed under capital, although the money-lender may well extort from him in the form of interest not only his entire surplus labour, but even – to put it in capitalist terms – a part of his wages), it would be quite wrong to seek to measure the national rate of profit by the level of the national rate of interest. Interest here includes both the entire profit and more than the profit, whereas in countries where capitalist production is developed it simply expresses an aliquot part of the surplus-value or profit produced. Moreover, in the former case the rate of interest is predominantly determined by factors such as the level of advances by money-lenders to the big landowners who are the recipients of ground-rent, which have nothing at all to do with profit but rather express the extent to which the money-lender himself appropriates this ground-rent.[26]

In the South before the Civil War slave labour *was* formally subsumed by capital, since the slave owners produced their crop to sell at a profit, but this was

26   Marx 1981, p. 321.

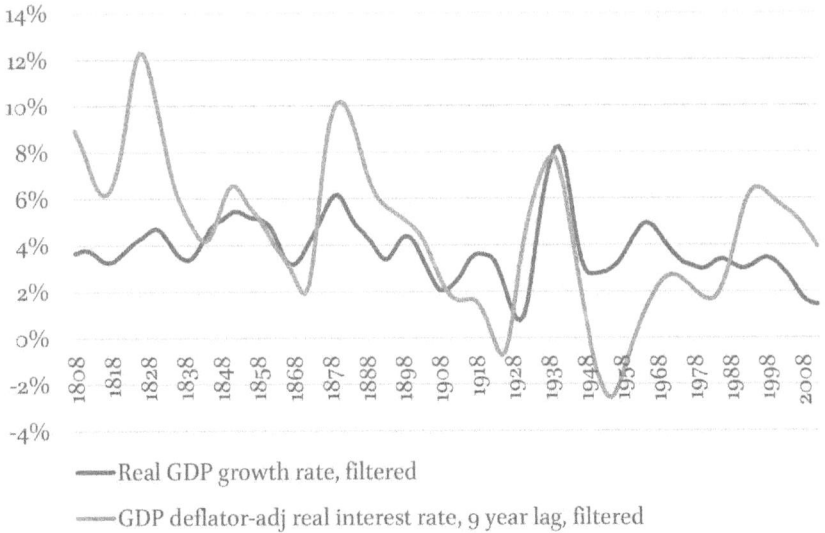

FIGURE 52   Filtered real interest rate with 9 year lag vs. filtered growth rate, long-term

arguably not a *real* subsumption, since it seems likely that these profits were overwhelmingly not invested in improving the means of production and re-organising production. So there was no strong basis for a tendency for the organic composition of capital to rise. It also seems likely that the interest rate would have been significantly influenced by the extent to which moneylenders appropriated the ground-rent from the plantations.

Third, and most importantly, it looks as though movements in the interest rate share a similar pattern to movements in real GDP growth, but that they are out of phase. We can see this more clearly still by taking the filtered series and applying a 9 year lag to the interest rate:

While the match is far from perfect, the cyclical movements in the two series do appear to roughly match up after applying the lag. As we would expect, the interest rate is generally more volatile than the rate of growth. It looks as though the appropriate lag is not fixed at 9 years: in the nineteenth century it looks more like 7 years while in the twentieth century it seems to extend to around 11 years. If we assume the interest rate is out of phase with the growth rate by half a cycle, as per Marx's hypothesis, then a lag of 7 to 11 years would correspond to business cycles of between 14 and 22 years.

In any case, Marx's two hypotheses concerning movements in the interest rate hold up well, if we interpret them as referring to the real interest rate. For the US, there does indeed appear to be a downward trend in the real interest rate over the long term, and a tendency for the interest rate to move between

7 to 11 years out of phase with movements in the business cycle. The long-term downward trend in the interest rate also fits with the evidence we have for a long-term downward trend in the rate of profit.

CHAPTER 8

Conclusions

1   The Rate of Profit and the Great Recession

The results strongly support the hypothesis that the Great Recession was the result of a prior decline in the rate of profit. By 2002, based on the more reliable measures, the rate of profit had declined over the long term, since its large increase after WWII, since its level immediately before the crises of the 1970s, and since its moderate recovery during the 1980s and 1990s, whether measured in terms of $s - u$, before-tax profits from production or after-tax profits from production.

But we do need to explain why, from 2003–05, rates of profit *on production* increased sharply, even though the rates of profit defined in terms of $s - u$ and rates of accumulation did not. This was overwhelmingly due to a stagnation in before-tax wages, which may have been compensated for to some extent by the Bush tax cuts. These tax cuts and low interest rates brought about an increase in the proportion of income spent on consumption, and may also have meant that although *wages* stagnated, the value of labour power did not. The tax cuts and low interest rates themselves were related to the falling rate of profit; specifically, they were responses to the weak economic conditions after the dot com crash, which was preceded by declines in all measures of rates of profit. Insofar as only the *gap* between the price and the value of labour power was narrowed, without actually driving down the value of labour power itself, this made no difference to the surplus value available for capitalists' consumption and investment; it improved the rate of profit on production that *appears* to capitalists, but not the rate of profit defined in terms of the actual *value* available to them. The general increase in the propensity to consume explains why the increase in rates of profit on production did not lead to a recovery in rates of accumulation. This analysis does not indicate that Bush and Greenspan were 'bad economic managers' but that, because their policies could not bring about a recovery in the rate of profit defined in terms of value, the boost their policies gave to the rate of profit on production could not indefinitely rescue US and world capitalism from a major crisis and recession.

Another consequence of the regime of low interest rates was to encourage the production of fictitious profit on property and financial markets, further creating the appearance of healthier economic conditions while driving down future rates of return on financial assets and property. These bubbles were therefore *symptoms* of the low underlying rate of profit. Compared to other bubbles, valuations in the property and financial markets relative to produced assets were not unusually high. Eventually these bubbles burst in the form of a property market crash combined with a credit crisis.

The results do not support the view that these financial and credit crises were the *underlying* cause of the Great Recession. The decline in the underlying rates of profit before 2007 is evidence against this explanation. Moreover, if the underlying cause of the Great Recession was the financial and credit crisis, then why did growth and employment not return to more 'normal' levels when financial and credit markets recovered? By 2010, the ratios of fictitious to genuine capital, for example, had recovered to around the same levels as before the financial crisis, indicating that investors' reluctance to buy shares and lend money had been overcome. Yet rates of employment and accumulation remained, and still remained by 2013, extremely low compared to other periods. While there had been a small recovery in measures of the rate of profit from their depths during the crisis, by 2013 capital has not been destroyed or devalued on a large enough scale to return rates of growth or employment to anywhere near 'normal' levels. The lack of devaluation of capital is a much more plausible explanation for the continuation of weak economic conditions than a financial and credit crisis which was severe but ended several years before the last years in the series analysed here (2012–13).

2   *Capital* and Marx's Value Theory

More importantly, what does this work establish concerning the usefulness and accuracy of Marx's analyses in *Capital*? Even some of Marx's most sympathetic critics regard *Capital* as at best a starting point from which to develop a superior or more complete theory. Mage, for example, who makes an early and perceptive critique of the Bortkiewicz-Sweezy non-solution to the transformation problem, completes his study of the falling rate of profit this way:

> It is plain, despite the scope, power, and basic clarity of his thought, that Marx left his system of economic analysis in a crude and unfinished form, that many vital concepts were poorly defined, and that essential parts of his model were not developed beyond the stage of artificial and unrealistic schemata. The endeavour to make an empirical test of one of the major 'laws' of this model, therefore, required the clarification and reformulation of these aspects of Marx's doctrine ...

The data developed through this test ... show clearly that Marx was no infallible prophet, that certain of his predictions proved to be invalid. But they also confirm that Marx was correct on the issues he regarded as decisive: the rising tendency of the organic composition of capital and the falling tendency of the rate of profit.

Confirmation on this vital score is not in any sense 'confirmation' of the Marxian economic theory as a whole – something which is in any case conceivable only through the integration of vast amounts of post-Marxian theory into the Marxian structure. What this study has shown is not that Marx is 'right' or 'wrong' – the point is, *that he is relevant.*[1]

We can of course agree that *Capital* is not perfect, and that Marx was not an infallible prophet. No one has ever reasonably argued otherwise. Can we agree, however, that Marx 'left his system of economic analysis in a crude and unfinished form'? This impression seems largely the result of Marx's 'failure' to translate all of his system into mathematical language. Marx touches on this issue when describing how his approach differs from that of classical political economy:

> Political economy has indeed analysed value and its magnitude, however incompletely, and has uncovered the content concealed within these forms. But it has never once asked the question why this content has assumed that particular form, that is to say, why labour is expressed in value, and why the measurement of labour by its duration is expressed in the magnitude of the value of the product. These formulas, which bear the unmistakable stamp of belonging to a social formation in which the process of production has mastery over man, instead of the opposite, appear to the political economists' bourgeois consciousness to be as much a self-evident and nature-imposed necessity as productive labour itself.[2]

Like Mage, this book has focused on Marx's development of the classicals' incomplete analysis of value and its magnitude. Marx does not 'complete' this analysis in the sense of developing a complete description of all of his concepts in mathematical language. Such a translation would have been useful. But mathematics is only a means through which arguments *might be* expressed more clearly. It is also possible to express arguments and concepts clearly

---

1   Mage 1963, pp. 231–2.
2   Marx 1976, pp. 173–5.

through ordinary language, or through more technical language which is non-mathematical. Where arguments or concepts refer to relationships between quantifiable concepts (e.g. value, surplus value, price, profit), it *should* be possible to express aspects of them mathematically, even if Marx himself does not do so, and this *can be* a more precise form in which to test the internal consistency of arguments.

On the other hand, too heavy a reliance on mathematical language or its misuse can reinforce the way in which the exchange of things makes capitalism appear natural or impossible to change; and it can obscure the fact that labour under capitalism has a *dual* nature, both abstract *and* concrete; that is, it can obscure the fact that capital is a *social relation*. Neoclassical economics harnesses this fetish-inducing power of mathematical language very effectively, in a way that takes it many steps backwards from the categories of bourgeois economics developed by the classicals. Ultimately, the point of Marx's value theory is to show that our domination by capital, the law of value and the LTFRP can be understood and can also *be changed*. Doubts about whether Marx's value theory really 'adds up' have held some Marxists back from embracing it, and this work has focused on exploring whether those doubts are justified. This should stimulate further study and concretisation of Marx's value theory *as a whole*, and *not only* its quantitative aspects.

The 'incomplete' nature of Marx's quantitative analysis may also be related to the limited statistics he had with which to analyse value. If better statistics *had* been available, he or Engels may well have gone further with the task of expressing their arguments in mathematical form, as Engels' following comment suggests:

> Since there are certainly only a few capitalists who make calculations of such a kind about their businesses, statistical material is almost completely absent on the ratio of the constant part of the total social capital to the variable part. Only the US Census gives what is possible under present-day conditions, the sum of the wages paid in each branch and the profits made. Dubious as these data are, owing to the way they rely on the unchecked information of the industrialists themselves, they are none the less extremely valuable and the only data that we have on the subject. In Europe we are far too kind-hearted to expect such revelations on the part of our great industrialists.[3]

---

3   Marx 1981, p. 169.

If it is valid, the interpretation offered in this book has shown that the most important quantitative aspects of Marx's value theory indeed *can be* expressed in mathematical language, without needing to make major 'corrections'. It has gone further than existing interpretations by showing:

1. how cost-reducing technological change can lead to a falling rate of profit *and* how this can be reversed by devaluation;
2. how the main influences Marx identifies on the rate of profit can be represented mathematically; and
3. how Marx's incomplete work on finance can be extended to explain the relationship between the rate of profit, rates of return on financial assets and the interest rate.

It has also shown that this interpretation is compatible with US national accounting statistics, which have allowed us to test important predictions of Marx's theory. Specifically, the results support Marx's hypotheses that, over the long term, as the forces of production develop:

1. the production of relative surplus value tends to increase the rate of surplus value;
2. the turnover time of variable capital tends to shorten;
3. the organic composition of capital tends to rise;
4. the value composition of capital tends to rise;
5. moral depreciation tends to devalue constant capital;
6. the rate of profit tends to fall; and
7. the (real) interest rate tends to fall.

In addition, over shorter time periods, the results support the hypotheses that:

8. the real interest rate tends to move in the opposite direction to the business cycle; and, most importantly
9. the rate of profit tends to fall in the lead up to major crises, and rise if and when they destroy or devalue sufficient capital.

This impressive list of accurate predictions is not evidence that Marx was clairvoyant, or that he made lucky guesses. In the cases of hypotheses 2–5, once they are formulated correctly, it is clear why Marx would have thought they were very likely to be consequences of the development of the forces of production. The hypothesis that the rate of surplus value tends to increase is perhaps a little bolder, but also strongly suggested by the history of capitalist development Marx had witnessed. The hypothesis that the rate of profit tends to fall over the long term was similarly consistent with the evidence Marx had available and, moreover, a consensus among classical political economists.

Yet without a better explanation of *why* the rate of profit tends to fall than that provided by the classicals, it would have been a mistake for Marx to make it such a central part of his theory of historical materialism. *Capital* provides this explanation by showing how the other hypotheses listed above make it likely that the rate of profit will fall over time and, crucially, how this will lead to recurrent economic crises while the capitalist mode of production remains. Marx's explanation of how crises devalue capital and can allow the rate of profit to recover also departs from classical political economy, by generalising from his experience and his dialectical conception of change. The remaining two hypotheses concerning the interest rate are also both generalisations from experience, and related to Marx's LTFRP. The success of Marx's analysis is therefore not an accident, but the result of years of careful intellectual labour.

The interpretation of Marx's system offered here may help to answer other questions about the nature of contemporary (or 'neoliberal') capitalism. For example, the results above suggest that, whatever 'neoliberal' capitalism is, it has not involved major *breaks* in the main tendencies mentioned above. Its symptoms are more likely to be a result of the continuation of these tendencies. One task that this work has not attempted is to give a concrete explanation of the link between these tendencies and the symptoms of 'neoliberalism'.

More generally, a more concrete explanation of the structure of contemporary capitalism, grounded in value theory, would be an important tool and guide for socialists. Like any social change, creating socialism depends on human beings making history 'under circumstances existing already, given and transmitted from the past'; unlike most other social change, it requires a high degree of consciousness of those circumstances and how to change them.[4] Marx was enthusiastic about the Paris Commune, despite its inevitable political defeat, because he saw it as 'the political form at last discovered under which to work out the economical emancipation of labour'.[5] At high points in struggle workers have since created an even more promising form of democratic political power: workers' councils. If workers create such political forms in future, we will not only need to confront the political problem of winning state power; we will also need to work out our economic emancipation. If we use its insights properly, *Capital* may have a great deal to teach us about doing that.

---

4   Marx 1995, chapter I.
5   Marx 1986, p. 334.

Bibliography

Albert, Michael 2003, *Parecon: Life After Capitalism*, London: Verso.

Arthur, Christopher 2004, *The New Dialectic and Marx's* Capital, Leiden: Brill.

Basu, Deepankar and Ramaa Vasudevan 2012, 'Technology, Distribution and the Rate of Profit in the US Economy: Understanding the Current Crisis', *Cambridge Journal of Economics*, 37, no. 11: 57–89.

Bortkiewicz, Landislaus 1952, 'Value and Price in the Marxian System', translated by J. Kahane, *International Economic Papers*, 2: 5–60.

Callinicos, Alex 2014, *Deciphering Capital*, London: Bookmarks.

Carchedi, Guglielmo 1984, 'The Logic of Prices as Values', *Economy and Society*, 13, no. 4: 431–55.

Carchedi, Guglielmo 1991, *Frontiers of Political Economy*, London: Verso.

Carchedi, Guglielmo 2009, 'From Okishio to Marx through Dialectics', *Capital & Class*, 99 (Autumn): 59–79.

Carchedi, Guglielmo 2011, 'Behind and Beyond the Crisis', *International Socialism*, 132.

Carchedi, Guglielmo and Alan Freeman (eds) 1996, *Marx and Non-Equilibrium Economics*, Cheltenham: Edward Elgar.

Carchedi, Guglielmo and Michael Roberts 2013a, 'A Critique of Heinrich's, "Crisis Theory, the Law of the Tendency of the Profit Rate to Fall, and Marx's Studies in the 1870s"', *Monthly Review Website*, 12 January, available at: http://monthlyreview.org/commentary/critique-heinrichs-crisis-theory-law-tendency-profit-rate-fall-marxs-studies-1870s.

Carchedi, Guglielmo and Michael Roberts 2013b, 'The Long Roots of the Present Crisis: Keynesians, Austerians, and Marx's Law', *World Review of Political Economy*, 4, no. 1: 86–115.

Cliff, Tony 1974 [1948], *State Capitalism in Russia*, London: Pluto Press.

Day, Richard 1981, *The Crisis and the Crash: Soviet Studies of the West (1917–1939)*, London: New Left Books.

Duménil, Gérard 1983, 'Beyond the Transformation Riddle: A Labor Theory of Value', *Science & Society*, 47, no. 4: 427–50.

Duménil, Gérard and Dominique Lévy 1994, 'The US Economy Since the Civil War: Sources and Construction of the Series' available at: http://www.cepremap.fr/membres/dlevy/dle1994e.htm.

Duménil, Gérard and Dominique Lévy 2002, 'The Field of Capital Mobility and the Gravitation of Profit Rates', *Review of Radical Political Economics*, 34: 417–36.

Duménil, Gérard and Dominique Lévy 2011, *The Crisis of Neoliberalism*, Cambridge, MA: Harvard University Press.

Duménil, Gérard and Dominique Lévy 2013, 'The US Economy Since the Civil War:

Database,' available at: http://www.jourdan.ens.fr/levy/uslt4x.txt accessed 02/09/ 2014.

Draper, Hal 2011 [1986], *Karl Marx's Theory of Revolution: Volume 3, The 'Dictatorship of the Proletariat'*, India: Aakar Books.

Dunayevskaya, Raya 1988 [1958], *Marxism and Freedom: From 1776 Until Today*, New York: Columbia University Press.

Engels, Friedrich 1976 [1847], *Principles of Communism*, in *Marx and Engels Collected Works*, Volume 6, New York: International Publishers.

Engels, Friedrich 1978a [1850], *The Ten Hours Question*, in *Marx and Engels Collected Works*, Volume 10, New York: International Publishers.

Engels, Friedrich 1978b [1850], *The English Ten Hours' Bill*, in *Marx and Engels Collected Works*, Volume 10, New York: International Publishers.

Engels, Friedrich 1985 [1870], *Preface to the Second Edition of the Peasant War in Germany*, in *Marx and Engels Collected Works*, Volume 21, New York: International Publishers.

Engels, Friedrich 1987 [1878], *Anti-Dühring*, in *Marx and Engels Collected Works*, Volume 25, New York: International Publishers.

Engels, Friedrich 1989 [1880], *Socialism: Utopian and Scientific*, in *Marx and Engels Collected Works*, Volume 24, New York: International Publishers.

Engels, Friedrich 1990a [1891], *A Critique of the Draft Social-Democratic Programme of 1891*, in *Marx and Engels Collected Works*, Volume 27, New York: International Publishers.

Engels, Friedrich 1990b [1892], *Reply to the Honourable Giovanni Bovio*, in *Marx and Engels Collected Works*, Volume 27, New York: International Publishers.

Engels, Friedrich and Karl Marx 1976a [1845–46], *The German Ideology*, in *Marx and Engels Collected Works*, Volume 5, New York: International Publishers.

Engels, Friedrich and Karl Marx 1976b [1848], *Manifesto of the Communist Party*, in *Marx and Engels Collected Works*, Volume 6, New York: International Publishers.

Engels, Friedrich and Karl Marx 1977 [1848], *Demands of the Communist Party in Germany*, in *Marx and Engels Collected Works*, Volume 7, New York: International Publishers.

Engels, Friedrich and Karl Marx 1978 [1850], *Address of the Central Authority to the League, March 1850*, in *Marx and Engels Collected Works*, Volume 10, New York: International Publishers.

Engels, Friedrich and Karl Marx 1989 [1882], *Preface to the Second Russian Edition of The Manifesto of the Communist Party*, in *Marx and Engels Collected Works*, Volume 24, New York: International Publishers.

Ernst, John 1982, 'Simultaneous Valuation Extirpated: A Contribution to the Critique of the Neo-Ricardian Concept of Value', *Review of Radical Political Economics*, 14, no. 2: 85–94.

Farjoun, Emmanuel, and Moshe Machover 1983, *Laws of Chaos: A Probabilistic Approach to Political Economy*, London: Verso.

Fine, Ben and Laurence Harris 1979, *Rereading Capital*, New York: Columbia University Press.

Foley, Duncan 1982, 'The Value of Money the Value of Labor Power and the Marxian Transformation Problem', *Review of Radical Political Economics*, 14, no. 2: 37–47.

Freeman, Alan 1996, 'Price, Value and Profit – A Continuous, General, Treatment', in *Marx and Non-Equilibrium Economics*, edited by Alan Freeman and Guglielmo Carchedi, Cheltenham: Edward Elgar.

Freeman, Alan 1999, 'The Limits of Ricardian Value: Law, Contingency and Motion in Economics', unpublished, available at: http://mpra.ub.uni-muenchen.de/2574/.

Freeman, Alan 2010a, 'Marxism without Marx: A Note towards a Critique', *Capital & Class*, 34, no. 1: 84–97.

Freeman, Alan 2010b, 'Trends in Value Theory since 1881', *World Review of Political Economy*, 4, no. 1: 567–605.

Freeman, Alan 2012, 'The Profit Rate in the Presence of Financial Markets: A Necessary Correction', *Journal of Australian Political Economy*, 70: 167–92.

Freeman, Alan and Andrew Kliman 2000, 'Two Concepts of Value, Two Rates of Profit, Two Laws of Motion', *Research in Political Economy*, 18: 243–67.

Friedman, Milton 1966, 'The Methodology of Positive Economics', in *Essays in Positive Economics*, Chicago: University of Chicago Press.

Gillman, Joseph 1957, *The Falling Rate of Profit*, London: Dennis Dobson.

Giussani, Paolo 1991, 'The Determination of Prices of Production', *International Journal of Political Economy*, 21, no. 4: 67–86.

Grossman, Henryk 1992, *The Law of Accumulation and Breakdown of the Capitalist System*, translated by Jairus Banaji, London: Pluto Press.

Harman, Chris 2009, *Zombie Capitalism*, London: Bookmarks.

Heinrich, Michael 2013, 'Crisis Theory, the Law of the Tendency of the Profit Rate to Fall, and Marx's Studies in the 1870s', *Monthly Review*, 64, no. 11, available at: http://monthlyreview.org/2013/04/01/crisis-theory-the-law-of-the-tendency-of-the-profit-rate-to-fall-and-marxs-studies-in-the-1870s.

Hodrick, Robert and Edward Prescott 1997, 'Postwar US Business Cycles: An Empirical Investigation', *Journal of Money, Credit and Banking*, 29, no. 1: 1–16.

Horngren, Charles (ed.) 2013, *Accounting*, 7th edn., Frenchs Forest, NSW: Pearson Australia.

Jones, Peter 2017, *Simple Reproduction and Falling Rate of Profit Examples Using a Temporalist Dual System Interpretation of Marx's Value Theory*, draft version, available at: https://anu-au.academia.edu/PeterJones.

Jones, Peter 2018, *A Falling Rate of Profit Due to Labour Saving Technical Change, at Both Temporalist and Simultaneist Unit Values and Prices*, draft version, available at: https://anu-au.academia.edu/PeterJones.

Keynes, John Maynard 1936, *General Theory of Employment, Interest and Money*, London: Harcourt.

Kliman, Andrew 1988, 'The Profit Rate Under Continuous Technological Change', *Review of Radical Political Economics* 20, nos. 2–3: 283–9.

Kliman, Andrew 1996, 'A Value-Theoretic Critique of the Okishio Theorem', in *Marx and Non-Equilibrium Economics*, edited by Alan Freeman and Guglielmo Carchedi, Cheltenham: Edward Elgar.

Kliman, Andrew 2007, *Reclaiming Marx's Capital: A Refutation of the Myth of Inconsistency*, Lanham, MD: Lexington Books.

Kliman, Andrew 2010, *The Persistent Fall in Profitability Underlying the Current Crisis: New Temporalist Evidence*, New York: Marxist-Humanist Initiative.

Kliman, Andrew 2011, *The Failure of Capitalist Production: Underlying Causes of the Great Recession*, New York: Pluto Press.

Kliman, Andrew 2014, 'The Whiggish Foundations of Marxian and Sraffian Economics', *Cambridge Journal of Economics* 38, no. 3: 643–61.

Kliman, Andrew, and Alan Freeman 2009, 'The Truthiness of Veneziani's Critique of Marx and the TSSI', *Marxism 21*, 6, no. 2: 277–300.

Kliman, Andrew, Alan Freeman, Nick Potts, Alexey Gusev, and Brendan Cooney 2013, 'The Unmaking of Marx's Capital: Heinrich's Attempt to Eliminate Marx's Crisis Theory', *MPRA Paper*, available at: http://mpra.ub.uni-muenchen.de/48535/.

Kliman, Andrew and Ted McGlone 1988, 'The Transformation Non-Problem and the Non-Transformation Problem', *Capital & Class*, 12, no. 2: 56–84.

Kliman, Andrew and Ted McGlone 1999, 'A Temporal Single-System Interpretation of Marx's Value Theory', *Review of Political Economy*, 11, no. 1: 33–59.

Lakatos, Imre 1968, 'Criticism and the Methodology of Scientific Research Programmes', *Proceedings of the Aristotelian Society*, New Series, 69: 149–86.

Lapides, Kenneth 1994, 'Henryk Grossmann on Marx's Wage Theory and the "Increasing Misery" Controversy', *History of Political Economy* 26, no. 2: 239–66.

Lee, Chai-on 1993, 'Marx's Labour Theory of Value Revisited', *Cambridge Journal of Economics*, 17, no. 4: 463–78.

Lenin, Vladimir Ilyich 1964 [1917], *The State and Revolution*, in *Lenin: Collected Works*, Volume 25, Moscow: Progress Publishers.

Mage, Shane 1963, *The 'Law of the Falling Tendency of the Rate of Profit': Its Place in the Marxian Theoretical System and Relevance to the US Economy*, New York: Columbia University Press.

Marx, Karl 1951 [1863], *Theories of Surplus Value*, edited by Karl Kautsky, translated by G.A. Bonner and Emile Burns, London: Lawrence & Wishart.

Marx, Karl 1963 [1863], *Theories of Surplus-Value (Volume IV of Capital)*, Moscow: Progress Publishers.

Marx, Karl 1970 [1859], *A Contribution to the Critique of Political Economy*, translated by S.W. Ryazanskaya, Moscow: Progress Publishers.

Marx, Karl 1973 [1858], *Grundrisse: Foundations of the Critique of Political Economy (Rough Draft)*, Harmondsworth: Penguin Books.

Marx, Karl 1976 [1867], *Capital, Volume I*, translated by Ben Fowkes, London: Penguin.

Marx, Karl 1978a [1850], *The Class Struggles in France*, in *Marx and Engels Collected Works*, Volume 10, New York: International Publishers.

Marx, Karl 1978b [1884], *Capital, Volume II*, translated by David Fernbach. London: Penguin.

Marx, Karl 1980 [1855], *The Association for Administrative Reform – People's Charter*, in *Marx and Engels Collected Works*, Volume 14, New York: International Publishers.

Marx, Karl 1981 [1894], *Capital, Volume III*, translated by David Fernbach, London: Penguin.

Marx, Karl 1986 [1871], *The Civil War in France*, in *Marx and Engels Collected Works*, Volume 22, New York: International Publishers.

Marx, Karl 1988 [1868], *Marx to Ludwig Kugelmann in Hanover*, in *Marx and Engels Collected Works*, Volume 43, New York: International Publishers.

Marx, Karl 1989a [1875], *Critique of the Gotha Programme*, in *Marx and Engels Collected Works*, Volume 24, New York: International Publishers.

Marx, Karl 1989b [1861–63], *Economic Manuscript of 1861–1863*, in *Marx and Engels Collected Works*, Volume 32, New York: International Publishers.

Marx, Karl 1994 [1861–63], *Economic Manuscript of 1861–1863*, in *Marx and Engels Collected Works*, Volume 34, New York: International Publishers.

Marx, Karl 1992 [1863–88], *Das Kapital III*, in *Karl Marx Friedrich Engels Gesamtausgabe II (MEGA II)*, edited by Manfred Müller, Jürgen Jungnickel, Barbara Lietz, Christel Sander, and Artur Schnickmann, Volume II, 4.2, Berlin: Internationales Institut für Sozialgeschichte Amsterdam.

Marx, Karl 1995 [1852], *The Eighteenth Brumaire of Louis Bonaparte*, marxists.org, available at: https://www.marxists.org/archive/marx/works/1852/18th-brumaire/.

Mill, John Stuart 1909 [1848], *Principles of Political Economy*, edited by W.J. Ashley, London: Longmans, Green, and Co.

Mohun, Simon 2006, 'Distributive Shares in the US Economy, 1964–2001', *Cambridge Journal of Economics*, 30, no. 3: 347–70.

Mohun, Simon 2009, 'Aggregate Capital Productivity in the US Economy, 1964–2001', *Cambridge Journal of Economics*, 33, no. 5: 1023–46.

Mohun, Simon 2014, 'Unproductive Labor in the US Economy 1964–2010', *Review of Radical Political Economics*, 46, no. 3: 355–79.

Moore, Geoffrey and Victor Narnowitz 1986, 'The Development and Role of the National Bureau of Economic Research's Business Cycle Chronologies', in *The American Business Cycle: Continuity and Change*, edited by Robert Gordon, 735–80, available at: http://www.nber.org/chapters/c10035.pdf.

Moseley, Fred 1993, 'Marx's Logical Method and the "Transformation Problem"', in *Marx's Method in Capital: A Re-Examination*, California: Humanities Press.

NBER 2010, 'US Business Cycle Expansions and Contractions', *National Bureau of Economic Research*, 20 September, available at: http://www.nber.org/cycles/cyclesmain .html.

Officer, Lawrence 2014, 'What was the Interest Rate Then?', *MeasuringWorth*, available at: http://www.measuringworth.com/interestrates/.

Officer, Lawrence and Samuel Williamson 2013, 'Annual Inflation Rate in the United States, 1775–2013, and United Kingdom, 1265–2013', *MeasuringWorth*, available at: http://www.measuringworth.com/inflation/.

Okishio, Nobuo 1961, 'Technical Changes and the Rate of Profit', *Kobe University Economic Review*, 7: 85–99.

Ramos M., Alejandro 1998, 'Value and Price of Production: New Evidence on Marx's Transformation Procedure', *International Journal of Political Economy*, 28, no. 4: 55–81.

Ramos M., Alejandro 2004, 'Labour, Money, Labour-Saving Innovation and the Falling Rate of Profit', in *The New Value Controversy and the Foundation of Economics*, edited by Alan Freeman, Andrew Kliman, and Julian Wells, Cheltenham: Edward Elgar.

Reuten, Geert and Peter Thomas 2011, 'From the "Fall of the Rate of Profit" in the *Grundrisse* to the Cyclical Development of the Profit Rate in Capital', *Science & Society*, 75, no. 1: 74–90.

Ricardo, David 1973, *The Principles of Political Economy and Taxation*, London and New York: Everyman's Library.

Roberts, Michael 2009, *The Great Recession*, available at: http://archive.org/details/ TheGreatRecession.ProfitCyclesEconomicCrisisAMarxistView.

Roberts, Michael 2012, 'A World Rate of Profit', *Paper Presented at the IIPPEE / AHE / FAPE Conference*, available at: http://thenextrecession.files.wordpress.com/2012/09/ a-world-rate-of-profit.pdf.

Rubin, Isaak Illich 1978 [1927], 'Abstract Labour and Value in Marx's System', translated by Kathleen Gilbert, *Capital and Class*, 2, no. 2: 107–39.

Rubin, Isaak Illich 1973 [1928], *Essays on Marx's Theory of Value*, translated by Miloš Samardžjia and Fredy Perlman, Montréal: Black Rose Books.

Shaikh, Anwar 1992, 'The Falling Rate of Profit as the Cause of Long Waves: Theory and Empirical Evidence', in *New Findings in Long Wave Research*, edited by Alfred Kleinknecht, Ernest Mandel, and Immanuel Wallerstein, London: Macmillan Press.

Shaikh, Anwar and Ertuğrul Ahmet Tonak 1994, *Measuring the Wealth of Nations: The Political Economy of National Accounts*, Cambridge: Cambridge University Press.

Smith, Adam 1976 [1776], *An Inquiry into the Nature and Causes of the Wealth of Nations*, edited by R.H. Campbell, A.S. Skinner, and W.B. Todd, Volume 1, Oxford: Clarendon Press.

Sohn-Rethel, Alfred 1978, *Intellectual and Manual Labour: A Critique of Epistemology*, translated by Martin Sohn-Rethel, Atlantic Highlands, NJ: Humanities Press.

Sweezy, Paul 1949a, 'Editor's Introduction', in *Karl Marx and the Close of His System*, New York: A.M. Kelley.

Sweezy, Paul 1949b, *The Theory of Capitalist Development*, London: Dobson.

Thorp, Willard Long and Hildegarde E. Thorp 1926, 'The Annals of the United States of America', *Business Annals, NBER*, 107–45, available at: http://www.nber.org/chapters/c4638.pdf.

Tobin, James and William C. Brainard 1976, 'Asset Markets and the Cost of Capital', *Cowles Foundation Discussion Papers*, no. 427, available at: http://econpapers.repec.org/paper/cwlcwldpp/427.htm.

US Bureau of Economic Analysis 2011, *Concepts and Methods of the US National Income and Product Accounts*, available at: http://www.bea.gov/national/pdf/chapters1-4.pdf accessed 05/11/2014.

US Bureau of Economic Analysis 2013, *BEA Depreciation Estimates*, available at: http://www.bea.gov/national/pdf/fixed%20assets/BEA_depreciation_2013.pdf accessed 05/11/2014.

US Bureau of Economic Analysis 2014, 'GDP-by-Industry Accounts', available at: http://www.bea.gov/iTable/index_industry_gdpIndy.cfm.

US Bureau of Economic Analysis 2015, 'Fixed Assets Accounts' and 'National Income and Product Accounts Tables', available at: http://www.bea.gov/iTable/index_FA.cfm and http://www.bea.gov/iTable/index_nipa.cfm.

Veneziani, Roberto 2004, 'The Temporal Single-System Interpretation of Marx's Economics: A Critical Evaluation', *Metroeconomica*, 55, no. 1: 96–114.

Weisskopf, Thomas 1979, 'Marxian Crisis Theory and the Rate of Profit in the Postwar US Economy', *Cambridge Journal of Economics*, 3, no. 4: 341–78.

Wells, Julian 2007, *The Rate of Profit as a Random Variable*, PhD Thesis, The Open University, available at: https://ideas.repec.org/p/pra/mprapa/98235.html.

Williamson, Samuel 2014, 'What was the US GDP then?', *MeasuringWorth*, available at: http://www.measuringworth.com/usgdp/.

Wolff, Richard D., Bruce Roberts, and Antonino Callari 1982, 'Marx's (not Ricardo's) "Transformation Problem": A Radical Reconceptualization', *History of Political Economy*, 14, no. 4: 564–82.

Index

CPSIA information can be obtained
at www.ICGtesting.com
Printed in the USA
JSHW032249281022
32324JS00002B/3